WITHDRAWN

CAMBRIDGE STUDIES IN
ANGLO-SAXON ENGLAND

23

BEOWULF AND OLD GERMANIC METRE

CAMBRIDGE STUDIES IN
ANGLO-SAXON ENGLAND

GENERAL EDITORS

SIMON KEYNES

MICHAEL LAPIDGE

ANDY ORCHARD

Volumes published

BEOWULF AND OLD GERMANIC METRE

GEOFFREY RUSSOM

Professor of English, Brown University

CAMBRIDGE
UNIVERSITY PRESS

PUBLISHED BY THE PRESS SYNDICATE OF THE UNIVERSITY OF CAMBRIDGE
The Pitt Building, Trumpington Street, Cambridge CB2 1RP

CAMBRIDGE UNIVERSITY PRESS
The Edinburgh Building, Cambridge CB2 2RU, United Kingdom
40 West 20th Street, New York, NY 10011–4211, USA
10 Stamford Road, Oakleigh, Melbourne 3166, Australia

© Geoffrey Russom 1998

First published 1998

Printed in the United Kingdom at the University Press, Cambridge

Typeset in Garamond 11/13pt [CE]

A catalogue record for this book is available from the British Library

Library of Congress cataloguing in publication data

Russom, Geoffrey.
Beowulf and Old Germanic metre / Geoffrey Russom.
p.   cm. – (Cambridge studies in Anglo-Saxon England: 23)
Includes bibliographical references
ISBN 0 521 59340 9 (hardback)
1. Beowulf – Versification.
2. English language – Old English, ca. 450–1100 – Versification.
3. English language – Old English, ca. 450–1100 – Rhythm.
4. Germanic languages – Versification. 5. Civilization, Anglo-Saxon.
6. Rhetoric, Medieval. 7. Alliteration.
I. Title. II. Series.
PR1588.R87   1998
829'.3 – dc21   97–13720   CIP

ISBN 0 521 59340 9 hardback

For Ray and Val

Contents

Preface

It has been my good fortune to pursue research on alliterative metre during a period when this subject attracted the attention of many Anglo-Saxonists and when questions of poetic form took on special importance for theoretical linguists. For valuable discussion of metrical problems by correspondence and at various conferences I owe thanks to Patricia Bethel, Mary Blockley, Thomas Cable, Robert Creed, Daniel Donoghue, Edwin Duncan, David Hoover, Constance Hieatt, Rand Hutcheson, Calvin Kendall, O. D. Macrae-Gibson, Bruce Mitchell, Haruko Momma, Eric Stanley and Jun Terasawa. A draft of the book was read by William Crossgrove, R. D. Fulk, Joseph Harris and two anonymous reviewers, for whose comments I am grateful. My approach to related linguistic problems began more than two decades ago in discussions with Roman Jakobson, Samuel J. Keyser and Paul Kiparsky. Since then I have also profited from conversation or correspondence with linguists Elan Dresher, Bruce Hayes, Richard Hogg, Pauline Jacobson, Roger Lass, David Lightfoot, C. B. McCully, Donka Minkova, Robert Noyer, Robert Stockwell, Seiichi Suzuki and Gilbert Youmans. Some of these researchers have published views differing from my own, but all have been courteous and helpful. They bear no responsibility, of course, for any errors I have made. To Jacqueline Haring Russom I owe special thanks for identifying computational procedures that greatly enhanced my control of the data. Allen Renear's Scholarly Technology Group found just the right software to implement these procedures and showed me how to use it most effectively. Kalev Peekna helped me navigate the internet to acquire valuable working materials, notably an electronic text of the *ASPR* with corrections by Bethel and Macrae-Gibson. Thanks are due to the Oxford Text Archive for making this version available. Finally, it has been a pleasure to work with Michael Lapidge and Sarah Stanton on problems of editing and book production.

Abbreviations

AGM	E. Sievers, *Altgermanische Metrik* (Halle, 1893)
ASPR	G. P. Krapp and E. V. K. Dobbie, eds., *The Anglo-Saxon Poetic Records*, 6 vols. (New York, 1931–53)
Behaghel–Taeger	O. Behaghel, ed., *Heliand und Genesis*, 9th edn rev. by B. Taeger (Tübingen, 1984)
BGDSL	*Beiträge zur Geschichte der deutschen Sprache und Literatur*
Bliss, *Metre*	A. J. Bliss, *The Metre of Beowulf*, rev. edn (Oxford, 1967)
Bostock–King–McLintock.	J. K. Bostock, *A Handbook of Old High German Literature*, 2nd edn rev. by K. C. King and D. R. McLintock (Oxford, 1976)
Braune–Ebbinghaus	*Althochdeutsches Lesebuch*, 16th edn rev. by E. A. Ebbinghaus (Tübingen, 1979)
Braune–Eggers	*Althochdeutsche Grammatik*, 13th edn rev. by H. Eggers (Tübingen, 1975)
CHEL I	R. M. Hogg, *The Cambridge History of the English Language I: The Beginnings to 1066* (Cambridge, 1992)
CSASE	Cambridge Studies in Anglo-Saxon England
DGV	W. P. Lehmann, *The Development of Germanic Verse Form* (Austin, TX, 1956)
ES	*English Studies*
Gordon–Taylor	E. V. Gordon, *An Introduction to Old Norse*, 2nd edn rev. by A. R. Taylor (Oxford, 1957), with Short Grammar, pp. 265–329 (cited by section number)

Hofmann, *Versstrukturen*	D. Hofmann, *Die Versstrukturen der altsächsischen Stabreimgedichte Heliand und Genesis*, 2 vols. (Heidelberg, 1991)
Klaeber	F. Klaeber, ed., *Beowulf and The Fight at Finnsburg*, 3rd edn with first and second supplements (Boston, 1950)
Kuhn, 'Wortstellung'	'Zur Wortstellung und -betonung im Altgermanischen', *BGDSL* 57 (1933), 1–109
MLR	*Modern Language Review*
Neckel–Kuhn	G. Neckel, *Edda: Die Lieder des Codex Regius nebst verwandten Denkmälern*, 5th edn rev. by H. Kuhn (Heidelberg, 1983)
Noreen	A. Noreen, *Altnordische Grammatik* I (Tübingen, 1884)
OEG	A. Campbell, *Old English Grammar* (Oxford, 1959)
OEM	*Old English Meter and Linguistic Theory* (Cambridge, 1987)
Pope, *Rhythm*	J. C. Pope, *The Rhythm of Beowulf: An Interpretation of the Normal and Hypermetric Verse-Forms in Old English Poetry*, rev. edn (New Haven, CT, 1966)
Sievers, 'Rhythmik'	'Zur Rhythmik des germanischen Alliterationsverses', *BGDSL* 10 (1885), 209–314 and 451–545
SN	*Studia Neophilologica*
TPS	*Transactions of the Philological Society*
ZDA	*Zeitschrift für deutsches Altertum und deutsche Literatur*

Abbreviated titles for Norse Eddic poems are those given in Neckel–Kuhn, pp. ix–x.

1

Introduction

The author of *Beowulf* composed in an ancient verse form also inherited
by Scandinavian and continental West Germanic poets. The oldest
surviving line in this form illustrates its essential features:

(1)   ekhlewagastiR : holtijaR : horna : tawido :[1]

Line (1) was carved in runes on a golden drinking horn. The character *R*
represents a sound derived from Germanic *z* that had not yet merged
with *r*. The language is probably an early form of Norse, and the artefact
dates from about 400 AD.[2] Like the lines employed in *Beowulf*, line (1)
falls into two natural syntactic constituents of about the same size. The
first constituent, a grammatical subject, contains a personal pronoun and
two proper nouns. The second constituent, a grammatical predicate,
contains a noun object and a finite verb. Word order is SOV (subject–
object–verb), generally regarded as the basic pattern for early Germanic.[3]
Each half of the line includes two stressed words separated by a boundary
marker, indicated above by a colon.[4] No punctuation appears between the
unstressed pronoun *ek* and the first stressed word. The stressed nouns in
the first half of the line both begin with *H-* and are said to *alliterate*.
These two words also alliterate with *horna* in the second half of the line.

---

[1] 'I, Hlewagast, Holt's son, made the horn.' The text is cited from Krause, *Runeninschriften*, p. 596. The translation is from Elliott, *Runes*, p. 80. Krause, *Runen*, p. 72,
gives essentially the same translation in German.

[2] Düwel, *Runenkunde*, pp. 15, 17 and 28; Krause, *Runen*, §52.

[3] See *CHEL I*, §2.6.

[4] Copies of the runic passage made before the horn was lost represent this marker as a
column of four points. See Krause, *Runeninschriften*, pp. 596–8; Morris, *Epigraphy*, §4.7.

THEORETICAL FRAMEWORK

In a work devoted to Old English metre, I proposed four fundamental principles to explain the verse form of *Beowulf*.[5] These principles can be stated in a general form applicable to the cognate Germanic traditions:

P1 *Foot patterns* correspond to native word patterns. The foot patterns most easily perceived correspond to the most common word patterns.

P2 The *verse* consists of two readily identifiable feet. Foot patterns corresponding to unusual word patterns add to the complexity of verses in which they appear.

P3 Assignment of *alliteration* corresponds to assignment of stress in Germanic compounds and serves to bind smaller metrical constituents into larger constituents. The integrity of the larger constituent is marked by alliteration on its first subconstituent.

P4 The *line* consists of two adjacent verses bound by alliteration. The first of these is the *a-verse*; the second is the *b-verse*.

The second half of line (1) obviously constitutes a well-formed b-verse of two *word feet*, since each of its subparts consists of a single stressed word. There are also two stressed words in the first half of the line. The runesmith's decision not to place a word boundary after the pronoun *ek* suggests that this unstressed constituent did not count as an additional word, i.e., that it was regarded as an anacrusis. The stress rule for Germanic compounds assigns primary stress to the first constituent and subordinates the second constituent. This linguistic rule reapplies at a higher level in compounds with more than two constituents.[6] Rule P3 applies to the metrical constituents of (1) in exactly the same way. As with stress assignment, assignment of alliteration confers special prominence on some constituents and subordinates neighbouring ones. At the level of the verse, P3 assigns alliteration to the first foot and subordinates the second foot. At the level of the line, P3 subordinates the b-verse to the a-verse. The subordinate foot of the dominant a-verse, occupied by *holtijaR*, remains fairly prominent, and may contain an alliterating syllable. A-verses with two alliterating syllables appear in all Germanic traditions, though there are also many a-verses in which the subordinate

---

[5] *OEM*, §0.2.   [6] *OEM*, §7.4; cf. Sauer, *Nominalkomposita*, §4.1.1.

foot fails to alliterate. Significantly less prominent is the subordinate foot of the subordinate b-verse, occupied in (1) by *tawido*. None of the early Germanic traditions permits alliteration in such a doubly subordinated foot.

Although example (1) has important affinities with lines from *Beowulf*, there are differences in detail. Personal pronouns comparable to runic *ek* do not appear as anacruses in the Old English epic. The *Beowulf* poet usually employs the least conspicuous unstressed constituents for anacrusis, such as verbal prefixes and preverbal negative particles.[7] In addition, the a-verse of (1), with its two long proper names, would be rejected as unacceptably large by the *Beowulf* poet.[8] The less strict constraints on verse size attested by (1) must result in part from the large average size of early Germanic words, as compared with words of the historical period. It is interesting to note, however, that the line remains deviant from an Old English point of view even when translated into Old Danish, a language later spoken in North Schleswig, where the runic horn was found. The Old Danish translation provided in a standard introductory text is *Ek, HlēgestR HøltiR, horn tāða*.[9] By Old English standards, *HlēgestR HøltiR* is a perfectly good a-verse, but we still have pronominal anacrusis, and the b-verse has become too short, falling below the absolute minimum of four syllables that applies in *Beowulf*. The detail rules evidently differed from one tradition to another. As we shall see, Old Norse metre of the historical period employs short verses of a type not found in *Beowulf*, and Old Saxon metre employs many non-prefixal anacruses.

PERCEPTION OF METRICAL FORM

In a literate tradition, rules for poetry can be published by acknowledged authorities and studied by poets who wish to conform. Germanic metre, on the other hand, clearly developed in a preliterate era. Although non-literate poets often adhere to strict standards of versecraft, they are typically quite unable to state the metrical rules they follow.[10] Rules of oral-traditional metre are acquired by intuition, like linguistic rules. Metrists can scan a written text at leisure, consulting reference works if

[7] See Cable, *Meter and Melody*, ch. 3.   [8] *OEM*, §2.5.
[9] Gordon–Taylor, p. 187.   [10] See Jakobson, *Selected Writings* V, 195–6.

3

necessary. When poetry of any kind is recited, scansion must take place at the speed of performance, like analysis of linguistic form during ordinary speech.[11] An explanatory account of Germanic versecraft is therefore subject to severe constraints. It would be quite implausible to argue, for example, that the poet's audience memorized a long, arbitrary list of acceptable patterns and checked each verse against the list during performance. Such mental operations could hardly take place with the necessary speed.[12] The detailed classifications of scholars like Bliss show that strict metrical constraints existed, but do not explain how such constraints could be appreciated or transmitted, as Bliss himself realizes.[13]

One way to explain fundamental principles of verse construction is to show that they correspond to linguistic principles already internalized by the native speaker. Principles P1–4 attempt this kind of explanation. Speakers of a language can identify native word units instantly in an acoustic signal, so it seems reasonable to suppose that they could identify metrical units comparable to native words at the speed of performance. Recognition of word feet is utterly trivial, of course, in the second half of example (1), where each foot consists of a single stressed word. Rule P3 operates exactly like the compound stress rule internalized by all native speakers of early Germanic languages and should have been quite easy to learn. In a metrical system with P3, moreover, P2 and P4 follow as a matter of course. Because linguistic compounding is a binary operation, the larger metrical domains bound together by alliteration are most naturally constructed in a binary fashion. Note that the units bound by alliteration (word feet) correspond to the units bound by the compound stress rule (words). In this sense, P1 also follows from P3. Thus P1–4

---

[11] The audience's ability to scan in real time is commonly presupposed even by metrists who confess that they are unable to account for it. Thus for example McLintock, 'Metre and Rhythm', p. 567: 'An educated audience (by a process which is difficult to describe) can recognize well-formed verses. It will be content (but no more) if it discerns such verses and can pronounce the poet competent in his craft; it will applaud him if he can exploit his craft in performance.'

[12] See Jackendoff, *Consciousness*, §4.2. This problem would arise in any verse form intended for recitation, even if poet and audience were fully literate and had received some explicit training in metrical analysis. According to Kendall, *Metrical Grammar*, p. 5, metrical constraints of the kind observed in *Beowulf* were unlikely to be codified as explicit rules, and the poet, though probably literate, used an oral-traditional metre.

[13] Bliss, *Metre*, §122.

4

have the kind of coherence that allows internalized rule systems to function at high speed.[14]

The detail rules of a coherent system follow from its general principles. In *Beowulf*, a number of detail rules guide the audience to correct interpretation of unstressed prefixes in anacrusis, preventing confusion about the number of feet in the verse.[15] These rules represent an intuitive rejection of verses that lack a clear two-foot structure, and thus follow from P2. Observe that a strong prediction is made about what would happen to a Germanic metre if unstressed prefixes were lost from the poet's language. In that case, the related detail rules would serve no purpose, and should be lost as well. We can test this prediction because Old Norse lost unstressed prefixes just before the Eddic poems were composed. As it turns out, the old detail rules were in fact lost, and verses of a kind avoided by the *Beowulf* poet began to appear in significant numbers.[16]

METRICAL COMPLEXITY IN THE WORD-FOOT THEORY

Good poets often deviate from standard verse patterns, in part because what they wish to say makes it necessary to do so and in part to avoid metrical banality.[17] In a poetic form intended for recitation, however, deviance must not create verses too complex for intuitive scansion. The complexity of an individual verse must be kept within tolerable limits, and a poem must not contain an intolerably high frequency of the most deviant verses. An ancient Germanic verse can be complex in two quite different ways. First, there may be one or more *mismatches* between the linguistic material occupying the verse and its underlying two-word pattern. A verse with more than two words may have an acceptable stress contour and the usual number of syllables, but it will not be a perfect match for the underlying pattern. Second, a verse may have an *inherently complex* pattern in which one of the feet corresponds to a word of relatively low frequency (see P1). Both types of complexity can occur in a single verse, but the more complex verse patterns are relatively intolerant of mismatches.[18]

---

[14] See Dresher and Lahiri, 'Germanic Foot', p. 283; *OEM*, p. 156.
[15] *OEM*, ch. 3 and §6.4.   [16] See below, ch. 4.
[17] See Kiparsky, 'Rhythmic Structure', p. 224.
[18] In general, a poet who deviates from the norm in one way is less likely to do so in other ways simultaneously. See Kiparsky, 'Rhythmic Structure', pp. 201–2. Deviations from the norm similar to those discussed here are recognized in *AGM* by Sievers, who

The two types of complexity are illustrated by the following examples:

(2) lange / þrāge[19]   (*Beo* 114a)
(3) sinc æt / symle[20]   (*Beo* 81a)
(4) hār / hilderinc[21]   (*Beo* 1307a)
(5) enta / ǣrgeweorc[22]   (*Beo* 1679a)

Sievers posits two trochaic feet in verses like (2), which he classifies as type A1 in *AGM*. A verse like (3), which has the same stress pattern as (2), would also be classified as type A1 within Sievers's system. Hofmann objects to Sievers's scansion as unnatural, pointing out that the caesura or major syntactic break in (3) does not coincide with the posited foot boundary (indicated above with a slash).[23] For similar reasons, Bliss would assign (2) and (3) to distinct classes.[24] The critiques of Hofmann and Bliss might at first glance seem applicable to the word-foot theory, which represents (2) and (3) as expressions of the same verse pattern and divides them as Sievers does. Unlike Sievers's theory, however, the word-foot theory distinguishes (2), the direct, two-word realization of the pattern, from (3), which is represented as deviant despite the fact that it has the normal stress pattern and number of syllables for an A1 verse. The difference between (2) and (3) is captured as a difference in metrical complexity. The preposition *æt* in (2) does stand closer syntactically to *symle* than to *sinc*, as Hofmann observes. Note, however, that the stressed syllable following *æt* is rendered more prominent by alliteration, which reinforces the foot boundary obscured by the syntax. Kendall proposes a categorical rule requiring a second alliteration in all Old English a-verses of type A1 with this kind of syntactic structure.[25] Kendall's rule has genuine empirical force because type A1 verses that are free of unstressed function words usually have single alliteration, like (2). If (2) and (3) represent unrelated verse patterns, there is no obvious explanation for their differing alliterative requirements. If (3) counts as a complex variant of the pattern expressed directly by (2), we can explain the second alliterating syllable as an aid to intuitive scansion.

ranks his verse types in approximate order of complexity (A–E) and identifies certain verses with an unusual stress contour (e.g. those in which anacrusis is posited) as complex variants of a given type.

[19] 'a long time ...'   [20] 'treasure at the feast'.
[21] 'old man of battle ...'   [22] 'ancient work of the giants ...'
[23] *Versstrukturen* I, 29.   [24] *Metre*, §43.   [25] *Metrical Grammar*, p. 208.

The kind of analysis applied to (2) and (3) can be applied to all verse patterns within the word-foot framework. In general, poets impose the fewest constraints on paradigmatic two-word realizations of a given pattern. Special constraints may apply to other variants of the pattern, since the effort of associating these variants with two-word paradigms must not become unpleasantly burdensome to the audience. In a metrical theory with explanatory ambitions, of course, a variant subject to a special constraint *should* have an unnatural scansion. The unnaturalness of the scansion notates the metrical complexity of the variant, illustrating the need for the constraint. This advantage of word-foot notation seems to require emphasis.[26]

The verse pattern corresponding to (2) and (3) is designated as type A1 by Sievers because of its high frequency. Within the word-foot framework, the priority of type A1 follows directly from P2, which states that feet corresponding to unusual word patterns add to the complexity of verses in which they appear. Since the most common Old English word pattern is trochaic, the verse pattern with the least inherent complexity will have two trochaic feet. Example (2), with a trochaic word in each foot, realizes the simplest pattern in the simplest way. Hofmann rejects the idea that type A1 has priority for metrical reasons. He claims that trochaic words are about as common in Germanic prose as in Germanic poetry, and argues that the high frequency of A1 verses results from unrestricted employment of a high-frequency word pattern.[27] This hypothesis might be difficult to refute with evidence from Old Saxon poetry, Hofmann's special interest, but it fails to explain some important facts about poetic word choice in other Germanic traditions. Natural syntactic constituents of exactly two trochaic words, with no clitics, have a far higher frequency in *Beowulf* than in a comparable prose text.[28] We

---

[26] Whitman, for example, rejects my scansion of *Beo* 1696a, *geseted ond gesæd*, which he characterizes, without argument, as incredible (*Comparative Study*, p. 156, n. 6); but the unnaturalness of the scansion usefully notates the unnaturalness of type B verses with an isolated verse-initial prefix, which are very rare in Old English poetry (as I had pointed out in *OEM*, §3.5). Sievers's notation for type B, which Whitman adopts, represents verses like *Beo* 1696a as natural realizations of a pattern with rising rhythm in each foot, predicting incorrectly that such verses will be common (as von See observes in *Germanische Verskunst*, p. 5).

[27] *Versstrukturen* I, 32–3.   [28] *OEM*, §10.5.

encounter verses like (2) so often not because they correspond to high-frequency grammatical constructions but because they have the kind of metrical simplicity defined by P1–2. In the heavier verse types, moreover, the poet usually pairs a stressed word of greater than average length with a lexical monosyllable rather than a lexical trochee.[29] If the frequency of verse patterns reduced to the frequency of word patterns, verses like (4) would occur less often than those like (5). In fact, the *Beowulf* poet employs about five verses like (4) for every verse like (5).

In general, we would expect metrical constraints to limit the placement, not the frequency, of words with a given pattern. Later English poets, at any rate, are quite reluctant to restrict their vocabulary, and will even stretch the rules slightly to accommodate an unusual word.[30] Ancient Germanic poets did not try to avoid words deviating from the trochaic norm. Instead, they made a significant effort to balance the less common word types against one another, increasing the frequency of verses comparable to (2) in length and stress count. It seems quite legitimate, therefore, to represent the pattern of (2) as a metrical norm. Other verse patterns will be represented as inherently complex to the extent that they deviate from this norm.

ORGANIZATION OF THE COMPARATIVE PROJECT

In this book I attempt to explain the development of Germanic verse form at the level of fine detail, using P1–4 as a theoretical framework. The anchor of our investigation is the Old English *Beowulf*, a unique long poem in traditional style dealing with traditional subject matter. Of equal importance are Eddic poems on native Scandinavian subjects in fornyrðislag, generally regarded as the Norse equivalent of Old English metre. Comparison of Old English and Old Norse materials occupies chs. 2–9 and yields a complete set of rules for fornyrðislag. Eddic poems based on material from south of Scandinavia are excluded from consideration, in part because they form a distinct metrical group possibly influenced by continental Germanic norms.[31] Such works also had to be excluded to

---

[29] *OEM*, §2.5.   [30] Kiparsky, 'Rhythmic Structure', p. 214.
[31] See Kuhn, 'Westgermanisches'.

provide a fair test for Kuhn's laws, which have received much attention in recent studies of Old English metre.[32]

The Old Norse materials show what happens to a Germanic metre when the natural language has an especially forceful primary stress, the kind of stress that weakens non-primary stresses within a word or phrase and tends to reduce the number of unstressed syllables. In chs. 10 and 11 we turn to continental West Germanic verse, which shows the metrical consequences of a weakened primary stress that allows unstressed syllables to proliferate.[33] The *Heliand* does not deal with heroic subject matter, and some traditional verse-making strategies seem to have been inconsistent with its sacred content. Nevertheless, this Old Saxon poem provides valuable evidence bearing on many issues that arise in analysis of cognate traditions. The length of the *Heliand* is a distinct advantage for the metrist, and parallel manuscripts of the poem make it possible to clarify some problems that are difficult to study in *Beowulf*, notably those associated with elision. The last poem to be considered is the continental West Germanic *Hildebrandslied*, a short, fragmentary work that does have traditional heroic content.

Treatment of Norse tradition is selective, emphasizing features with obvious comparative significance. Readers interested in the whole range of Norse metres can consult *AGM* and a number of other studies.[34] In dealing with the *Heliand* and *Hildebrandslied*, I have founded my arguments primarily on clear cases, sidestepping some notorious difficul-

---

[32] See Kendall, *Metrical Grammar*, and Donoghue, *Style*, which provide references to previous work. According to Kuhn, 'Wortstellung', pp. 36 and 46, his laws are well observed in native Eddic fornyrðislag but are frequently violated in fornyrðislag with exotic content. Kuhn provides ample evidence to show that legendary matter from the south was expressed in a distinct metrical dialect. His claim that heroic poems of the Edda were translations of West Germanic originals is controversial, however. See Fulk, *History of Old English Meter*, §273. H. Momma kindly allowed me to see page proofs of *The Composition of Old English Poetry*, forthcoming as CSASE 20, an important study of Kuhn's laws as they apply (or fail to apply) within the whole corpus of Old English verse. Here I will be concerned with Kuhn's-law effects in the cognate Germanic traditions and with the purely metrical issues systematically excluded by Momma from her study (p. 182).

[33] See *DGV*, ch. 3.

[34] See especially Árnason, *Rhythms of Dróttkvætt*; Faulkes, *Háttatal*; Frank, *Old Norse Court Poetry*; Heusler, *Deutsche Versgeschichte*; and Kuhn, *Dróttkvætt*. For a brief overview of Eddic forms, see Russom, 'Eddic Meters'.

ties of metrical classification.[35] I have not reiterated all the evidence for the word-foot theory provided in *OEM*, but I use similar headings here and adopt a similar order of presentation. The reader can often find additional Old English evidence for theoretical claims made below by consulting the table of contents in *OEM*. As in *OEM*, rules introduced during the argument are repeated at the end of the book for the reader's convenience. Unless the reader is notified to the contrary, verses are scanned as they appear in Klaeber (for *Beowulf*), Neckel–Kuhn (for Eddic verse), or Braune–Ebbinghaus (for *Hildebrandslied*). Verses from the *Heliand* are usually cited from Behaghel–Taeger.[36] Citations of Old English poems other than *Beowulf* come from the *ASPR*. Indications of vowel length are sometimes added when not supplied by the editor, and editorial punctuation is deleted occasionally. In many cases, the word-foot theory isolates as particularly complex or unmetrical a verse emended by modern editors. I often cite emendations as independent witnesses to the problematic character of a verse, though usually without attempting to justify or critique them as emendations.

Some function words in each manuscript were probably added by the scribes, though it is difficult to achieve certainty about particular cases. My counts of unstressed syllables may be slightly too high for all the poems studied here, but such imprecision probably has no comparative significance. It has seemed most important to ensure that statistics for a given tradition should be derived from a consistently edited body of material. My Norse statistics are based exclusively on poems in Neckel–Kuhn, which yield a corpus of material about half the size of *Beowulf*. This is perfectly adequate for our comparative purposes because the Norse poems differ quite dramatically from West Germanic poems.[37] Our corpus certainly includes works by several Norse authors, and the metrical

---

[35] For informative discussion of these difficulties, see Hofmann, *Versstrukturen* I, ch. 5.
[36] Variants, however, are routinely cited from the parallel-text edition, *Heliand*, ed. Sievers.
[37] The corpus contains the following poems in fornyrðislag with native content: *Vǫlospá (Vsp)*, *Hymisqviða (Hym)*, *Þrymsqviða (Þrk)*, *Helgaqviða Hundingsbana in fyrri (HH)*, *Helgaqviða Hiorvarðzsonar (HHv)*, *Helgaqviða Hundingsbana ǫnnor (HH II)*, *Baldrs draumar (Bdr)*, *Rígsþula (Rþ)*, *Hyndlolióð (Hdl)*, and *Grottasǫngr (Grt)*. The Helgi poems have an *ad-hoc* connection with Southern legend, but are based primarily on Norse material and are classified as native Eddic fornyrðislag in Kuhn, 'Wortstellung', pp. 25–8. *Heliand* is abbreviated as *Hel* and *Hildebrandslied* as *Hld*.

features shared by these works are consistent with Snorri's paradigmatic example of fornyrðislag, which regularizes them.[38] Verse counts for the *Heliand* are derived from the extremely precise scansion in Hofmann, *Versstrukturen* II, which the reader may wish to consult independently. Statistics for the other poems are derived from electronic scansions that cannot be captured on the printed page. Readers interested in obtaining copies of these scansions should write to the author.[39]

VERSE RHYTHM

Little is known about the performance of alliterative poetry. We do know that Germanic poets sometimes accompanied themselves on a kind of lyre, though evidently not in Norse tradition.[40] The only significant clues to verse rhythm are provided by constraints on poetic language, as evaluated within the context of research on musical cognition.

Some scholars have suggested that Germanic verse was hardly more rhythmical than Germanic prose.[41] If that were true, we might imagine a performance of *Beowulf* accompanied by something like Gregorian chant or the opening alap section of a North Indian raga.[42] It seems inappropriate, however, to ignore efforts made by the poet to control stress and syllable count, which point towards some type of regular rhythm. Although a limited degree of rhythmic regularity sometimes occurs in prose, the clear cases involve repetition of similar stress patterns within the phrase or within adjacent phrases.[43] Such prose poetry is nothing like *Beowulf*, in which adjacent verses normally have contrasting stress patterns.[44]

P1–4 make no mention of rhythm. If these fundamental principles hold true, the rhythms of Germanic words would have provided the basis

---

[38] See below, pp. 85–6.

[39] Currently at the Department of English, Box 1852, Brown University, Providence, RI 02912, USA.

[40] Hofmann, *Versstrukturen* I, 20–1.

[41] See especially Daunt, 'Speech Rhythm', p. 64. In *History of Old English Meter*, pp. 27–8, Fulk critiques 'Speech Rhythm' and other publications expressing similar views.

[42] These rhythmically irregular traditions are discussed by Lerdahl and Jackendoff in *Tonal Music*, §2.2.

[43] For good examples and discussion see Traugott and Pratt, *Linguistics for Students of Literature*, pp. 77–9.

[44] See R. Lehmann, 'Broken Cadences'.

for poetic rhythm, and an artistic approach to rhythm would have involved scoring the linguistic givens effectively for performance.[45] Because Germanic simplexes have a predominantly falling rhythm, with stress on the first syllable, the most convenient verse rhythms would be falling. These are the preferred rhythms of later Western music and also seem to be preferred across traditions. According to Lerdahl and Jackendoff, genuinely rising rhythms like those of gamelan music are exceptional.[46] What seems quite impossible is direct rhythmical interpretation of Sievers's five-types system, which posits two falling feet in type A, two rising feet in type B, and one foot of each kind in type C, supposedly an example of rising-falling rhythm.[47] Certain rhythmical shifts in verse do have musical parallels. Stravinsky, for example, will change from 4/8 to 5/8 time and back again within a few bars.[48] This might be compared to the shift from normal to hypermetrical patterns in West Germanic poetry.[49] Lerdahl and Jackendoff have not found a traditional idiom that shifts abruptly back and forth between rising and falling rhythms of equal status, however.

If Germanic verse patterns had a genuinely rhythmical interpretation, we would expect the most common pattern, type A1, to serve as the rhythmical norm. Other verse patterns would then be perceived as syncopated departures from the norm rather than as shifts from one rhythm to another. This is essentially the hypothesis advocated by Pope, which seems to me quite plausible, though like all such hypotheses it is still disputed.[50]

---

[45] Like a number of other metrists, I distinguish *metrical competence* (the ability to recognize metrical verses) from *metrical performance* (the ability to exploit metrical competence in production of a complete work with significant rhetorical and artistic qualities of a non-metrical kind). Effective scoring of verses seems to be related quite indirectly to metrical competence. For further discussion, see McLintock, 'Metre and Rhythm'.

[46] *Tonal Music*, §7.7.   [47] *AGM*, §12.5.

[48] Lerdahl and Jackendoff, *Tonal Music*, pp. 64–5.   [49] See Pope, *Rhythm*, p. 122.

[50] For a recent critique of Pope, *Rhythm*, see Hofmann, *Versstrukturen* I, 16–30.

2

The foot

Let us begin by considering the definition of 'word' that underlies the foot patterns of Old English metre:

D1a   All stressed simplexes count as words.
D1b   Unstressed prefixes count as function words.
D1c   A compound may count as one word or as two.
D1d   A function word may count as a word or as undefined linguistic material.

Provision D1a hardly requires comment. The simple equation *foot* = *word* would not be communicated to the audience if some ordinary stressed lexical items did not count as words. Provision D1b goes against modern word spacing conventions, but is justified by the fact that Old English unstressed prefixes still look like prepositions in most cases and behave exactly like prepositions from a phonological point of view. Provision D1c acknowledges that word-level linguistic rules sometimes take a whole compound as their domain and sometimes apply to the subconstituents of a compound as if each were a separate word. Provision D1d is justified by the fact that prepositions, conjunctions, and similar unstressed constituents have a rather weak identity as words, an identity often lost altogether when they are absorbed by neighbouring stressed words. In general, the metrical interpretation of words will vary only in the way that linguistic interpretation varies.[1]

Provisions D1a, D1c, and D1d should apply to Eddic as well as to Old English poetry, but provision D1b will seldom apply because Old Norse has hardly any unstressed prefixes. All Germanic languages had unstressed

---

[1] For more detailed justification of D1a–d, see *OEM*, §§1.1–1.1.4.

prefixes originally.[2] When attached to following words, primarily verbs, these prefixes created extended or epistemic senses. Because epistemic senses were not related to root senses in any predictable way, a common prefix could take over the function of a marginal prefix, which would then be lost from the language. In Old Norse, this process continued until a single prefix, spelled *of* or *um*, became dominant. As a catch-all, the dominant prefix had acquired a sense so vague as to be practically useless. Bragi Boddason, the first known skald, used past participles (normally prefixed in early Germanic) only when the metre would allow *of* / *um* to be inserted before them; but later skalds felt free to disregard this constraint, and employed *of/um* simply for metrical convenience. According to Kuhn, *of/um* then ceased to be a prefix and became a *Füllwort* or filler word.[3] The Eddic corpus used for this comparative study contains only one unstressed prefix of the ordinary Germanic kind: *fyr-*, which occurs with a handful of Old Norse verbs.[4] The only other trace of an unstressed prefix surviving in Old Norse is the cognate of OE *ge-*, which appears in forms such as ON *glíkr* 'like' (cf. OE *gelíc*). This relic, which has lost its vowel due to the subordinating effect of the following stress, no longer bears any resemblance to a word. Loss of prefixes was accompanied by substitution of new enclitic forms for other closely bound Norse proclitics such as definite articles and preverbal negatives.[5]

WORD PATTERNS

In early Germanic languages, the significant features of word patterns are syllable length, syllable count and stress. The length of an Old Norse syllable depends partly on the relation of its consonants to the vocalic element, which constitutes the syllabic *nucleus*. Consonants placed before the nucleus occupy the *onset*. These consonants have no effect on the length of their syllable. Consonants placed after the nucleus occupy the *coda*. A syllable with one or more consonants in the coda is *closed*, and all closed syllables are long. Some examples of closed syllables are mono-

---

[2] See Kuhn, *Füllwort*.
[3] Ibid., p. 94. In Neckel–Kuhn, filler words appear as independent constituents flanked by word spaces.
[4] Ibid., p. 97. Neckel–Kuhn prints this as part of the following word in *Vsp* 1/6, *vel fyrtelia*.
[5] See Samuels, *Linguistic Evolution*, p. 85.

syllabic words like ON *stað* 'place' (short i-stem, accusative singular) and *gest* 'guest' (long i-stem, accusative singular). A syllable with no consonants in the coda is *open*. Open syllables can be long if they have a long vowel in the nucleus. A monosyllabic word like ON *kné* 'knee' consists of a long, open syllable. A short syllable is an open syllable with a short vowel.[6]

Germanic languages tend to maximize onsets.[7] In Old Norse, a single consonant between vowels always occupies the onset of the following syllable, leaving the preceding syllable open, as for example in the short-stemmed nominative plural *sta.ðir* (where the point indicates the syllable boundary).[8] The stem syllable of short-stemmed words (as they are somewhat misleadingly called) is short only when its final consonant occupies the onset of a following syllable. In the accusative singular form *stað*, the final consonant necessarily occupies the coda of the stem syllable, which is therefore long. The first of two intervocalic consonants normally occupies the coda of the preceding syllable. In inflected long-stemmed forms like nominative plural *ges.tir* (cf. *gest*), the initial syllable remains long.[9] Poets sometimes make a distinction between an ordinary long syllable and an ultra-long syllable (a closed syllable containing a long vowel, e.g. *bók* 'book'). Old Norse has fewer ultra-long syllables than Old English due to early shortening of long vowels before most double consonants and some consonant groups.[10]

Isolated short syllables could not bear stress in early Germanic languages such as Old Norse. There were no short stressed monosyllables, and short stressed syllables did not occur word-finally. If a word-final consonant was lost after a short stressed vowel, the vowel was lengthened.[11] The smallest words containing a short stressed syllable had the

---

[6] Since the nucleus and the coda both affect syllable length in Germanic languages, they are often placed together in a higher-level constituent called the *rhyme*. See *CHEL I*, §3.3.2.1. In recent theoretical research, syllables are designated heavy or light rather than long or short. I use the older terms here because they prevail in standard works on Germanic metre.

[7] See Fulk, *History of Old English Meter*, §109.

[8] See Gordon–Taylor, §28; *AGM*, §37. My syllabication follows Dresher and Lahiri, 'Germanic Foot', which comments on earlier proposals in Lass, 'Quantity', and Suzuki, 'Syllable Structure'. See also Árnason, *Rhythms of Dróttkvætt*, p. 118.

[9] The cluster *st* occasionally acts like one consonant in Old English verse. See *OEM*, §10.2, examples (98b)–(98c).

[10] Gordon–Taylor, §55.   [11] Ibid., §53.

pattern of *saga* 'story', with a short stressed syllable followed by an unstressed syllable. Sievers observes that the sequence of syllables in a word like *saga* often substitutes for a long syllable on a strong metrical position or arsis in Germanic verse patterns.[12] The syllabic sequence is then said to be *resolved*. This type of substitution seems natural, since resolved sequences and long syllables are both minimal domains of stress assignment. Recent work on Germanic languages in metrical phonology suggests that resolution is a direct expression of phonological structure. According to Dresher and Lahiri, for example, resolved sequences and long stressed syllables occupy the same type of higher-level phonological constituent, called a *metrical position*.[13] Like the arsis of Sievers, this stress-bearing position is the strong element of a domain called the foot. The purely linguistic foot, called the *Germanic foot*, also has a weak element in the simplest or *unmarked* case. Whenever possible, the syllables of Germanic words are organized into linguistic trochees; one-position feet arise by default, in monosyllables like *gest* and in resolved disyllables like *saga*. Use of the Germanic foot to represent linguistic environments enables Dresher and Lahiri to account for high-vowel deletion and j-vocalization (Sievers's law) as well as stress assignment.[14]

The resolvable sequence was a complex or *marked* alternative to the long syllable normally associated with stress.[15] Both English and Icelandic eliminated most resolvable sequences during the later Middle Ages by lengthening the vowels of stressed open syllables. Because long vowels underwent shortening in ultra-long closed syllables, most stressed syllables then had standard length.[16] In Old Norse, resolvable sequences had already become significantly less common than in Old English due to widespread syncopation of unstressed medial vowels, generally attributed to the influence of a particularly strong primary stress.[17] Norse inflectional

---

[12] *AGM*, §9.1.   [13] See 'Germanic Foot'.

[14] Hanson and Kiparsky regard the Germanic foot as a theoretical necessity, but represent it as a 'maximal foot' derived from a 'minimal foot' of a kind more widely employed in phonological theory ('Poetic Meter', p. 305). For our purposes here, the view of resolution advocated by Hanson and Kiparsky does not differ significantly from that of Dresher and Lahiri.

[15] Ibid., p. 282.   [16] Ibid., pp. 279–83.

[17] *DGM*, pp. 78–88. These syncopated vowels had often provided the second syllable for a resolvable sequence.

vowels had also been lost in some cases.[18] Old Norse probably resembled forceful style registers in which phonologically subordinate constituents are especially vulnerable to reduction or elimination.[19] It is particularly difficult to find Norse analogues for Old English forms like *werodes* 'of the troop' (gen. sg.), which can acquire a trochaic value by resolution of the first two syllables.

Secondary constituents of common Old Norse compounds often undergo stress reduction, and a long vowel in such a constituent may then be shortened, as in forms of *af-ráð* 'tribute', which often show shortening of the radical *á*.[20] Unstressed vowels are always short in Old Norse. Vowels of Old Norse inflections are never marked long, unlike Old High German inflectional vowels, which retained etymological length in some cases.[21] Some Norse function words contain etymologically long vowels (e.g. *hón* 'she', *hónum* 'to him'). The length indicated in editorial spelling was retained only when the function word bore phrasal stress, however.[22] Word-final vowels in function words had to be long under significant stress, but were short otherwise. In standard editions of Eddic poetry, a final root vowel in a function word is always marked with the acute accent, but in many cases the word clearly lacked stress and the marked vowel would have been shortened. Closed unstressed syllables could become short by consonant loss. Loss of word-final *-m* in *frá* 'from', for example, was compensated in stressed usage by lengthening of the vowel, but in unstressed usage the shortening went through to completion. Vowels also underwent shortening in function words that became enclitic to a stressed word. Thus the final vowel in ON *þú* 'thou' lost its length (and distinctive height) in *vildo* 'thou wilt'. The initial consonant of *þú* was affected by enclisis as well, becoming *d* by the usual word-level rule for the sequence *lþ*.[23] In forms like *vantattu* 'you did not hinder', word-final *þú* assimilated to the preceding negative enclitic form *-at-*. Since word-level rules express the native speaker's intuitive concept of word-hood, forms like *vildo* and *vantattu* are best regarded as single words in which enclitics have the status of secondary affixes or inflectional endings.

---

[18] Cf. tetrasyllabic OE *middangeardes*, disyllabic ON *miðgarðs* ('of middle earth', gen. sg.).

[19] Samuels, *Linguistic Evolution*, pp. 21–2, 25 and 89. On the relation between stress and heavy usage (lexicalization), see *OEM*, §1.1.2.

[20] Noreen, §151.1.

[21] Prokosch, *Comparative Germanic Grammar*, p. 139.

[22] Gordon–Taylor, §§44 and 109; Noreen, §151.   [23] Gordon–Taylor, §66.

DERIVATION OF FOOT PATTERNS FROM WORD PATTERNS

The elements of foot patterns are metrical positions and boundaries, which are derived from the syllables and boundaries of words. The *primary arsis*, represented by a capital *S*, is a metrical position derived from a syllable with primary stress. A lower-case *s* represents the *secondary arsis*, derived from a syllable with secondary stress. S and s positions are derived only from the unmarked type of Germanic stressed syllable, which is long. Ordinarily, an arsis will be filled by a single syllable (the unmarked case in poetic metre as in metrical phonology). Like the strong metrical position of Dresher and Lahiri's Germanic foot, however, the primary arsis will sometimes be occupied by a resolvable sequence (the marked case). This happens most frequently when the resolvable sequence bears primary stress, the degree of stress most strongly associated with length. Stress and length are less strongly associated on subordinate s positions and in resolvable sequences that have undergone linguistic subordination. As the degree of subordination increases, the bias towards an unmarked, one-to-one assignment of syllables to metrical positions takes precedence over considerations of length, and the short stressed syllable may stand unresolved on an arsis of its own. A *weak position*, represented by a lower-case *x*, is derived from a syllable with weak or zero stress. Weak positions can represent unstressed syllables of stressed words, as for example in the foot pattern Sx, which corresponds to words like *bróðir* 'brother'. Early Germanic metres also employ feet corresponding to unstressed words. The x foot is derived from words like ON *oc* 'and'. The xx foot is derived from words like *yfir* 'over'. As we have observed, unstressed syllables are characteristically short rather than long. Because a strong expectation of length is required to overcome the initial bias towards one-to-one correspondence between syllables and metrical positions, adjacent unstressed syllables cannot undergo resolution.[24] In its use of distinct x positions, word-foot notation departs from the five-types system, which assigns adjacent weak syllables to an undifferentiated metrical position called the *Senkung*, translated into English as *thesis* or *dip*.[25]

---

[24] Resolution or *Auflösung* is distinct from *elision* of adjacent unstressed vowels (see *OEM*, §1.8). Adjacent weak syllables not eligible for elision are sometimes assigned to one weak metrical position in skaldic poetry by *Verschleifung*, but this cannot be assumed for Eddic metres (see Kuhn, *Dróttkvætt*, p. 41).

[25] See *AGM*, §10.1.

Table 2.1 *Old Norse foot patterns*

Feet	Corresponding words
x	*oc* 'and'
	um (filler word)
S	*kné* 'knee'
xx	*yfir* 'over', prep.
Sx	*dróttinn* 'lord'
Ss	*miðgarðr* 'middle earth'
xxx	*ertattu* 'you are not'
Sxx	*jafnaði* 'he trimmed'
	vantattu 'you did not hinder'
Ssx	*heilræði* 'wholesome counsel'
Sxs	*hveitiakr* 'wheat field'
	bekkjunautr 'bench companion'

A LIST OF FOOT PATTERNS

The lexical inventory of Old Norse yields the inventory of foot patterns shown in table 2.1. The Norse lexical inventory differs in certain important respects from the corresponding Old English inventory.[26] The *Beowulf* poet employs prefixes as very light feet in some verses, but related Old Norse verses have filler words instead. Characteristic Norse forms with enclitics include xxx words and Sxx words with no Old English equivalents.[27] Since

[26] *OEM*, §1.4.

[27] Although they have long medial syllables, forms like *vantattu* clearly have the value Sxx in verses like *vantattu / vígi* (HH II 28/5), which cannot be Ssx/Sx, a forbidden pattern in fornyrðislag as in Old English poetry. In *Beowulf*, trisyllabic simplexes with long medial syllables like *murnende* must normally be interpreted as Ssx rather than Sxx, since a number of verses like *murnende / mōd* (50a) would otherwise constitute a forbidden pattern Sxx/S. Because the Sxx/S pattern is employed in fornyrðislag, there is no metrical test of this kind for light stress on the long medial syllable *-at-* in forms like *vantattu*. It seems likely, however, that stress was assigned to long medial syllables in simplexes only, and that words like *vantattu* were derived at another level of the phonology. On this analysis, the enclitics *-at-* and *-tu* would have the synchronic status of secondary rather than primary affixes or inflections, as suggested above, p. 17. In a systematic treatment, which I cannot undertake here, it would be desirable to account for the fact that long medial syllables occasionally count as unstressed in *Beowulf* (*OEM*, §3.4).

Old Norse lost most infixes along with prefixes, it eliminated most Sxs compounds comparable to OE *handgeweorc* 'handiwork', with infixed *-ge-*. ON *bekkjunautr* is one of very few compounds with infixed *-u-*, a reduced form of prefixal *um*.[28] There are no Norse Sxxs compounds analogous to OE *sibbe-ge-driht* 'kindred band'. Norse words with short stressed syllables will occupy one or another of the foot patterns listed above, depending on whether resolution occurs.[29]

WORD GROUPS WITHIN THE FOOT

A story consisting entirely of two-word phrases would be impossibly difficult to compose. In Eddic verse, as in *Beowulf*, the foot sometimes contains a word group that mimics the structure of an individual word. One of the most important challenges facing the audience was to see the analogy between such a word group and the type of larger word for which it substituted. Consider the following two verses:

(1)	snýz / iormungandr[30]	(*Vsp* 50/3)
(2)	gengr / Óðins sonr[31]	(*Vsp* 56/3)

In word-foot notation, the slash represents the boundary between the two feet of the verse. Example (1) is a two-word realization of the pattern x/ Sxs, with a weakly stressed, non-alliterating verb followed by an Sxs compound. Example (2) has the same syntax, but the noun phrase *Óðins sonr* substitutes for an Sxs compound in the second foot. It must have been easy to associate this particular phrase with a corresponding compound word. Many proper nouns in Old Norse consist of the father's name in the genitive case followed by a compounded form of *sonr* (e.g. *Haraldsson, Sigurðarson*).

---

[28] See Kuhn, *Füllwort*, p. 92.

[29] My reasons for representing *jafnaði* as Sxx rather than Ssx will be given below (pp. 114–16). Large compounds excluded from the list are discussed in ch. 3. Spellings in the list follow the usual conventions for Norse words mentioned in linguistic analysis, but citations of Eddic verse will adhere more closely to the style of the manuscript. The initial *j-* of *jafnaði*, for example, is printed as *i-* in Neckel–Kuhn.

[30] 'The great wand (i.e., the Midgard Serpent) coiled ...'

[31] 'Óðinn's son goes ...'

LABELLING MISMATCHES

In the simplest type of foot, syllables with primary stress occupy all S positions, syllables with secondary stress occupy all s positions, and syllables with zero stress occupy all x positions. Syllables do not always match metrical positions in a foot that contains a word group, however.[32] In *Beowulf*, mismatches between syllables and labelled metrical positions stay within limits imposed by the following detail rules:

R1a   A syllable with primary stress normally occupies an S position. When such a syllable occupies an s position, the S position of the same foot normally contains an alliterating syllable.

R1b   A syllable with zero stress must occupy an x position unless it shares an arsis with the short stressed syllable of a resolved sequence. Adjacent unstressed vowels may share a single x position by elision.

R1c   A syllable with secondary stress may occupy an s position or an S position.

The alliterative constraint mentioned in R1a operates as a categorical rule in *Beowulf*, but applies less strictly in native Eddic fornyrðislag. Rule R1c applies to the secondary constituents of compounds and also to words with an equivalent phrasal stress, primarily clause-final finite verbs and clause-final function words.[33] Syllables with reduced or unstable secondary stress usually occupy s positions, but are not categorically restricted by R1a–c, and sometimes occupy x positions.[34]

BRACKETING MISMATCHES

Kiparsky's analyses of modern verse forms represent the boundaries of poetic feet as analogous to the boundaries of linguistic constituents,

---

[32] Note the distinction between the type of syllable from which a given metrical position is derived and the syllable occupying that position in a given verse. Since the s position is derived from a syllable of secondary stress, for example, it is normally occupied by such a syllable. Occupation of an s position by a syllable with primary stress constitutes a mismatch and adds to metrical complexity.

[33] For detailed discussion of R1a and R1c in Norse metrical practice, see below, ch. 7.

[34] See *OEM*, §§9.1–9.4.

notably words.[35] Such boundaries are often notated by brackets.[36] When a foot boundary in the verse pattern does not coincide with a word boundary in the linguistic material, a *bracketing mismatch* occurs. Such mismatches are allowed rather freely in familiar metres with a single foot pattern and a single verse pattern.[37] In the metres that concern us here, however, the location of foot boundaries is much more difficult to deduce from the stress contour of the verse alone, and bracketing mismatches are likely to contravene the fundamental principle P2, which requires feet to be readily identifiable.

Like the *Beowulf* poet, Old Norse poets adhere to an especially strict set of *bracketing rules*:

R2a Every foot boundary must coincide with a word boundary. Note: the internal boundaries of compounded forms count as word boundaries for the purposes of this rule.

R2b In verses with three or more stressed words, assignment of stressed words to feet must respect syntactic constituency. Note: compounds count as two words for the purposes of this rule.

The treatment of compounds in R2 follows from provision D1c in the definition of 'word', which allows a compound to count as two words. Rule R2a allows for use of large compounds as complete two-foot verses. Rule R2b will not allow the foot boundary to fall within a compound when the verse contains another stressed word, however.

Three-word verses of the form S/Sxs pose special problems for intuitive scansion. According to P2, foot patterns corresponding to unusual word patterns add to the complexity of verses in which they appear. Even in Old English, Sxs compounds have a rather low frequency, and such compounds are still rarer in Old Norse due to syncopation and loss of infixes. Confronted with a three-word realization of S/Sxs, the audience might well be tempted to group the words in a pattern Ssx/S (Sievers type E), with a first foot corresponding to the more common type of trisyllabic compound. The labelling and bracketing rules make it possible to

---

[35] See 'Rhythmic Structure' and previous articles by Kiparsky in its list of works cited.

[36] See, for example, Chomsky and Halle, *Sound Pattern*. Kiparsky sometimes employs a notation in which foot brackets are replaced by branching foot nodes, but I reserve this style for patterns of compound stress and alliteration (discussed in ch. 6).

[37] 'Rhythmic Structure', pp. 201–11.

interpret such verses in a straightforward way, however. Consider the following S/Sxs variants:

(3) Haraldr / hilditǫnn[38]   (*Hdl* 28/1)
(4) óc / Óðins sonr[39]   (*Þrk* 21/7)
(5) brúðr / orð um qvað[40]   (*Grt* 24/2)

No problem arises in example (3), a direct expression of the underlying two-word pattern. In (4), the foot boundary falls at the major syntactic break, between predicate and subject, as required by bracketing rule R2b. Although this verse has a fully stressed word on its s position (a significant labelling mismatch), the leftward boundary of its second foot is clearly marked by an alliterating syllable, as required by rule R1a. Such alliteration gives metrical prominence to the first word in the foot, indicating that the second word occupies a less prominent arsis. Metrical subordination of non-alliterating words is of course expected in a metrical system with a fundamental principle like P3, which links the alliterative patterns of the verse and line to linguistic subordination in compounds. In (5), the foot boundary falls between subject and predicate. The s position of the second foot is occupied by a finite verb, which undergoes subordination within its phrase, as in Modern German.[41] Because both stress and syntax indicate the subordinate status of the verse-final word, the poet does not need a second alliterating syllable in (5).

LIGHT FEET

In Norse poetry, the x foot appears most often in verses classified by Sievers as type C:

(6) né / upphiminn[42]   (*Vsp* 3/6)
    [x/Ssx]
(7) oc / tól gorðo[43]   (*Vsp* 7/8)
    [x/Ssx]

---

[38] 'Harald War-tooth ...' The first word in this verse occupies a single S position by resolution.

[39] 'Óðinn's son drove ...' The S/Sxs scansion presupposes, with Sievers and Kuhn, that an alliterating main verb always occupies an arsis, though some metrists would disagree. I take up this issue in ch. 9.

[40] 'the woman uttered words ...'   [41] See Kiparsky, 'Akzent'; *OEM*, §8.2.

[42] 'nor heaven above ...'   [43] 'and they made tools'.

Two-word verses like (6) have an especially high frequency in the Old Norse corpus, lending support to the x/Ssx analysis.[44] Sievers's analysis of type C as an iamb followed by a trochee, on the other hand, seems particularly inappropriate for Eddic metre, since it has no two-word manifestations. In (7), the word group *tól gorðo* conforms well to the Ssx foot pattern. As in example (5), the root syllable of the finite verb has a subordinate phrasal stress that provides a good match for an s position.

A light x foot also appears in the type B pattern x/Sxs. The *Beowulf* poet obtains many Sxs words for the second foot of type B by coining poetic compounds, but this technique is not employed systematically in fornyrðislag, and the relative scarcity of Sxs compounds in Old Norse further restricts realization of the Sxs foot as a single word. The practice of skaldic poets makes it clear, however, that the Sxs compound was still perceived as the ideal occupant of the Sxs foot. It is well known that most a-verses in dróttkvætt metre consist of an embedded fornyrðislag verse followed by a trochaic word. Kuhn classifies such a-verses according to the Sievers type of the embedded verse. Consider the following examples in which the fornyrðislag segments preceding the double slash correspond to type B verses:

(8) lǫtum / kenni-Val // kanna[45]   (F39/3)[46]
     [xx/Sxs//Sx]

(9) við / góma sker // glymja[47]   (F11/3)
     [x/Sxs//Sx]

Kuhn states that the most characteristic realization of the type B segment is as in (8), with an unstressed function word followed by an Sxs compound.[48] In (9), the Sxs foot of the verse is occupied by the genitive phrase *góma sker*. Kuhn analyses a phrase employed in this way as a word group that corresponds to a *Nominalkompositum* (a compound with nominal or adjectival constituents).[49] This is exactly the correspondence posited in the word-foot analysis of type B, which consists of a function

---

[44] There are about 100 of these in *Beowulf* and over 200 in the smaller Norse corpus.

[45] 'Let us cause the adventurous horse (i.e., the ship) to explore . . .'

[46] For the reader's convenience, I supply examples from Frank, *Old Norse Court Poetry*, which provides full glossing and commentary. The notation 'F39/3' indicates line 3 of Frank's stanza 39.

[47] 'to resound against the skerries of the gums (i.e., the teeth) . . .'

[48] *Dróttkvætt*, p. 141.   [49] Ibid.

word and a compound in the simplest case. Dróttkvætt is a notoriously strict metre, imposing constraints on deviation from underlying metrical patterns much more narrow than those of fornyrðislag. The skalds give us valuable information about underlying patterns when they incorporate fornyrðislag verses as subconstituents. The technique of poetic compounding, though little used in Eddic poetry, is extremely productive in dróttkvætt. Many skaldic neologisms are Sxs compounds that fill the complex Sxs foot in the most desirable way. Although type B verses had become more difficult to associate with underlying two-word patterns, they clearly remained viable.

The preferred realization of a type C segment in skaldic verse corresponds to two-word Eddic verses like example (6), with a function word followed by an Ssx compound. Evidence is even clearer for this pattern, no doubt because compounds that filled the Ssx foot were ready to hand and required no special neologistic efforts. According to Kuhn, variants with a word group in the Ssx segment occur so rarely that they might have been regarded as lapses.[50]

EXTRAMETRICAL WORDS

Sievers assigns syllables with zero stress to an undifferentiated thesis, which may contain two or more such syllables. Within the theory proposed here, on the other hand, each unstressed syllable normally occupies its own distinct x position. The only exceptions are for cases of elision or resolution sanctioned by labelling rule R1b, which allows two syllables to occupy one metrical position under special conditions. If these special conditions do not obtain, an unstressed syllable of a stressed word must occupy an x position in the metrical pattern proper. Unstressed function words, however, may occupy extrametrical x positions as undefined linguistic material, in accord with the definition of 'word' (provision D1d). For our comparative purposes, the following extrametricality rule will suffice:

---

[50] Ibid., p. 142. An example of skaldic type C with an Ssx word group is *Heyr / Míms vinar // mína* (F11/1), which appears in the same stanza as example (9), the complex variant of skaldic type B with an Sxs word group. Tolerance for word groups within the foot evidently varied from one skald to another. Kuhn's paradigmatic form of skaldic type C is exemplified by *at / forsnjallir // fellu* (F7/5).

25

R3 Unstressed words may appear before either foot (as consistent with P2).

The parenthesized phrase in R3 is a reminder that feet must be readily identifiable. As with other deviations from the norm, employment of extrametrical syllables must not make it impossibly difficult to recover the underlying two-word pattern of the verse. Extrametrical words clearly stand before rather than after an adjacent foot, since they often appear verse-initially and never appear verse-finally.[51]

The following example illustrates employment of an extrametrical word in verse-medial position:

(10) Heiði / (hana) héto[52]   (*Vsp* 22/1)
      [Sx/(xx)Sx]

Here the inflectional -*i*, as part of the stressed word *Heiði*, occupies an x position in the first foot. The unstressed pronoun *hana* stands outside the foot, however. No Sxxx foot pattern can exist in Eddic metres because no Old Norse words have this pattern. With *hana* excluded, the verse has the common type A1 pattern Sx/(xx)Sx, where the parentheses enclose extrametrical positions before the second foot (note that parentheses are also used to enclose the extrametrical word in the marked-up citation of the corresponding verse above). The parenthesized material is placed after the slash to indicate that it stands before the second foot of example (10) rather than after the first foot.

As we have observed, the forceful primary stress of Old Norse had a strongly subordinating effect on unstressed function words, reducing prefixes to root onsets and enclitic forms to secondary affixes or inflections. Metrical subordination of comparable strength would be expected to restrict employment of extrametrical constituents in fornyrðislag. If Norse linguistic stress promoted incorporation of clitics into words like *vildo* and *vantattu*, Eddic metrical stress should promote incorporation of x positions into feet. The terseness of the Eddic form is in fact one of its most conspicuous stylistic features.[53] Strings of function words employed by the *Beowulf* poet are significantly longer, on average, than those employed by the Norse poets.[54] As we shall see in ch. 4, Eddic poets

---

[51] Any extrametrical words in the middle of the line will obey constraints on the b-verse. See *OEM*, §2.2.

[52] 'They called her Heiði ...'   [53] *DGV*, p. 41.   [54] See *AGM*, §§43 and 82.

The foot

Table 2.2 *Old Norse verse patterns*

Pattern	Sievers type	Example	
x/Sxx	C	oc / fnásaði[55]	(*Þrk* 13/2)
x/Ssx	C	oc / morðvarga[56]	(*Vsp* 39/4)
x/Sxs	B	þótt / óscabyrr[57]	(*HH II* 32/3)
xx/Sx	A3	verða / flestir[58]	(*Hdl* 49/3)
xx/Ss	A3	þeir er / miðgarð[59]	(*Vsp* 4/3)
xx/Sxx	C	verða / ǫflgari[60]	(*HH II* 51/5)
xx/Ssx	C	mundo / einheriar[61]	(*HH* 38/5)
xx/Sxs	B	Biðiom / Heriafǫðr[62]	(*Hdl* 2/1)
xxx/S	none	Þá qvað þat / Þórr[63]	(*Þrk* 17/1)
xxx/Sx	A3	Ertattu / vǫlva[64]	(*Bdr* 13/5)
xxx/Ss	A3	Kiósattu / Hiorvarð[65]	(*HHv* 3/1)
S/Sxx	Da	mǫn / iafnaði[66]	(*Þrk* 6/6)
S/Ssx	Da	briótr / berg-Dana[67]	(*Hym* 17/7)
S/Sxs	Db	Haraldr / hilditǫnn[68]	(*Hdl* 28/1)
Sx/S	none	krása / beztr[69]	(*Rþ* 4/10)
Sx/Sx	A1	tangir / scópo[70]	(*Vsp* 7/7)
Sx/Ss	A2	Sótti / Sigrún[71]	(*HH II* 14/1)
Sx/Sxx	Dax	bíta / hvassara[72]	(*Þrk* 25/4)
Sx/Ssx	Dax	fello / eitrdropar[73]	(*Vsp* 38/5)
Ss/Sx	A2	harðráðr / Hymir[74]	(*Hym* 10/3)
Ss/Ss	A2	vindǫld, / vargǫld[75]	(*Vsp* 45/9)
Sxx/S	none	kǫlloðo / Karl[76]	(*Rþ* 21/3)
Sxx/Sx	A1	vantattu / vígi[77]	(*HH II* 28/5)
Sxx/Ss	A2	svort verða / sólscin[78]	(*Vsp* 41/5)
Ssx/S	E	gullhyrndar / kýr[79]	(*HHv* 4/3)

[55] 'and she snorted ...' [56] 'and murderous wretches ...'
[57] 'though the wind (follows) ...' Parenthesized elements will be supplied occasionally from neighbouring verses to make the translations comprehensible.
[58] 'most of them are destined ...' [59] 'those who (made) the earth ...'
[60] 'they become stronger ...' [61] 'Óðinn's host would have (fought) ...'
[62] 'Let us ask Óðinn ...' [63] 'Then Þórr said the following ...'
[64] 'You are not a sybil ...' [65] 'Do not choose Hiorvarð ...'
[66] 'he trimmed (horses') manes'. [67] 'destroyer of giants ...'
[68] 'Harald War-tooth ...' [69] 'best of delicate foods ...'
[70] 'they made smith's tongs ...' [71] 'Sigrún sought ...'
[72] 'eat more voraciously'. [73] 'poison drops fell ...' [74] 'cruel Hymir ...'
[75] 'an age of storm, a wolf-age ...' [76] 'they named him Karl ...'
[77] 'you could not stop the battle ...' [78] 'the sun's light will be dimmed ...'
[79] 'gold-horned cattle ...'

27

eliminated an entire category of extrametrical syllables, the anacruses, at the earliest opportunity.

A LIST OF ATTESTED FOOT PAIRINGS

Table 2.2 provides a simple example for each reliably attested verse pattern in our Old Norse corpus. Patterns are arranged according to length (number of metrical positions) and weight (number of S and s positions), beginning with those in which the first foot is relatively light and short. The familiar Sievers type is provided for each pattern routinely employed by Old English as well as Old Norse poets. The notation 'none' indicates that the pattern falls outside the five-types system and is not reliably attested in *Beowulf*. Not included in the table are some extremely rare short patterns (discussed in ch. 3) that may have been acceptable only in *Rígsþula* and *Hyndlolióð*.

3

The verse

The *Beowulf* poet had to maintain the sense of a two-word verse norm while employing extrametrical words before the foot and word groups within the foot. This task was particularly challenging because verse patterns were so numerous and because they occurred at unpredictable intervals.[1] With no advance knowledge of the poet's metrical intentions, the audience had to recover the underlying two-word pattern in each case from the linguistic material of the verse. Old English poets were willing to limit the frequency of complex variants, and they did exclude some verse patterns from the metrical system altogether (e.g. Sxs/S, Ssx/Sx, Sxx/S). Such constraints were imposed only when there was a serious threat to metrical coherence, however. The poets seem to have exploited every viable two-word pattern available to them.

Linguistic developments could affect the way in which metrical variety was reconciled with a clear two-foot structure. If changes in Old Norse made a given pattern more difficult to recover from linguistic material, we would expect that pattern to be used less often or eliminated. If linguistic obstacles to scansion of a given pattern disappeared from Old Norse, on the other hand, we would expect that pattern to be exploited for metrical variety. Old Norse poets did employ verse patterns not found in *Beowulf*, and they did minimize or abandon use of certain patterns attested in Old English poems. Within the word-foot framework, these differences between the two traditions can be seen as shrewd artistic responses to divergent linguistic histories.

---

[1] See R. Lehmann, 'Broken Cadences'.

SOME IMPOSSIBLE VERSE PATTERNS

Employment of proclitics in verse-final position is blocked by a universal principle of syntactic integrity:

U1 When identification of verse boundaries is problematic, verses corresponding to natural syntactic units are preferred.

This principle applies quite strictly to Germanic metres, with their problematic variety of foot patterns and verse patterns. Any proclitic after the last stressed word of a verse belongs to the following verse, and will obey all rules applying to that verse. A Norse verse can end with an enclitic, but this counts as part of the stressed word to which it is attached.[2] If an enclitic occupied an x foot in verse-final position, the verse-medial foot boundary would fail to coincide with a word boundary, in violation of bracketing rule R2a. Because U1 excludes light feet from final position independently, we do not need additional rules to block reversed type B and C patterns such as Sxs/x and Ssx/x.[3]

Skaldic practice shows that reversed B and C patterns do arise when proclitics can occupy an x foot in second position:

(1) Miklagarðs / fyr // barði[4]   (F41/6)
     {Sxs/x//Sx}
(2) harðmúlaðr / es // Skúli[5]   (F29/4)
     {Ssx/x//Sx}

The fornyrðislag segment to the left of the double slash in (1) consists of an Sxs compound followed by a preposition. If this segment appeared as a complete verse, *fyr* would violate the requirement of syntactic integrity; but in dróttkvætt, a preposition in the second foot may be proclitic to the trochaic word in the third foot. Kuhn associates the fornyrðislag segment in examples like (1) with type A2 (Sx/Ss), but this seems quite unnatural.[6] Prepositions are normally unstressed when they appear immediately before the governed noun, and would not be expected to occupy s positions. It seems most plausible to scan (1) as Sxs/x//Sx, with the fornyrðislag segment derived by reversal of the type B pattern x/Sxs.

---

[2] See above, p. 17.
[3] A general discussion of reversal will be provided later in this chapter.
[4] '(The roofs) of Constantinople before the prow ... '
[5] '(Duke) Skúli is hard-mouthed (i.e., callous) ... '   [6] *Dróttkvætt*, §59.

Example (2) seems to scan most plausibly as Ssx/x//Sx, with the fornyrðislag segment derived by reversal of the type C pattern x/Ssx. Although Kuhn associates the fornyrðislag segment with type E in examples like (2), assigning the function word to a primary arsis, he observes that such segments are reversals of infelicitous type C segments.[7] Analysis of the fornyrðislag segment as reversed type C is thus supported by stylistic evidence. I know of no independent linguistic evidence that would justify stressing *es* in (2).

OVERLAP, HYPERMETRICAL PATTERNS, AND SHORT PATTERNS

In Old English poetry, the verse pattern Sxx/S is eliminated by an overlap constraint, which I formulate as a universal principle:

U2 Avoid feet that resemble verses and verses that resemble feet.

Whenever a poetic audience is required to count the number of feet per verse, violation of U2 will obviously be perceived as a faltering of the metre. Consider the following, for example:

$$(3) \quad *\text{fundode} / \text{secg}^8 \qquad\qquad (cf.\ Beo\ 1137b)$$
$$[*\text{Sxx/S}]$$
$$(4) \quad \text{wæs him} / \text{Bēowulfes sīð}^9 \qquad\qquad (Beo\ 501b)$$
$$[\text{xx/Sxxs}]$$

If the *Beowulf* poet employed verses like (3), with the pattern Sxx/S, many long type B verses would look like unmetrical structures of three feet. Verse (4), for example, might then be interpreted as *xx/Sxx/S. Because verses like (3) do not occur, however, the audience has no precedent for a three-foot analysis of verses with a second foot of the form Sxxs.[10] In general, verse patterns are excluded from the metrical system if they would look too much like foot patterns that the poet chooses to employ. Complex variants of acceptable verse patterns may also be excluded if they provide false precedents for analysis of more highly valued variants.

---

[7] *Dróttkvætt*, §62.   [8] 'the man was eager to go ... '
[9] 'to him Beowulf's journey was ... '
[10] The syntactically problematic *Beo* 6a is emended in Klaeber, and I assume that it is due to scribal error.

Although it has a relatively low frequency, the verse pattern Sxx/S occurs too often in our Eddic corpus to ignore.[11] Consider the following:

(5)	kǫlloðo / Karl[12]	(*Rþ* 21/3)
	[Sxx/S]	
(6)	Látumat / okkr[13]	(*Wk Ang* 29a)
	[Sxx/S]	
(7)	Freyio at / qvæn[14]	(*Þrk* 8/8)
	[Sxx/S]	
(8)	né / niðia in heldr[15]	(*HH* 12/3)
(9)	sem / biorg eða brim[16]	(*HH* 28/5)
(10)	um / lǫnd oc um lǫg[17]	(*Hdl* 24/7)

The paradigmatic example (5) has a trisyllabic finite verb in the first foot. The first foot in (6) is occupied by the special Norse type of Sxx word, a finite verb with incorporated enclitics.[18] Verse (7) represents the variant of Sxx/S that has a word group in the first foot. Within the word-foot framework, the appearance of Norse Sxx/S verses follows predictably from elimination of the Sxxs foot, which no longer corresponds to a word. Norse poets can employ an Sxx/S verse type because they have no need to be concerned about precedents for interpretation of long type B variants. The five putative examples of long type B in our fornyrðislag corpus seem quite doubtful. Verse (8) reduces to x/Sxs, since R1b allows the adjacent unstressed vowels of *niðia* and *in* to occupy a single x position. In (9), a scribe probably substituted bisyllabic *eða* for the earlier monosyllabic form *eðr*. In (10) and two similar examples, a scribe may have reintroduced a preposition that the poet felt free to omit.[19] It seems reasonable to conclude that the Sxxs foot had been eliminated from this system.

[11] With the examples cited below cf. *Vsp* 20/3, 29/2; *Hym* 3/4, 10/5, 34/4; *Þrk* 11/8 (= 8/8), 22/6 (= 8/8), 18/3; *HH* 2/1, 33/2, 50/2; *HHv* 33/1, 33/12, 42/1; *HH II* 32/1, 32/5, 33/1, 36/1, 36/3, 50/1; *Rþ* 4/8 (repeated once), 6/1 (repeated twice), 26/4, 27/1; *Hdl* 14/1, 20/5; and *Grt* 7/3. Since verses of this sort are repeated in several poems, their authenticity is well established. For discussion of putative examples with weakly stressed finite main verbs, see below, p. 134.

[12] 'they named him Karl . . . '   [13] 'Let us not allow (corpses to frighten) us . . . '
[14] 'Freyia as a wife.'   [15] 'nor kinsmen more quickly (get wergild) . . . '
[16] 'as if the cliffs or the sea (were breaking) . . . '   [17] 'by land and by sea . . . '
[18] Verses like (6) do not happen to occur in the corpus proper. This example is supplied from *The Waking of Angantýr*, as printed in Gordon–Taylor, p. 143, where the text is set out in the long-line format employed by editors of Old English poems.
[19] The other two putative examples of an Sxxs foot are *sá hon vítt oc um vítt* (*Vsp* 29/5) and

The *Beowulf* poet cannot employ an xxx foot because no Old English function words have this pattern. In Old Norse, however, xxx function words like *ertattu* arise from word groups through enclisis, and a new xxx foot is licensed:

(11) Ertattu / vǫlva[20]   (*Bdr* 13/5)
[xxx/Sx]

(12) Þá qvað þat / Þórr[21]   (*Þrk* 17/1)
[xxx/S]

In (11), the xxx foot is realized in the simplest possible way, with an xxx word. In (12), the xxx foot is realized as a word group. If an xx foot replaced the xxx foot in (11), an acceptable type A3 pattern would result. The xxx foot seems indispensable in (12), however, since the pattern xx/S is otherwise avoided.[22]

The overlap constraint (U2) represents an intuitive rejection of verses that lack a clear two-foot structure. U2 is satisfied whenever the poet finds a way to distinguish feet from verses. If U2 is a poetic universal, we would expect it to apply in full generality, and this expectation is confirmed by what may look at first like outright violations. The *Beowulf* poet does not ordinarily employ feet of the form Sxsx, for example, since they would overlap high-frequency A1 verses of the form Sx/Sx. Old

of lopt oc um lǫg (*HH* 21/3). In the latter example, *of* and *um* are simply variant spellings of the same preposition. Both exceptions might be explained as scribal restoration of the second preposition, which could have been deleted by the poet. The *Heliand*, which makes extensive use of type B, provides a good example of the deleted preposition: *âno / uuîf endi kind* 2871a. Here deletion of the second *âno* reduces what would otherwise be an Sxxxs foot to Sxxs, which has lexical support in Old Saxon (see below, p. 140). The deleted element has evidently been reintroduced by a scribe in *Heliand* 4483a, *âno / uuîg endi âno uurôht*. Deletion of syntactically parallel function words was probably most common when conjoined items were felt to constitute a natural unit (wife and child, land and sea) or to be identical (war and strife). Since Old Norse long B verses are extremely rare if not forbidden, it would be implausible to posit a pattern x/Sxxxs for a single verse in our corpus, *oc kýs ec, þatz ec vil* (*HHv* 2/7). This may originally have been something like *oc / kýzk þatz vil*, with the first instance of the pronoun contracted and the second instance deleted.

[20] 'You are not a sybil ...'   [21] 'Then Þórr said the following ...'

[22] Like (11) are *HHv* 42/5; *Bdr* 13/5; *Grt* 8/1, 17/5 and 20/7. Like (12) are *Vsp* 33/1; *Þrk* 22/1, 25/1, 30/1; *HH* 16/5; *HH II* 11/1, 19/5, 33/5, 33/7, 48/9, 51/1; *Rþ* 26/3; *Hdl* 25/3; and *Grt* 15/1. Possible examples of xxx/Ss are *HHv* 3/1 and 10/1, but in both cases the Ss word is a proper name that might also be analysed as Sx.

English Sxsx compounds can count as two words (see D1c), and may appear as complete Sx/Sx verses. In hypermetrical clusters, however, the same type of compound constitutes the second foot of verses with the pattern Sx/Sxsx.[23] This is tolerable because the strategy of clustering isolates the Sxsx foot from the Sx/Sx verse, enabling the audience to shift its metrical expectations appropriately.[24]

Native Eddic fornyrðislag is a concise, light metre, with relatively few long or heavy verses. Poets who used this metre learned how to generalize the overlap constraint, but they employed small verses resembling normal feet rather than large feet resembling normal verses. We might refer to the short Norse verses as *hypometrical*, capturing their symmetric relationship to hypermetrical verses; but it seems less awkward simply to call them *short*, like Gordon. Some short patterns have doubtful status due to extremely low frequency, but one pattern in particular, Sx/S, occurs too often to ignore:

> (13) krása / beztr[25]   (*Rþ* 4/10)
>   [Sx/S]
>
> (14) Þræll oc / Þír[26]   (*Rþ* 11/7)
>   [Sx/S]

Example (13) is a two-word paradigm. In (14), a word group occupies the first foot. Gordon derives such short patterns from normal patterns in earlier verses.[27] 'After the syncope of unaccented vowels in the eighth century', he says, 'lines originally containing the minimum number of syllables were reduced below that minimum, and the reduced lines then came to be regarded as permissible variants and were imitated in later poems.' This type of reanalysis may account not only for the origin of short patterns but also for the loss of hypermetrical patterns, which probably did occur in prehistoric Norse poetry, since they are represented in cognate traditions. Overlap at both ends of the scale would have made

---

[23] A characteristic Sx/Sxsx verse is *Beo* 2996a, *mon on / middan-gearde* '(any) man on middle-earth'. Cf. the normal verse *middan- / geardes* 'of middle earth' (*Beo* 504b and 751b). A strikingly large proportion of Sxsx compounds appear as the main part of a hypermetrical verse rather than as a complete normal verse (*OEM*, §6.2). This is very much as expected, since compound words are in general most naturally interpreted as single feet. Once the danger of overlap is removed, a large compound is predicted to behave like any other compound.

[24] *OEM*, ch. 6.   [25] 'best of delicate foods ... '   [26] 'Þræll and Þír ... '

[27] Gordon–Taylor, §178.

it impossibly difficult to determine the number of feet in the verse. When small foot-like verses were introduced, large verse-like feet would have to be abandoned. The remaining problem is to explain the acceptability of the Sx/S pattern, however derived. Tradition alone might account for a few short verses as archaic survivals, but no pattern could be used systematically in a word-foot metre unless its two-foot structure was emphasized in some way.

Some poets in our fornyrðislag corpus may not have accepted the Sx/S pattern. No examples occur in *Grottasǫngr*. A single example in *Hymisqviða* (7/2) seems doubtful; and the three examples in the Helgi poems might also be questioned.[28] Only *Rígsþula* and *Hyndlolióð* make genuinely systematic use of Sx/S verses. If such verses created serious problems of metrical ambiguity, they would certainly do so in *Rígsþula*, which has twenty-five examples.[29] Here, if anywhere, employment of Sx/S verses would warrant interpretation of type B verses as unmetrical sequences of the form *x/Sx/S. The poet differentiates the Sx/S verse carefully from the Sxs foot of type B, however, by imposing unusually strict constraints on labelling mismatches:

(15)	Gecc / Rígr at þat[30]	(14/1)
	[x/Sxs]	
(16)	oc / hiorvi brá[31]	(37/8)
	[x/Sxs]	
(17)	oc / keyra plóg[32]	(22/8)
	[x/Sxs]	
(18)	mœtti / hann[33]	(39/5)
	[Sx/S]	

Examples (15) and (16) show the poet's characteristic handling of type B. These verses end in a function word or finite verb with a subordinate stress appropriate to a verse-final s position. More than half of the type B

---

[28] Manuscript A (Codex Arnamagnæanus 758, 4⁰) has *dag fráliga*, an ordinary type Da variant, rather than *dag þann fram* for *Hym* 7/2. *HHv* 7/7 and 43/2 would scan as Sxx/S if the pronouns were contracted. *HH II* 33/11 is emended from *hefðir eigi mat* to *hefðira mat* in two early editions. The emendation scans as Sxx/S rather than Sx/S. See Neckel–Kuhn, pp. 89 and 157.

[29] *Rþ* 4/2, 4/10, 7/4, 8/4, 10/6, 11/7, 11/8, 12/14, 16/2, 16/3, 16/10, 23/7, 27/3, 29/1, 31/2, 31/4, 34/5, 37/2, 37/3, 37/6, 39/5, 41/4, 41/7, 41/8 and 41/9.

[30] 'Rígr left then ...'   [31] 'and brandished the sword ...'
[32] 'and to plough'.   [33] 'he met ...'

verses in *Rígsþula* (12/22) end with the phrase *at þat*, and five of these are outright repetitions.[34] After the first such verse was analysed, the others would be easy to interpret. Only three other type B verses are like (17), which ends with a fully stressed noun.[35] The poet fills the Sx/S pattern quite differently. In twenty-four examples, there is a strongly stressed noun or adjective on the verse-final S position, as in (13) and (14). The only anomaly is (18), which ends with a function word, presenting the appearance of an Sxs foot rather than an Sx/S verse. The conspicuous effort to mitigate overlap in *Rígsþula* gives us a kind of insight into Germanic versecraft not available from a poet who stays well away from areas of potential ambiguity.

The author of *Hyndlolióð* employs the Sx/S pattern with similar care. In five examples, a strongly stressed noun or adjective fills the second foot.[36] Verse 29/3, the one putative example ending in a finite verb, is a site of editorial emendation, and the similar *Bdr* 11/5 is generally regarded as inauthentic.[37] Neckel and Kuhn record no emendations for the characteristic variety of Sx/S with a strongly stressed word occupying the S foot.

The priority of Sx/S among short patterns was observed long ago by Heusler.[38] This pattern has a straightforward explanation within our theoretical framework. As we have observed, syncopation and loss of infixes eliminated many Sxs compounds from Old Norse.[39] When it became more difficult to associate word groups with the marginal Sxs foot pattern, there would have been an increasing tendency to regard such groups as two-word expressions of an Sx/S verse pattern, especially when the last word had prominent stress.

SHORT VERSE PATTERNS OF RESTRICTED DISTRIBUTION

Some short patterns may have been acceptable only in *Rígsþula* and *Hyndlolióð*:

[34] *Rþ* 2/1 is repeated as 6/3, 20/3 and 33/7. *Rþ* 6/5 is repeated as 20/5 and 33/9. The other verses with *at þat* are *Rþ* 4/5, 9/1, 9/5, 14/1 and 38/1. The remaining type B verses are *Rþ* 24/3, 31/8, 37/4, 37/8, 39/4, 45/6, 47/2, 48/1 and 48/5.

[35] Cf. 24/3, 31/8 and 48/1.   [36] *Hdl* 6/8, 7/9, 17/3, 22/1 and 25/9.

[37] See Neckel–Kuhn, pp. 279 and 293. *Vsp* 31/8, the one putative Sx/S verse in the poem, is extremely problematic, since it consists of an Sxs compound. The remaining clear cases of Sx/S in our corpus have a fully stressed word on the S foot (*Þrk* 17/2 and 18/3; *Bdr* 2/2 and 13/4).

[38] *Versgeschichte*, §235.   [39] See above, p. 17, n.18, and p. 20.

(19)	Breiðr, / Bóndi[40] [S/Sx]	(*Rþ* 24/5)
(20)	sonr / húss[41] [S/S]	(*Rþ* 11/4)
(21)	oc / Hiordís[42] [x/Ss]	(*Hdl* 26/3)
(22)	Reið / Konr ungr[43] [x/Ss]	(*Rþ* 46/1)

Five examples like (19) appear in the two poems with the largest number of short variants.[44] These verses seem acceptable to the editors, but Neckel–Kuhn records emendations for four of six putative examples in other poems.[45] The high frequency of Ssx compounds gives high priority to the Ssx foot in fornyrðislag, repressing employment of the overlapping S/Sx verse pattern. Ss compounds are also most naturally interpreted as feet, and employment of S/S verses is accordingly repressed. The very short (20) is one of just two S/S verses in the corpus. Verse (21) is a two-word expression of the pattern x/Ss. Two other x/Ss variants like (22) occur in *Rígsþula*.[46]

Short patterns that raise doubts in fornyrðislag would not do so in ljóðaháttr, which capitalizes on stanzaic structure to facilitate scansion. The characteristic half-stanza in this metre is a set of three verses with gradually increasing syllabic count. As the first member of such a set, a short verse is isolated about as effectively as a hypermetrical Old English verse in a cluster.[47]

DEVIATION FROM THE NORM AND RELATIVE FREQUENCY

The most common type of Old Norse word has a trochaic pattern, with a long root syllable followed by an overt inflectional ending. This corre-

[40] 'Breiðr and Bóndi ...' [41] 'the son of the house ...' See *Rþ* 8/9.
[42] 'and Hiordís ...' [43] 'Young Konr rode ...'
[44] Cf. *Rþ* 8/7; *Hdl* 9/2, 10/2 and 29/7.
[45] Cf. *Vsp* 16/8; *HH* 21/5 and 25/1; *HH II* 3/7; *Bdr* 4/4 and 6/8.
[46] Cf. 28/2 and 43/1.
[47] The first ten stanzas of *Hávamál*, for example, contain seven short verses, each placed first in its half-stanza (2/1, 2/4, 3/1, 4/1, 5/1, 8/1 and 9/1). Snorri's paradigmatic stanza in *Háttatal* regularizes this arrangement, with the first verse of the half-stanza always short, the second always longer, and the third always longest. See Faulkes, *Háttatal*, p. 39; Russom, 'Eddic Meters'.

sponds to the unmarked or simplest form of the Germanic foot, represented by Dresher and Lahiri as the privileged pattern of word-level phonology.[48] In native Eddic fornyrðislag, Sx is accordingly the *standard foot*. In relation to this standard, a foot with one metrical position is *short* and a foot with three metrical positions is *long*. A foot with no S position is *light* in relation to the Sx standard. A foot with an S position and an s position is *heavy*. The *standard verse* iterates the standard foot to produce the pattern Sx/Sx, which has four metrical positions (Sievers type A1). A *short verse* has fewer than four metrical positions; a *long verse* has more than four. Due to elimination of Sxxs from the fornyrðislag system, no Norse foot has the length of a standard verse. In relation to the Sx/Sx standard, a verse with only one arsis is *ultra-light*. A verse with two S positions and an s position is *heavy*. The Ss/Ss pattern is *ultra-heavy*. I refer to verses with a light foot and a heavy foot as *balanced*.

In Old English poetry, a short foot always pairs with a long foot to produce a verse pattern with at least four metrical positions.[49] We must allow for short Old Norse patterns, however, at least in some poems. The following detail rules are presented in a generalized form applicable to native Eddic fornyrðislag as well as *Beowulf*:

R4a A short foot is normally balanced by a long foot and vice versa.
R4b A light foot is normally balanced by a heavy foot and vice versa.
R4c Only one foot may be long.

As we have seen, Norse poets impose especially strict constraints on labelling mismatches in verses that are abnormally short by the standard of R4a.

TYPE A

The standard pattern Sx/Sx has the highest frequency, comprising about 32 per cent of the verses in *Beowulf* and about 33 per cent of the verses in our Norse corpus. Of the Sx/Sx verses employed in *Beowulf*, about 45 per cent consist of two trochaic words, with no extrametrical syllables. The corresponding figure for the Norse corpus is 51 per cent. Obviously, both Old Norse and Old English poets returned with great frequency to the metrical centre. The two traditions also show similar frequencies for the

---

[48] See above, p. 16.   [49] *OEM*, §2.5, rule 13a.

38

remaining patterns classified as A1 or A2 by Sievers (Sxx/Sx, Ss/Sx, Sx/Ss, Ss/Ss, Sxx/Ss).[50] There is a significant contrast with respect to type A3. The pattern xx/Sx has a frequency of 5 per cent in *Beowulf*, but in the Norse corpus its frequency is doubled, rising to 10 per cent. The A3 subtype xx/Ss is not uncommon in fornyrðislag, with a frequency of about 2 per cent, whereas in *Beowulf* the figure is less than half of one per cent. Here fornyrðislag shows its well-known bias toward the lighter patterns.

TYPE B

As expected, weak support for the Sxs foot in the Norse lexical inventory has produced a sharp drop in the frequency of type B. In *Beowulf*, x/Sxs and xx/Sxs patterns have a combined frequency of 13 per cent, but about half that, 7 per cent, in the Norse corpus. In *Beowulf*, the long type B patterns x/Sxxs and xx/Sxxs have a combined frequency of 3 per cent, with about 170 instances; in fornyrðislag, complete lack of support for the Sxxs foot in the lexical inventory has reduced long B to a few doubtful examples like (9) and (10) above.

An independent estimate of complexity can be derived from the proportion of a-verses to b-verses, which is affected by a principle of closure:

U3 Minimize complexity toward the end of the line.

This seems quite clearly to be a poetic universal.[51] Because of U3, a verse pattern that becomes more complex due to language change will be more likely to appear in the first half of the line. In *Beowulf*, 28 per cent of the type B variants are a-verses (excluding variants with a second foot of the form Sxxs, which have no Eddic equivalents). In the Norse corpus, the figure jumps quite remarkably, to 75 per cent.

---

[50] The Ss/Sx pattern has a frequency of about 4 per cent in *Beowulf* and about 6 per cent in our Norse corpus. Sx/Ss: *Beowulf* 2 per cent, Norse corpus 1 per cent. Sxx/Sx: 1 per cent in both corpora. Sxx/Ss and Ss/Ss: less than 1 per cent in both corpora. In deriving these statistics, complex feet of the form xx and Sxx are posited only where a simpler scansion would result. Otherwise, the sequences xx and Sxx are analysed as relatively simple feet of the form x, S, or Sx accompanied by extrametrical unstressed words (see *OEM*, §5.5). Only a rough statistical overview of verse types will be provided in this chapter, with figures rounded to the nearest per cent in most cases. For more detailed treatment, see chs. 6 and 8.

[51] See Hayes, 'Grid-based Theory', p. 373; *OEM*, §5.3.

TYPE C

In *Beowulf*, the type C patterns x/Ssx and xx/Ssx have a combined frequency of 17 per cent. In the Norse corpus, their combined frequency rises to 23 per cent. The simplicity of the Ssx foot relative to the Sxs foot is particularly evident in the Norse corpus. The word-foot theory posits a distinct ultra-light type C pattern with a second foot of the form Sxx. In *Beowulf*, 72 per cent of the variants with this pattern are a-verses; in the Norse corpus, about 70 per cent.[52] Distribution of the more common x/Ssx and xx/Ssx patterns goes the other way. In *Beowulf*, about 46 per cent of these are a-verses; in the Norse corpus, only about 32 per cent. It seems clear that the patterns x/Sxx and xx/Sxx were distinguished from x/Ssx and xx/Ssx. Since the ultra-light patterns deviate from standard weight, they would naturally tend to appear more often in the first half of the line, the preferred site for complex verses (see U3).

TYPE D

Although they are less concerned than Old English poets about the substandard weight of verses with a light foot and a normal foot, Old Norse poets adhere more scrupulously to the 'vice versa' provision of R4b, which promotes employment of a light foot to offset the extra weight of a heavy foot. Recall that the decline in the frequency of type B (x/Sxs, xx/Sxs) is accompanied by a rise in the frequency of type C (x/Ssx, xx/Ssx). On this analogy, we might expect the frequency of S/Ssx verses to rise if there is a decline in the frequency of S/Sxs verses. The frequency of S/Sxs (type Db) does fall significantly. In *Beowulf*, this pattern occurs with a frequency of 2 per cent; in the Norse corpus, its frequency is no more than 1 per cent. The number of Norse Db verses genuinely comparable to those in *Beowulf* is very small. Most putative examples can be analysed as

---

[52] The Old English examples are *Beo* 96a, 115a, 144a, 480a, 536a, 630a, 1363a, 2177a, 2766a, 2933a, 2985a, 3159a, 3178a; 292b, 560b, 1819b, 2619b and 3103b. Putative additions to this list are 898a, 3042a, 1944a, 2253a and 379b. The Old Norse a-verses are *Þrk* 11/1; *HH* 23/7; *HHv* 5/1; *HH II* 4/5, 5/5, 5/7, 6/7, 22/7, 51/5; *Rþ* 45/5; *Hdl* 29/1, 50/7; and *Grt* 6/5. Old Norse b-verses: *Hym* 30/6; *Þrk* 1/2, 1/4, 10/2, 13/2; and *Grt* 9/4. With regard to *HH II* 5/5, 5/7 and 6/7, which have Sxx word groups, see below, pp. 134–5. A general discussion of the Norse Sxx foot is provided below on pp. 114–16.

Sxx/S or S/Sxx instead.[53] The frequency of S/Ssx (type Da) does not rise, however. In *Beowulf*, this pattern accounts for 6 per cent of total verses, but the figure actually falls slightly in the Norse corpus, to 5 per cent. The more severe restriction on the frequency of the Norse Sxs foot is accompanied by an independent restriction on heavy verses generally. The word-foot theory posits a distinct Da pattern S/Sxx with standard weight. As expected, this is immune to the Norse bias against heavy verses, holding at slightly more than 2 per cent in the Norse corpus, as compared with slightly less than 2 per cent in *Beowulf*.

TYPE E

A heavy foot usually follows the light foot of a verse with the normal number of stresses (see R4b). Heavy feet also stand second in type D patterns, which have restricted frequency due to their extra weight. Type E pattern Ssx/S is heavy, like type D, and the unexpected position of its compound foot adds additional complexity. I refer to patterns with a compound foot in first position as *reversed*.

About 7 per cent of total verses in *Beowulf* have the pattern Ssx/S. It is difficult to compute total figures for Norse type E due to uncertainty about the stress of medial finite verbs.[54] The relatively severe restrictions on this type show up clearly in the distribution of unambiguous two-word examples, however:

(23)   sincfāge / sel[55]   (*Beo* 167a)
(24)   gullhyrndar / kýr[56]   (*HHv* 4/3)

Two-word E verses like (23) account for about 5 per cent of total verses in *Beowulf*. Analogous examples like (24) account for only about 2 per cent of total verses in the fornyrðislag corpus, where Ssx compounds are more often combined with a light foot to form balanced type C variants. The increased complexity of Norse type E interacts with the principle of closure (U3). In *Beowulf*, verses with the structure of (23) appear in the second half of the line about two times out of three. Only half of the comparable Norse verses appear in this location. As with Norse type B, an

---

[53] See below, p. 134.   [54] See below, pp. 133–5.
[55] 'hall shining with treasure . . . '   [56] 'gold-horned cattle . . . '

41

increase in metrical complexity is accompanied by a decline in the frequency of b-verses relative to a-verses.[57]

The *Beowulf* poet always accompanies a short foot with a long foot, but as we have seen, some Norse poets employ a short pattern Sx/S. On the other hand, Norse poets less often disregard the 'vice versa' provision of R4a, which promotes employment of a short foot to offset the abnormal length of a foot with three metrical positions. About 2 per cent of the verses in *Beowulf* have the expanded Da pattern Sx/Ssx or Sx/Sxx, with a long foot accompanied by a standard foot rather than a short foot. In the Norse corpus, the figure falls to less than one-half of one per cent, with ten examples in all.[58] About thirty expanded Db verses of the form Sx/Sxs appear in *Beowulf*. To Norse poets, however, the special complexity of the Sxs foot seems to have been unacceptable in verses that were also complex with respect to length and weight.[59]

Both Old Norse and Old English poets adhered to the following constraints:

---

[57] The higher frequency of b-verses in type E, as compared with type Da, is due to constraints on alliteration. Any type E variant may be used with single alliteration in the b-verse, whereas many variants of type Da require double alliteration and are restricted to the a-verse for that reason alone (*OEM*, §8.2). Unlike type D variants, type E variants often end with finite verbs, which are especially appropriate on a line-final arsis (see below, p. 126). Assignment of type E to the b-verse is thus promoted by factors independent of metrical complexity. The comparative evidence allows us to see that type E does indeed respond to the principle of closure (U3), though this is not obvious from inspection of one tradition. Within each tradition, the complexity of type E can be deduced from especially strict constraints imposed on deviation from the two-word norm (*OEM*, §7.5.3).

[58] Examples of the pattern Sx/Ssx in the a-verse are *HH* 51/1, *Hdl* 46/1 and *Prk* 30/7. In the b-verse: *Prk* 21/4, *HH* 16/4, *Hdl* 13/5 and *Hdl* 32/2. *Prk* 25/4 and 25/6 have the Sx/Sxx pattern, and are long but not heavy. *Prk* 25/6, a b-verse, is unmetrical because it has double alliteration.

[59] Clear cases of Sx/Sxs in *Beowulf* are 358a, 400a, 421a, 625a, 726a, 938a, 1274a, 1312a, 1359a, 1447a, 1450a, 1452a, 1617a, 1627a, 1679a, 1729a, 1757a, 1837a, 1854a, 2044a, 2286a, 2422a, 2451a, 2478a, 2731a, 2964a, 3115a, 3123a; 1424b and 2941b. Uncertain cases are 402a, 2107a and 2687a. The only putative Norse example of Sx/Sxs is *HH* 20/1, *Uggi eigi þú*, but division before *eigi* would probably violate R2b, which requires the foot boundary to fall at the major syntactic break of a heavy verse. Perhaps *HH* 20/1 is a scribal trivialization of *Uggi þú eigi*, which would be an unremarkable A1 variant. Cf. *uggi ek eigi* (*The Waking of Angantýr* 111a), Gordon–Taylor, p. 146.

The verse

R5a Reversed heavy patterns may not contain a foot of the form Sxs or
Sxxs.

R5b Reversed heavy patterns may not exceed normative length.

Provision R5a rules out heavy patterns such as Sxs/S in which the
complexity of the Sxs foot pattern is aggravated by its placement in the
less usual location (see U4). Regulation of Sxxs is of course unnecessary in
fornyrðislag, which does not employ this foot pattern. Provision R5b
forbids use of patterns such as Ss/Sxx and Ss/Ssx. When a compound
occupies the first foot, the second foot must not have more than two
metrical positions. Note that R5a does not rule out reversal of the less
complex types B and C, which have the normal number of stresses. As we
have observed, this sort of reversal does occur in dróttkvætt, and its
absence in fornyrðislag can be attributed to the principle of syntactic
integrity (U1).

SUMMARY

Viewed in isolation, Old Norse poetry provides limited insight into
problems of overlap. Only in West Germanic poetry do we find such a
strict rule against verses that resemble feet. This rule provides a well-
defined context for analysis of Norse short verses, which obey strict
constraints on labelling that facilitate recovery of the underlying two-
word pattern. If we confined our attention to *Beowulf*, it would be harder
to study the gradations of deviance predicted by P2, which states that feet
corresponding to unusual words add to the complexity of verses in which
they appear. The usefulness of type B to the Old English poet as a site for
word groups with rising stress tends to mask the complexity of the Sxs
foot, which corresponds to a relatively unusual compound word pattern.
In *Beowulf*, this complexity has salient effects only when the verse is also
complex in other ways, as for example in the long, heavy pattern Sx/Sxs,
which is excluded from the second half of the line by the principle of
closure (U3), in contrast to the pattern Sx/Ssx.[60] Measuring the complexity of Sxs would be equally difficult if we confined our attention to
fornyrðislag, since the type B pattern is also useful to Norse poets and has
an elevated frequency at a lower level. What cannot be ignored is the

---

[60] *OEM*, §5.3.

43

sharply restricted employment of fornyrðislag type B relative to Old English type B. As predicted by P2, further marginalization of the Sxs word pattern in Old Norse increases the complexity of the corresponding foot pattern, constraining use of Sxs word groups and establishing a remarkably strong preference for placement of type B verses in the first half of the line. Elimination of the Sxxs word pattern results in abandonment of long type B, with its Sxxs foot pattern. These developments prepare the way for new verse patterns of the form Sx/S and Sxx/S.

4

Light feet and extrametrical words

Rule R3 allows unstressed function words, including prefixes, to appear before the foot as extrametrical constituents (see D1b and D1d). Such constituents add to the complexity of the verse, however, and their employment must not make it too difficult to recover the underlying two-word pattern at the speed of performance (see P2). Extrametricality is most problematic at the beginning of the verse, where a function word normally signals the presence of a light foot. If an extrametrical constituent in anacrusis is mistaken for a light foot, the first alliteration of the verse will be assumed to mark the beginning of the second foot, and the verse will appear to consist of three feet. If a light foot is mistaken for an anacrusis, on the other hand, the first alliteration will be assumed to mark the beginning of the first foot, and the verse will appear to consist of one foot. Verses most naturally analysed as one or three feet would impose a heavy analytical burden on the audience. Occasional variants of this kind might be scanned successfully on a second try, but a high frequency of such variants would obviously be intolerable. The *Beowulf* poet, who needed to employ some anacruses, facilitated intuitive scansion by imposing special constraints on light feet.[1] Linguistic change in Old Norse made anacrusis unnecessary, and the poets seem to have abandoned it at the earliest opportunity. Since constraints on light feet were no longer required in fornyrðislag, new possibilities of verse construction arose.

---

[1] Due to syntactic change in the natural language, Old Saxon poets had a significantly greater need to employ anacruses, and their efforts to control related problems of metrical ambiguity were not entirely successful, as we shall see in ch. 10. The consequent rise in average verse complexity was apparently intolerable to the audience, throwing the alliterative tradition into rapid decline (*DGV*, p. 50).

Beowulf *and Old Germanic metre*

ANACRUSIS AND LIGHT FEET

Germanic metres are somewhat unusual in employing light feet that correspond to unstressed words. Old Irish alliterative metre, which is similar in many respects, allows all stressed words, but only stressed words, to constitute feet.[2] Denial of foot status to unstressed words betrays a concern that an enumerated structural element of the verse should not be too inconspicuous, and Germanic poets share this concern to a significant extent. Although they use conjunctions and prepositions freely as light feet, they rarely employ closely bound proclitics such as prefixes, articles or preverbal negatives for that purpose. Such proclitics make relatively ineffective word feet because they have a rather weak identity as words, often losing their wordhood entirely when incorporated into neighbouring stressed words as secondary inflections or root onsets.

Articles seldom suffice to constitute a light foot. Prefixal elements occasionally constitute light feet in the relatively simple type C pattern, but hardly ever in the more complex type B. Consider the following:

(1)	in / konungborna[3]		(*HH II* 48/10)
(2)	se / scynscaþa[4]		(*Beo* 707a)
(3)	um / sacnaði[5]		(*Þrk* 1/4)
(4)	be- / lēan mihte[6]		(*Beo* 511b)

Verses like (1) and (2), with an isolated article as the first foot, have an extremely low frequency. I found only four other Norse verses like (1), three of them in the Helgi poems.[7] *Beowulf* contains only five other verses like (2).[8] Old Norse verses like (3), with an isolated filler word for a light foot, are about as rare as those like (1).[9] The *Beowulf* poet is somewhat more willing to use a prefixal element as a light foot, but does so primarily to obtain useful type C variants like (4) that consist of a prefixed

[2] Travis, *Celtic Versecraft*, pp. 1–14. [3] 'the royal one . . . .'
[4] 'the injurious demon . . . ' [5] '(filler word) he sought . . . '
[6] 'might dissuade . . . ' [7] Cf. *HH* 1/6, 55/6; *HHv* 32/4; and *Hdl* 19/7.
[8] Cf. *Beo* 416a, 1685a, 3122b (type C); 639a (type B); and 1105a (probably type C rather than type B).
[9] Cf. *Vsp* 32/6; *Þrk* 24/2, 32/4; and *Bdr* 7/2. The smallness of this sample is particularly striking because the percentage of two-word type C verses is very high in Eddic verse and because the filler word is more likely than any other unstressed constituent to appear on the x position of the Norse Sxs foot.

non-finite verb and its auxiliary. Variants of this kind are usually b-verses.[10]

Norse poets could remove verse-initial clitics quite freely. The prefix-like filler word was optional, and the pre-nominal definite article was optional as well. Preverbal negatives were replaced by enclitic negatives when a verse-initial verb had to be negated.[11] In Old English poetry, articles could be deleted, but there were no enclitic negatives, and prefixes could be dispensed with only in a limited number of cases.[12] When an Old English prefix or preverbal negative had to appear verse-initially, it was normally excluded from the verse pattern as an anacrusis.

The following examples illustrate special constraints imposed by the *Beowulf* poet to distinguish syllables in anacrusis from light feet:

(5)	(ofer-)wearp þā / wērigmōd[13]		(*Beo* 1543a)
	[(xx)Sx/Sxs]		
(6)	*ofer- / wearp bā		
(7)	*ofer / ȳðe[14]		(cf. *Beo* 46a)
(8)	ðē wē / ealle[15]		(*Beo* 941a)
	[xx/Sx]		
(9)	þǣr þā // gōdan / twēgen[16]		(*Beo* 1163b)
	[xx//Sx/Sx]		

Anacrusis allows for verse-initial placement of alliterating verbs preceded by negative particles or prefixes, and is seldom used for any other purpose

[10] Only eight clear cases of type B in *Beowulf* have an isolated prefix as the light foot: 34a, 620a, 1408a, 1696a, 1870a, 2345a, 2516a and 3156a. An additional putative example (emended) is 652a. There are sixty-five type C verses with this kind of foot. The other b-verses like (4), with verb-auxiliary structure, are *Beo* 106b, 117b, 220b, 308b, 355b, 414b, 562b, 571b, 648b, 738b, 780b, 804b, 910b, 961b, 990b, 1078b, 1140b, 1196b, 1277b, 1350b, 1462b, 1472b, 1496b, 1535b, 1561b, 1599b, 1628b, 1875b, 1911b, 1919b, 1928b, 1998b, 2090b, 2104b, 2145b, 2186b, 2397b, 2400b, 2588b, 2630b, 2707b, 2726b, 2770b, 2954b, 3147b and 3165b. Cf. the damaged 2218b. The remaining b-verses are *Beo* 288b, 304b, 526b, 922b, 997b, 1395b, 1412b, 1595b, 2497b, 2569b and 2740b. There are only seven comparable a-verses: *Beo* 139a, 424a, 659a, 1034a, 1073a, 1703a and 2766a. A prefix will do in a pinch as a light foot because its kinship with prepositions and adverbs is still recoverable in Old English (*OEM*, §1.1.1).

[11] Kuhn, *Füllwort*, p. 127.   [12] *OEM*, §10.3, example 107a.

[13] '(she) then unbalanced the weary one ...'   [14] 'over the waves ...'

[15] 'which we all ...'   [16] 'where the two noble ones (sat) ...'

in *Beowulf*.[17] Selective placement of verses within the line keeps metrical ambiguity to a minimum. Examples like (5), with prefixal anacrusis, normally appear in the a-verse, but as we have just observed, the b-verse is the normal location for variants like (4), which employ the prefix as a light foot. In all but a handful of cases, the audience will be able to make a correct guess about the metrical value of a verse-initial prefix without having to evaluate the following linguistic material. The poet avoids variants of type A3 that would resemble the first foot of a verse such as (1) with preceding anacrusis. There are no A3 verses in *Beowulf* like (6), and there is accordingly no precedent for interpretation of (5) as a normal verse followed by an unmetrical third foot. In the first half of the line, the verse-initial sequence xxSx is almost entirely reserved for type A or D verses with anacrusis. There are no two-word variants like (7) in which the verse-initial function word might be confused with a prefix in anacrusis. In type A3, then, concern about metrical ambiguity overrides the usual bias towards two-word expression of the underlying metrical pattern. Old English poets occasionally employ four-syllable A3 verses like (8), but the vast majority of A3 verses have at least one extrametrical syllable. Since the maximum number of syllables in anacrusis corresponds to the maximum number of syllables in an Old English prefix (two), an initial sequence xxx signals the presence of a light foot unambiguously.[18] In the second half of the Old English line, the verse-initial sequence

[17] See Cable, *Meter and Melody*, p. 35. In *Metrical Grammar*, Kendall argues that alliterating verbs count as unstressed particles, and attempts to eliminate anacrusis from his metrical system. Arguments against this approach can be found in Russom, Review, which critiques some of Kendall's explanatory attempts while drawing attention to the value of his observations. On the similarity between prefixes and negative particles in Old Irish, see Lehmann and Lehmann, *Introduction to Old Irish*, p. 100.

[18] Rule P2 requires the light foot to be readily identifiable, but it is not necessary to distinguish extrametrical constituents from constituents of the light foot in strings of verse-initial function words. Anyone with an intuitive understanding of the alliterative requirement would have known that a verse cannot consist of two light feet, since each verse must contain an alliterating syllable, and alliteration occurs only on an arsis (*OEM*, §7.5, rule 50c). Having determined (intuitively) that a light foot was signalled by a verse-initial string, the audience could immediately assume that the second foot began with the first alliterating syllable, and scansion could proceed straightforwardly. In type A3, and in the special Norse pattern xxx/S, it would be necessary to verify that the thesis had a certain number of syllables, but not to determine which of any additional syllables were the extrametrical ones (see *OEM*, §5.5). Sievers's concept of an undifferentiated thesis would be quite adequate for scansion of types B and C, where

xx/Sx . . . is reserved for hypermetrical b-verses like (9), which consist of a light foot followed by an embedded normal verse, usually of type A1. In such b-verses, the poet often emphasizes the light foot by adding extrametrical syllables.[19] When this occurs, the verse-initial sequence of the hypermetrical b-verse often looks exactly like a type A3 verse. Because the *Beowulf* poet excludes all A3 variants from the b-verse, however, the audience will not be misled by the false resemblance.

ELIMINATION OF ANACRUSIS IN NORSE TRADITION

If anacrusis serves primarily to allow for initial placement of prefixed verbs, loss of prefixes should be accompanied by elimination of anacrusis. That is the result we observe in the Norse corpus. There are a few putative examples of non-prefixal anacrusis, but most of these are regarded as corrupt by Sievers.[20] As we have observed, the Germanic prefixes were reduced in Old Norse to *of / um*, which could be omitted even in careful skaldic practice at a time shortly after Bragi's floruit. Later skalds used *of / um* only as 'filler', that is, only to obtain some metrical improvement.[21]

In fornyrðislag type B variants, *of / um* often appears where we would find a prefix in analogous Old English variants:

(10) þau er / fremst um man[22]   (*Vsp* 1/8)
      [xx/Sxs]
(11) sē ðe / eall geman[23]   (*Beo* 2042b)
      [xx/Sxs]

Without the filler word, (10) would constitute an unusual variant of heavy type A3 (xx/Ss). The *Beowulf* poet never places an Ss word group in the second foot of this pattern. A few Norse xx/Ss variants do contain such a word group (e.g. *Vsp* 21/5), but these are much rarer than type B verses, so the filler word creates a more highly favoured metrical pattern

any sort of light foot is acceptable, but this concept cannot explain the kind of thesis in which the unstressed syllables have to be enumerated.
[19] See *OEM*, §§6.4 and 8.7; Pope, *Rhythm*, p. 125.
[20] *AGM*, §43.8. I found only seven examples in our corpus: Þrk 4/2; Rþ 32/6; Hdl 9/6, 23/6, 42/8, 44/3 and 45/6. Note that all but one of these are b-verses, whereas Old English variants with anacrusis are normally a-verses.
[21] See above, p. 14.   [22] 'the earliest that I remember . . . .'
[23] 'he who remembers all . . . '

in (10). Observe that loss of prefixes does not prevent Norse poets from constructing verses analogous to (11). The precipitous drop in the frequency of type B cannot result solely from a dearth of appropriate linguistic material. Although they are used to maintain the old formulaic pattern of (10), filler words never appear in the old positions of anacrusis.[24]

With anacrusis eliminated, there would be a reduction in the complexity of two-word A3 verses like (7) and minimal A3 verses with four syllables like (8). Moreover, since fornyrðislag had abandoned hypermetrical patterns for short ones, the absolute prohibition against type A3 in the b-verse could be relaxed. Norse poets made use of these opportunities. Our corpus contains thirty examples of two-word A3 (about 8 per cent of the total for this type). Another 112 A3 verses, about 28 per cent of the total, have the minimum number of syllables. There are nineteen A3 b-verses.[25] Although *Beowulf* is about twice the size of our Norse corpus, it contains no two-word A3 verses, no A3 b-verses, and only eight A3 variants with the minimum number of syllables.[26] The Eddic xx/Ss pattern tolerates a word group in the second foot, but the *Beowulf* poet always realizes the second foot of this pattern in the simplest way, with an Ss compound.[27]

---

[24] The Norse data tell against the hypothesis of Bliss (*Metre*, p. 43) that anacrusis improves the metre by balancing the breath groups on either side of his caesura. This hypothesis incorrectly predicts that Eddic poets would use *of* / *um* to balance breath groups in the cognate verse patterns.

[25] Norse two-word A3: *Vsp* 7/1, 57/5, 60/1; *Hym* 7/1, 11/7, 13/1, 14/1, 16/1, 31/3, 35/1, 37/1; *Þrk* 30/5; *HH* 11/1, 12/1 (probably heavy A3, xx/Ss), 14/1, 21/1, 23/5, 29/3, 50/1 (probably xx/Ss); *HHv* 3/5, 5/5; *HH II* 6/3; *Rþ* 40/1; *Hdl* 49/3; *Grt* 10/1, 11/5, 11/7, 12/1, 14/3 and 23/3. Norse A3 in b-verse: *Vsp* 6/4, 9/4, 23/4, 25/4, 35/6, 48/2; *Hym* 20/8; *Þrk* 4/4, 7/2, 7/6 (with unstressed predicate adjective), *HH II* 32/2, 32/6, 33/2, 33/10, 42/6, 46/12; *Bdr* 6/2 (probably xx/Ss), 6/4, 14/2; and *Grt* 9/8.

[26] *Beo* 391a, 632a, 898a (assuming syncopation), 941a, 1175a, 2036a, 2587a and 2977a.

[27] See *OEM*, §5.4.2. A Norse example of xx/Ss with a heavy word group is *era þat* / *karls ætt* (*HH II* 2/3). Cf. *Vsp* 6/1, 9/1, 19/7, 23/1, 23/7, 25/1, 25/5; *Þrk* 4/1, 12/7, 20/5; *HH* 50/3; *HH II* 8/1, 9/1, 9/3, 18/5, 40/1; *Rþ* 45/1 and 47/3. In similar variants with clause-final monosyllabic pronouns, the pronouns seem to have been enclitic rather than stressed (see below, p. 135). The Old English poet probably avoided variants of xx/Ss with a word group in the second foot because they would have provided false precedents for scansion of verses like *þæt ic sweord here* (*Beo* 437a). This would be xx/Ss with resolution of the verse-final word, but is most naturally interpreted as a variant of type C with an extrametrical syllable (see rule R9b, discussed in ch. 8). Since the poet

In *Beowulf*, extrametrical words placed before the first stress in a type B or C verse help to distinguish the light foot from anacrusis. A third unstressed syllable makes the light foot unmistakable because anacrusis never extends beyond two syllables. A second unstressed syllable provides almost as much information because most anacruses are monosyllabic. Although the majority of Old English function words have only one syllable, more than half of the two-word B and C verses in *Beowulf* have a disyllable as the light foot. In fornyrðislag, where the poet has no need to be concerned about anacrusis, two-word B and C verses have monosyllabic light feet much more often.[28]

Norse poets usually employ a conspicuous xx word for the light foot of a two-word A3 verse:

(12)	spurði / Helgi[29]	(*HH* 23/5)
	[xx/Sx]	
(13)	verða / flestir[30]	(*Hdl* 49/3)
	[xx/Sx]	
(14)	(í) inom / mæra[31]	(*Vsp* 28/9)
	[(x)xx/Sx]	
(15)	né inn / meira mioð[32]	(*Þrk* 25/7)
	[xx/Sxs]	

In (12), the xx foot has been filled in the most conspicuous way, with a non-alliterating main verb. This represents the most common two-word realization of the type. Less common are examples like (13), with an xx foot filled by a colourless function word.[33] The xx foot of two-word A3 is never filled by clitics such as articles. An article occupies an xx foot in

avoids clear cases of xx/Ss with a word group in the second foot, the type C scansion is forced. This problem of metrical ambiguity does not arise in Old English type C variants with a compound in the second foot, where scansion is forced by Kaluza's law (see Fulk, *History of Old English Meter*, §172). A Norse xx/Ss variant with a word group in the second foot cannot provide a false precedent for analysis of type C because the Norse poets never place resolved sequences on the secondary arsis (see below, p. 108).

[28] There are about 250 two-word B and C verses in *Beowulf*. The light foot is monosyllabic in only about 44 per cent of these. In the smaller Norse corpus, there is a much higher frequency of two-word B and C verses, with about 260 total examples (mostly of type C). The light foot is monosyllabic in about 89 per cent of these.

[29] 'Helgi asked ...'   [30] 'most of them are destined ...'   [31] 'in the great ...'

[32] 'nor more mead ...'

[33] The light foot also seems rather colourless in *Þótti / három* (*Hym* 16/1), *varðat / hrǫnnom* (*HH* 29/3), *Létað / buðlungr* (*HH* 12/1), *urðom / síðan* (*HHv* 5/5).

(14), but the weak realization of that foot is strengthened by an extrametrical preposition here. The preposition is particularly useful because (14) has an unusual sort of enjambment. Normally the adjective and the noun phrase it modifies occupy the same verse, but here the adjective stands in verse-final position and its large associated noun phrase occupies the whole following verse. Without the preposition, (14) would look like an incomplete type B verse of the common sort represented by (15). As it stands, (14) gives a much stronger impression of completeness, since Norse type B seldom has more than two unstressed syllables verse-initially.[34] Extrametrical syllables remain useful in Norse type A3 because they signal that the verse-final Sx word constitutes a foot by itself rather than sharing an Sxs foot with a following word.

THE LIGHT FOOT RULE

Let us define closely bound proclitics (prefixes, filler words, preverbal negatives and definite articles) as *minor function words*.[35] Other unstressed or weakly stressed constituents, such as prepositions, auxiliaries, conjunctions and pronouns, will be *major function words*. Using these terms, we can capture constraints on placement of function words with the following rules:

R6a Minimize use of minor function words as light feet.

R6b Minimize use of major function words for anacrusis.

R6c Minimize use of major function words in complex foot patterns as substitutes for unstressed word-internal syllables.

---

[34] I found only four other B variants in the Norse corpus like *þá er inn / aldni kom* (*Vsp* 28/2). Cf. *Vsp* 62/5, *HHv* 32/1, *Bdr* 2/8 and *Hdl* 48/3. The role of long dips in preventing confusion between Old English A3 and B verses was pointed out to me by Mary Blockley (personal communication).

[35] Linguists treat closely bound proclitics as members of the same word class for analysis of problems that have nothing to do with poetic metre (see Samuels, *Linguistic Evolution*, p. 85). These proclitics form a natural set, and are not classified *ad hoc* according to their metrical behaviour. Note that the defining characteristic of minor function words, close binding, is a syntactic rather than a morphological one. Many prefixes are morphologically identical to prepositions, but prepositions do not qualify as minor function words. Shortcomings of purely morphological classification systems in analyses of poetic word order are well illustrated by Momma (*Composition of Old English Poetry*, ch. 3).

As we shall see in ch. 9, finite main verbs behave like major function words in some ways but in other ways like nouns and adjectives.

Both traditions adhere to R6a, as we have seen. R6b is of course irrelevant to Eddic poetry. The force of R6c shows up clearly in Old English metre and to a significant extent in Old Norse metre as well. Consider first some long variants of Old English type Db in which the second foot has the most complex pattern, Sxxs:

> (16) sēon / sibbegedriht[36]   (*Beo* 387a)
>   [S/Sxxs]
>
> (17) Þegn / nytte behēold[37]   (*Beo* 494b)
>   [S/Sxxs]
>
> (18) sibb' / æfre ne mæg[38]   (*Beo* 2600b)
>   [S/Sxxs]

In *Beowulf*, word groups occupying the Sxxs foot of a long Db verse conform very closely to the morphological structure of Old English Sxxs compounds, all of which are derived from an initial trochaic constituent and a following prefixed constituent. There are perhaps four examples like (16), a two-word paradigm. In twelve of thirteen other long Db verses, the Sxxs foot is occupied by a word group with a trochaic constituent and a prefixed constituent, as in (17).[39] The only apparent exception is (18), but its closely bound preverbal negative is very much like a prefix. As we have observed, negative particles are quite acceptable to Old English poets as substitutes for prefixes in anacrusis, though non-prefixal anacrusis is otherwise rare. In long Db verses, then, the poet obviously avoids assignment of major function words to foot-internal x positions of the complex Sxxs foot.

Complex verses like those in (20) are of course absent in fornyrðislag, along with all other patterns containing Sxxs. It is worth noting, however, that the prefix-like *of/um* appears more frequently than any other

---

[36] 'to see the band of kinsmen ... '   [37] 'The thane performed his task ... '
[38] 'never can (anything hold back) kinship ... '
[39] See *Beo* 2367a (with extrametrical syllables), 2527a; 1080b, 1122b, 1132b, 1214b, 1503b, 1520b, 1569b, 2396b and 2692b (with elision). Somewhat less clear cases with a medial adverb are 390b, 721b and 2296b. All three of these have a trochaic word and a prefixed monosyllable in the Sxxs foot. Additional examples like (16), with an Sxxs compound in the second foot, are 848a and (probably) 2717a and 2774a (see *OEM*, §8.4). As expected, the same care is exercised in an instance of the still more complex expanded Db pattern, *oncȳð / eorla gehwǣm* 1420a (Sx/Sxxs).

monosyllabic word on the x position of the Sxs foot, the position that would be occupied by the internal prefix of an Old English compound like *hand-ge-weorc*. The x position of the Sxs foot is also frequently occupied by the unstressed, non-root syllable of a trochaic word that is followed by a stressed monosyllable.[40] In such cases the Sxs word group mimics the structure of compounds with a trochaic first constituent (e.g. OE *middan-geard*, ON *iormun-gandr*).

KUHN'S-LAW EFFECTS WITHIN THE VERSE

In formulating his well-known laws of poetic syntax, Kuhn divides weakly stressed words into two categories, *Satzpartikeln* (clitics to a clause) and *Satzteilpartikeln* (clitics to a clausal subconstituent). Satzpartikeln include all the major function words mentioned in R6 except for prepositions, which Kuhn classifies together with our minor function words as Satzteilpartikeln. These laws impose the following constraints:

K1 First Law: Unstressed Satzpartikeln must be grouped together before the first or second stressed word of the clause.

K2 Second Law: Any unstressed constituents situated before the first stressed word of the clause must include a Satzpartikel.

Kuhn's laws predict relative placement of words within the verse and relative placement of verses within the clause. For the present I confine attention to verse-internal effects. Effects within larger domains will be considered in ch. 9. K1–2 are repeated for the reader's convenience in the appendix.

Momma's critique of Kuhn's laws clarifies many points of terminological confusion and takes the whole *ASPR* corpus into account. She finds that K1 applies quite generally, whereas adherence to K2 varies from one Old English poem to another.[41] Momma also points out serious flaws in Kuhn's attempt to ground K1–2 in linguistic history.[42] Although her study underscores the importance of Kuhn's observations (appropriately sharpened), it also draws attention to the lack of a plausible explanation for them. Momma is not the only researcher to criticize Kuhn's laws. Mitchell voiced significant concern at a relatively

---

[40] See von See, *Germanische Verskunst*, p. 5.
[41] *Composition of Old English Poetry*, pp. 182–3.   [42] Ibid., pp. 72–5.

early date.[43] According to a recent study by Blockley and Cable, 'One effect of the taxonomy of Kuhn's Laws is to obscure the need for further investigation that might reveal the more general principles regulating the opening of clauses.'[44] In this comparative study I shall be primarily concerned to show that Old Norse, Old Saxon, and Old High German verse texts pose somewhat different problems for K1–2 and that many, perhaps all, of the Kuhn's-law effects not attributable to ordinary prose syntax can be explained by general principles of the word-foot theory.

K1 predicts relative placement of unstressed words in verses with two distinct sites for them. Most of the crucial cases have the type B pattern, which accommodates unstressed words on initial and medial x positions. In type B, two or more Satzpartikeln are almost always grouped together by the poet in the first thesis, before the first stress, as predicted by K1–2. This is perhaps Kuhn's most important result. The special status of the first thesis cannot be captured by Sievers, who makes no distinction between initial and medial x positions in his analysis of type B. Hence K1–2 are necessary adjuncts to the five-types theory. Within the word-foot theory, on the other hand, the initial x positions of type B verses constitute light feet, while the medial x positions correspond to weak internal syllables of compounds. The effects of K1 are captured by the light foot rule (R6), which deploys major function words toward the beginning of the verse, where they make the first foot more conspicuous. The light foot rule accounts for some facts that resist analysis within Kuhn's framework. Since Kuhn must place prepositions and minor function words together in the category of Satzteilpartikeln, he has no way to explain why a verse-initial preposition suffices to fill the first thesis in many verses of types B and C, whereas minor function words normally require support from extrametrical constituents to do so, whether or not the verse is clause-initial. The boundary between major and minor function words is more distinct than the boundary between Kuhn's categories, which is blurred to protect K1–2 from refutation. Articles, for example, are reclassified as quasi-relatives by Kuhn when they exhibit the behaviour predicted for Satzpartikeln.[45]

---

[43] *Old English Syntax* II, §3947.

[44] 'Kuhn's Laws', p. 269. Similar concerns are expressed in several of the recent publications for which references are provided in this article (p. 279, n. 2).

[45] 'Wortstellung', p. 44. For a critique of this *ad-hoc* procedure, see Momma, *Composition of Old English Poetry*, pp. 72–3.

Some complex verses may appear at first glance to justify Kuhn's classification system. If prepositions are Satzteilpartikeln, for example, Kuhn's laws allow them to be placed in the second thesis of type B, as sometimes happens.[46] This thesis is much more frequently occupied by prefixes and filler words, however, as predicted by R6c. The light foot rule does not explain why prepositions are the only major function words ordinarily assigned to the second thesis of type B, but that is expected on other grounds. Assignment of a clausal conjunction or relative pronoun to the second thesis would require the poet to begin a new clause there, something that rarely happens because verses with a high degree of syntactic integrity are preferred (see U1).[47] No special explanation is required for the fact that personal pronouns and sentential adverbs occupy the first thesis so consistently in type B. Unstressed prepositions are confined to proclitic position before the governed noun by a constraint of ordinary prose syntax, but there is no such constraint blocking leftward movement of unstressed personal pronouns or sentential adverbs.[48] With so little effort required, the poet might well achieve perfect consistency in assignment of free-moving unstressed words to their most appropriate locations, as defined by R6.[49]

The remaining variants in which K1 applies crucially are seldom or never found in Old Norse poems, so they cannot detain us long. The

[46] There are nine diverse examples in the Eddic corpus, e.g. *enn / áðr í tvau* (*Hym* 12/7). Cf. *Hym* 13/2, 21/5; *Þrk* 13/9, 20/3; *HH* 27/3, 44/8; *HHv* 10/7; and *Hdl* 4/3. Twelve additional examples in *Rígsþula* result from formulaic repetition of the phrase *at þat* (2/ 1, 4/5, 6/3, 6/5, 9/1, 9/5, 14/1, 20/3, 20/5, 33/7, 33/9 and 38/1).

[47] Note that a relative pronoun does occupy the second thesis in *var / karls, er kom* (*Hym* 10/7), a rare example of type B with a clause boundary between the stresses. It would be perfectly legitimate, and may be necessary, to establish an intermediate category for function words like prepositions, which are loosely bound clitics to a phrase, as distinct from clitics to a clause on the one hand and closely bound proclitics on the other (see Russom, 'Metrical Replacements for Kuhn's Laws'). In Old Saxon poetry (ch. 10) we will be able to observe a wider variety of unstressed word classes with distinct metrical values in a regular gradation from those most suitable as light feet to those most suitable as anacruses.

[48] To put it another way, a preposition can be unstressed only when it occupies a proclitic position before a noun, whereas a pronoun or sentential adverb can be unstressed in a proclitic position toward the beginning of any clause.

[49] The two instances of *ec* in *oc kýs ec, þatz ec vil* (*HHv* 2/7) are probably scribal (see above, p. 33, n. 19). The Old English and Old Norse corpora contain no other examples of type B with a personal pronoun in the second thesis.

following list will suffice to exhibit possible sites for unstressed Satzpartikeln in verses with two such sites:

Type A1 with anacrusis	(x)Sx/(x)S[x]
Type A2 with anacrusis	(x)Sx/(x)Ss
Type Da with anacrusis	(x)S/(x)Ss[x]
Type Dax with anacrusis	(x)Sx/Ss[x]
Type Db with anacrusis	(x)S/(x)Sxs
	(x)S/(x)Sxxs
Type Dbx	Sx/Sxs
	Sx/Sxxs
Type Dbx with anacrusis	(x)Sx/Sxs
	(x)Sx/Sxxs

Bracketed verse-final positions in the listed patterns have no significance
here, since they are closed to unstressed words generally, with a few
possible exceptions involving enclitics that would not be governed by
Kuhn's laws in any case.[50] With verse-final positions excluded, type C (x/
Ss[x], xx/Ss[x]) accommodates unstressed syllables only before the first
stress, and is therefore omitted from the list above. We do not of course
need K1 to explain why unstressed words cluster at the only available site
in this type. Likewise omitted from the list is the type E pattern Ssx/S.
Because anacrusis never occurs in this type, it provides only one site for
unstressed syllables. The number of crucial cases arising in the listed
patterns is actually quite small, even in *Beowulf*. The Old English poem
contains only about eighty instances of anacrusis, for example.[51] When a
verse with anacrusis has two or more major function words, these words
usually cluster in the verse-medial thesis, as permitted by K1. Clustering

---

[50] For discussion of enclitics, see below, p. 135.

[51] *Beo* 25a, 94a, 107a, 109a, 141a, 217a, 234a, 399a, 409a, 501a, 723a, 758a, 772a,
827a, 1027a, 1108a, 1125a, 1150a, 1151a, 1169a, 1248a, 1274a, 1304a, 1384a,
1390a, 1451a, 1453a, 1460a, 1485a, 1518a, 1537a, 1543a, 1545a, 1549a, 1557a,
1563a, 1610a, 1665a, 1667a, 1711a, 1724a, 1751a, 1758a, 1837a, 1977a, 1987a,
2044a, 2093a, 2252a, 2284a, 2367a, 2455a, 2525a, 2529a, 2538a, 2591a, 2628a,
2629a, 2697a, 2703a, 2705a, 2717a, 2738a, 2756a, 2769a, 2878a, 2930a, 2936a,
3062a, 3121a, 3141a; 93b, 666b, 1223b, 1504b, 1773b, 1877b, 2247b and 2592b.
Doubtful examples are 368a, 1068a and 9b. Assignment of a verse-initial function
word to the preceding a-verse might eliminate the putative anacruses in 402b, 2481b
and 2592b. Many examples of anacrusis with a prefixed alliterating verb would be
disallowed by defenders of Kuhn's laws, further reducing the number of crucial cases.

is explained more precisely, however, by the light foot rule, which discourages employment of major function words for anacrusis and identifies the verse-medial thesis as the most appropriate location for them in types A and D. Even within the small group of crucial cases, K1 encounters an exception, further indication that stylistic preferences rather than categorical rules are in play.[52]

Theoretically, type D variants have two or even three locations for unstressed words, but the heavy foot is usually filled by a compound rather than a word group, and hardly any D variants contain more than one major function word. A rare crucial case in *Beowulf* exhibits clustering of Satzpartikeln after the first stress, as permitted by K1, but this also has an isolated Satzteilpartikel clause-initially, and violates K2.[53] Our Norse poets, of course, use no anacrusis, hardly any extrametrical syllables in type Da, a mere handful of Dax verses and no Dbx verses. Kuhn claims that K1–2 were well observed in native Eddic fornyrðislag.[54] To a considerable extent, however, the appearance of conformity results from limited employment of expanded verse types and extrametrical syllables in this concise form.

In a verse that initiates a clause, K2 forbids placement of a Satzteilpartikel in the first thesis unless a Satzpartikel is also placed there. Although R6a and K2 both predict that isolated minor function words will be avoided before the first stress of a type B verse, R6a covers a wider range of cases:

(19) Ymb- / ēode þā[55]   (*Beo* 620a)

(20) ge- / seted ond gesǣd[56]   (*Beo* 1696a)

The clause-initial (19) violates K2, but (20) should be unexceptionable, since it appears later in the clause. As it turns out, there are six or seven other verses like (19) in *Beowulf* but no others like (20).[57] Kuhn cannot explain why verses like (20) should be rarer than those that violate K2.

---

[52] An unstressed adverb is split from a personal pronoun by an alliterating main verb in *Hū lomp ēow on lāde* (*Beo* 1987a). The exception is removed if such alliterating verbs are defined as sentence particles rather than stressed words (see Kendall, *Metrical Grammar*, p. 281); but then it is difficult to explain why variants like *Beo* 1987a are so rare.

[53] *Tō* is clearly proclitic to *lang* in *Tō lang ys tō reccenne* (*Beo* 2093a).

[54] 'Wortstellung', pp. 26 and 46.   [55] 'Then she went around ...'

[56] 'set down and stated ...'

[57] Like (19) are *Beo* 34a, 1408a, 1870a, 2345a, 2516a and 3156a; cf. also 652a.

On the other hand, provision R6a of the light foot rule identifies both (19) and (20) as deviant verses of a kind that should have low frequency. Additional problems with K2 will be considered in ch. 9.

SUMMARY

The light foot rule (R6) returns to Kuhn's earliest classification of particles, in which he assigns prepositions and conjunctions to the same category. R6 is anticipated by Kuhn's observation that prefixes and filler words, as the lightest speech material, were not well suited for a certain kind of thesis, whereas prepositions and conjunctions sufficed to fill any thesis.[58] The same classification of particles plays a crucial role in Kuhn's elision rule for skaldic poetry.[59] Kuhn does not provide means to capture these results when he discards his original classification.[60]

Placement of unstressed constituents in fornyrðislag takes the turn predicted by the word-foot theory. Loss of unstressed prefixes from the Eddic poet's language triggers a complete elimination of anacrusis from the metrical system. The optional filler words derived from prefixes, though exploited systematically to obtain a more desirable verse pattern, never appear in anacrusis. Elimination of anacrusis makes it much easier to recover the metrical pattern of Norse type A3. Two-word variants of this type never occur in *Beowulf*, but are clearly acceptable to Old Norse poets; and we observe a strikingly high frequency of Norse A3 variants with the minimum number of syllables. The *Beowulf* poet never places an A3 variant in the second half of the line, where it might be confused with the opening segment of a hypermetrical b-verse. This possibility of confusion cannot arise in fornyrðislag, however, since the Norse poets have abandoned hypermetrical patterns in favour of short ones. As expected, Norse b-verses of type A3 begin to appear.

---

[58] 'Präfixe und Füllwort waren das leichteste Sprachmaterial . . . ; sie scheinen für einige Senkungen zu leicht gewesen zu sein, in denen Präpositionen und Konjunktionen genügten' (*Füllwort*, p. 55). Kuhn may have abandoned this view because prevailing theories of Germanic metre treated all *Senkungen* as equivalent.

[59] 'Vor Füllwort und bestimmten Artikel wird oft elidiert, vor Präpositionen und Konjunctionen selten' (*Füllwort*, p. 73).

[60] 'Wortstellung', p. 47, n. 107.

5

Metrical archaisms

An unmetrical verse in our Norse corpus often becomes perfectly regular when the scribal form of a word is replaced by an earlier form.[1] Similar cases arise in *Beowulf*. The Old English poet evidently used older or newer phonological values of certain words according to metrical convenience. In some cases, the newer value would make the verse unmetrical; in others, the corresponding older value would do so.[2] Variation of this sort does not seem to occur in native Eddic fornyrðislag. When metrical evidence points to an archaic value in one instance, there are no clear cases of the corresponding newer value elsewhere.

POSTCONSONANTAL RESONANTS AND VOWEL CONTRACTION

Variant Old English spellings testify to development of an epenthetic vowel before the postconsonantal resonants *l*, *m*, *n*, *r* in word-final position. Thus *tācn* 'token' has a variant spelling *tācen*. The *Beowulf* poet ordinarily uses such a word with its old monosyllabic value, but exploits the newer disyllabic value in some cases. Norse languages underwent a similar epenthesis (cf. ON *maðr* 'man', Modern Icelandic *maður*), but this took place after the date of the Codex Regius manuscript. Throughout our period of interest, Old Norse words like *teikn* 'token' were spelled as monosyllables and so treated in the syllable-counting skaldic metres.[3]

In Old English poetry, a contract form like *sēon* 'to see' sometimes has the disyllabic value of the archaic form **seohan*. Norse sound changes also

---

[1] *AGM*, §§36–9.   [2] *OEM*, §§4.2–4.6.
[3] See Fulk, *History of Old English Meter*, §83.

reduced disyllabic forms to monosyllables, and metrical evidence points to the older value in a significant number of cases:

(1)	at / þeir sé {séi}[4]	(*HH II* 11/2)
	[x/Ssx, not x/Ss]	
(2)	ok / grióz griá {gréa}[5]	(*Grt* 2/3)
	[x/Ssx, not x/Ss]	
(3)	nefgiold / fá {fáa}[6]	(*HH* 12/4)
	[Ss/Sx, not Ss/S]	
(4)	dagsbrún / siá {séa}[7]	(*HH* 26/6)
	[Ss/Sx, not Ss/S]	

The pre-contract forms in curly brackets make normal scansion possible when substituted for the manuscript forms of examples (1–4). Such archaisms do not appear in the main text of Neckel–Kuhn, but are supplied in the apparatus at the bottom of the page, where they are attributed to particular editors, or to 'hgbb' (*Herausgeber*) when there is an editorial consensus. If the contract form of the manuscript is assumed in (1), the verse has a short pattern x/Ss, which would be particularly doubtful in a poem that seems to avoid short patterns otherwise.[8] If the pre-contract form is assumed, (1) becomes a common variant of the type C pattern x/Ssx.[9] The etymologically long vowels of the bracketed forms are marked with an acute accent according to standard editorial practice. They would be subject, however, to a general rule shortening a long vowel in hiatus before another vowel.[10] Hence the older forms have the metrical value of words like *gata* 'road', with a short stressed syllable followed by an unstressed syllable. In Neckel–Kuhn, the metrical values of the old forms appear within parentheses after the editorial spellings. For the manuscript form *sé* in (1) above, the editorial spelling *séi* is supplied in the apparatus, followed by its metrical value (*seï*), with the diaeresis used in this particular case to distinguish the pair of adjacent short vowels from the Old Norse diphthong *ei*. In (2), the monosyllabic

---

[4] 'that they may be ...' [5] 'and of the grey (mill)stone ...'
[6] 'to get compensation ...' [7] 'to see daybreak ...'
[8] As we observed above (p. 35), the Helgi poems contain only three doubtful examples of the most common short pattern Sx/S, and the two other short verses in these poems are sites of editorial emendation. Examples (3) and (4) also come from a Helgi poem.
[9] Other type C verses with contract forms: *Vsp* 64/4; *Hym* 1/6; *Þrk* 29/3, repeated as 32/3; *HH II* 11/2; and *Grt* 5/3.
[10] See Bugge and Sievers, 'Vocalverkürzung'; *AGM*, §37.1; Noreen, §129.

form *griá* results from shift of stress to the second element of an originally disyllabic sequence *-éa*. As in (1), the monosyllabic form creates the doubtful pattern x/Ss, but the disyllabic form *gréa* (metrically *grea*) yields a perfectly regular type C pattern. Similar analyses have been proposed for verses like (3) and (4). If the newer monosyllabic value is assumed for these verses, the result is a short reversed pattern Ss/S of doubtful authenticity. The older forms yield the most common A2 subtype (Ss/Sx).[11] Shortening of hiatus vowels leaves pre-contract forms perfectly appropriate to their metrical contexts in examples (1)–(4). As we shall see in ch. 8, short syllables appear very frequently on the s position of type C and on the second S position of the pattern Ss/Sx.

THE PROSODIC SIGNIFICANCE OF NORSE ARCHAISMS

The archaic forms of (1)–(4) are resolvable sequences, since they consist of a short stressed syllable followed by an unstressed syllable. In *Beowulf*, resolvable sequences often substitute for stressed monosyllables in verses of type B or E, but this never happens in native Eddic fornyrðislag.[12] If words like *siá* (later spelled *sjá*) could be scanned according to their newer monosyllabic value, we would expect them to appear occasionally in a B or E verse; but they do not. Sievers states flatly that words like *sjá* always count as disyllabic.[13] If so, they would naturally be excluded from types B and E along with other resolvable sequences. We do find one apparent example of the newer value at the end of a type B verse, the form *bjó* 'built' (spelled *bió* in *Rþ* 39/4). This has little value for dating, however, since the development of strong class VII preterites like *bjó* is less well understood than the development of ordinary contract forms like *sjá*.[14]

The metrical facts would have an obvious explanation if our corpus dated before the advent of forms like *sjá*. Yet as Sievers points out, some skalds continued to use the old disyllabic value after others had begun to exploit the monosyllabic value.[15] Alliteration could provide a helpful clue to the old metrical value of rising diphthongs. Well after the date of the Codex Regius, forms like *jǫrð* 'earth', with an initial y-glide,

[11] Contract forms in other Ss/Sx verses like (3) and (4): *HH* 52/8 and *HH II* 43/8 (identical to *HH* 26/6).
[12] See below, p. 104. [13] *AGM*, §36.1.
[14] Prokosch, *Comparative Germanic Grammar*, §62.
[15] Bugge and Sievers, 'Vocalverkürzung', p. 395.

Metrical archaisms

continued to alliterate with words that had initial vowels. This convention must have been established when *j*- was still a vowel rather than a y-glide.[16] If forms from the earlier period survived as underlying forms in the native speaker's grammar, alliteration might identify the level of abstraction at which metrical rules applied.[17] The mere presence of archaic forms does not, then, suffice to date our corpus before the period of vowel contraction and stress shift, though the apparent absence of later metrical values points in that direction.

[16] Gordon–Taylor, §179.

[17] In this case the syllable with the y-glide developed out of a falling diphthongal monosyllable rather than out of a disyllabic sequence (cf. OE *eorðe*). The older value of words like ON *jǫrð* can be employed anywhere in the line without requiring an unusual type of resolution.

6

Alliteration

In native Eddic fornyrðislag, as in *Beowulf*, the phonological equivalence called alliteration gives special prominence to certain stressed syllables. Within a given verse, the syllable with the strongest stress is the most likely to alliterate. The second constituent of a compound, for example, never alliterates in preference to its first constituent.[1] The concept of equivalence for alliteration derives from native-speaker intuitions about syllable structure, and corresponds to the concept of equivalence for early Germanic reduplication.[2] In most cases, stressed syllables alliterate if they have the same initial consonant, regardless of other consonants in the onset. Thus the -*r*- of ON *brim* 'sea' plays no role in alliterative matching, and this word may be used to alliterate with *blindr* 'blind' or *bekkr* 'bench'. However, when the onset begins with the group *sp-*, *st-*, or *sk-* (usually spelled *sc-* in the Codex Regius), both elements of the group must be matched. Thus *steinn* 'stone' alliterates with *strangr* 'strong', but not with *sonr* 'son' or *spakr* 'wise'. Only consonants participate in alliterative matching. When a stressed syllable begins with a vowel, the quality of the vowel is ignored, and the empty onset is treated as a 'zero consonant' equivalent to any other empty onset. Thus *áss* 'god' (Ø*áss*) alliterates with *eldr* 'fire' (Ø*eldr*) and *iorð* 'earth' (Ø*iorð*). Observe that the *i*- of words like *iorð* (usually spelled *j*- in linguistic discussions) counts as a syllable-initial vowel in Eddic poetry.

---

[1] *OEM*, §§7.2 and 8.6.

[2] See Kuryłowicz, *Grundlagen; OEM*, §7.1.

LINGUISTIC COMPOUNDING AND ALLITERATION

The Germanic compound rule adds prominence to the leftmost stressed syllable within its linguistic domain of application and subordinates every other stressed syllable. The effect is to bind smaller words into larger words. In Germanic poetry, principle P3 adds prominence to the leftmost arsis within its metrical domain of application and subordinates every other arsis within that domain. The effect is to bind smaller metrical constituents (word feet) into larger metrical constituents (verses and lines). Prominence is realized as stress within linguistic domains and as alliteration within metrical domains. Otherwise, the metrical rule operates exactly like the linguistic rule from which it derives.[3]

Metrical phonologists employ tree diagrams to represent hierarchies of linguistic subordination.[4] Consider the tree for a large Norse compound like *Gullin-kambi* 'Golden-comb' (name of a rooster):

(1)

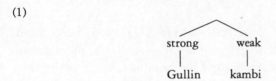

The unlabelled node at the top of the tree branches into two lower nodes, one labelled strong and the other labelled weak. The lower nodes are called *terminal nodes* because they do not branch. Each terminal node attaches to a stressed syllable in the constituent below. No terminal nodes are provided for the non-radical syllables *-in*, *-i* because the compound stress rule ignores such syllables. Only two types of branching are allowed, strong–weak and weak–strong. This constraint expresses the generalization that stress assignment is a binary operation making one constituent more prominent than another. Branching is strong–weak in (1) because the compound stress rule elevates the prominence of the leftmost stress-bearing constituent within the domain of the large word.

---

[3] For further discussion of the linguistic issues, see Russom, 'Metrical Evidence'. The choice of alliteration as an artistic substitute for stress seems natural, since reduplication, on which alliteration is based, often has intensifying function.

[4] This notation was introduced in Liberman and Prince, 'Linguistic Rhythm'.

Assignment of stress to the leftmost syllable marks wordhood in Germanic compounds as in other Germanic words of major category. The less salient wordhood of the weak constituent is marked by secondary stress on its leftmost syllable.

In a metrical tree structure, terminal nodes attach to metrical constituents derived from stressed syllables (S or s positions). The domains represented in metrical trees are feet, verses and lines. A type A1 verse pattern has the following representation:

(2)

In linguistic trees like (1), as we just observed, only root syllables attach to terminal nodes. In metrical trees like (2), accordingly, no nodes are provided for subordinate x positions of the word foot, which derive from non-radical syllables. Representations (1) and (2) might both be characterized as metrical in the sense that both employ the notation of metrical phonology. I will reserve the term 'metrical' for poetic rules and structures, however.

The nodes in (2) are labelled by the metrical equivalent of the compound stress rule:

R7a When two S positions appear within the same metrical domain, alliteration is assigned obligatorily to the first S position, beginning with the smallest domain.

R7b Assignment of alliteration to a given constituent subordinates all other constituents within the domain of application.

In representation (2), the first constituent containing an S position is the leftmost Sx foot, which is accordingly marked for alliteration by R7a. By R7b, the first foot is labelled strong and the second is labelled weak. Alliteration marks the integrity of the verse just as stress on the leftmost syllable of *Gullin-kambi* marks the integrity of the compound. In some cases, a verse is compounded both linguistically and metrically. Thus *Gullin-kambi* appears as a type A1 verse in *Vsp* 43/2, where its integrity is doubly marked on the left by an alliterating syllable that also has the most prominent stress. In many cases, however, the verse will have a strongly stressed constituent to the right, and alliteration will give a purely metrical prominence to a preceding constituent.

LINGUISTIC EMBEDDING

Branching constraints make it necessary to employ embedding when a representation contains three or more terminal nodes. Consider the linguistic tree for the multiple compound *mið-viku-dagr* 'mid-week day, Wednesday':

(3)

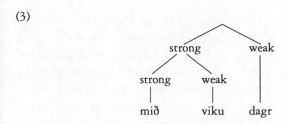

Here *mið* and *viku* are embedded under a higher-level node to produce the well-formed representation (3), which has binary branching at all levels, as required. Embedding must respect inherent relations among the constituents of multiple compounds.[5] In *mið-viku-dagr*, the first two constituents are the more closely related. Grouping of the second constituent with the third would satisfy the constraints on branching, but would imply an incorrect meaning 'middle of a week-day' for the triple compound, which is derived by combining *mið-viku* with *dagr*. Labelling in (3) results from two applications of the compound stress rule. Within the smaller domain, *viku* undergoes subordination to *mið*. Within the larger domain, *dagr* undergoes subordination to the complex constituent *mið-viku*. Both *viku* and *dagr* attach to weak nodes, but the twice-subordinated *viku* has the lesser prominence.

---

[5] See Sauer, *Nominalkomposita*, §4.1.1.

METRICAL EMBEDDING

As the binding operation for metrical constituents, R7 applies within all metrical domains, including the line. Consider the metrical tree for a line composed of two type A1 patterns:

(4)

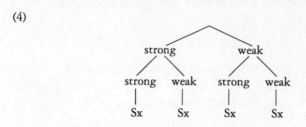

Here, as in the linguistic representation (3), constraints on branching require us to embed, and our choice from among the well-formed structural possibilities must respect inherent relations of constituency. The first two feet are embedded under a strong node that represents the integrity of the a-verse as a metrical constituent of the line. The second two feet are embedded under a weak node representing the b-verse. Metrical compounding applies within each verse domain, subordinating the second foot to the first. At the higher level, the b-verse is subordinated to the a-verse. Since the x positions of the feet play no role in compounding, diagram (4) could be used to represent the metrical stress pattern of any line with four S positions and no s positions. In any such line, alliteration is obligatory on the first and third S positions, optional on the second, and forbidden on the fourth. The positions of obligatory alliteration are represented in (4) as the strongest two S positions of the line. The position of optional alliteration is the weak second S of the stronger verse (the a-verse). Alliteration is forbidden on the weak second S of the weaker verse (the b-verse).[6]

Constraints on alliteration for all verse types are expressed by the following rules:

---

[6] The skaldic poet's concept of the 'chief stave' or 'head stave' turns out to be unsuitable for representation of alliterative patterns in Eddic and Old English poetry. I discuss this issue below after introducing the patterns.

R8a The strongest two metrical positions within the line must contain alliterating syllables.
R8b A weak constituent of a weak constituent may not contain an alliterating syllable.
R8c No alliterating syllable may occupy an x position.
R8d Within a compound foot, the S position has priority for alliteration.

R8a–d operate on hierarchies of relative prominence created by R7a–b. Some positions in a given hierarchy may be ineligible for alliteration after R7a–b have applied, but others may be eligible for optional alliteration. R8d forbids assignment of optional alliteration to the s position of a compound foot unless alliteration has been assigned to the S position of that foot. This is a more general form of the rule that forbids alliteration on the secondary constituent of a compound when the primary constituent does not alliterate.[7] Rule R7b applies with optional as well as obligatory alliteration. When the S position of a compound foot alliterates optionally, the following s position will undergo another cycle of metrical subordination.

Optional alliteration provides a valuable opportunity for comparative analysis. As we have observed, weakly stressed syllables were lost more often in Old Norse than in Old English due to the more forceful character of the Norse primary stress, which had a more powerful subordinating effect.[8] If alliteration mimics stress assignment in the natural language, we would expect an alliterating arsis to have an especially powerful subordinating effect in fornyrðislag, inhibiting optional alliteration on an arsis to the right.

PATTERNS OF NORMAL WEIGHT

The following Norse examples illustrate verse patterns with two S positions and no s position. The rare Norse pattern Sx/Sxx is represented by a b-verse. All other examples are a-verses with the maximum allowable number of alliterating constituents:

(5) grára / geira[9]　　　　　(HH 12/7)
[Sx/Sx]

[7] *OEM*, §8.6.　　[8] See above, p. 16.　　[9] 'of (steel-)grey spears ...'

69

(6)	vantattu / vígi[10] [Sxx/Sx]	(*HH II* 28/5)
(7)	tungls / tiúgari[11] [S/Sxx]	(*Vsp* 40/7)
(8)	bíta / hvassara[12] [Sx/Sxx]	(*Þrk* 25/4)
(9)	kǫlloðo Karl[13] [Sxx/S]	(*Rþ* 21/3)
(10)	Þræll oc/ Þír[14] [Sx/S]	(*Rþ* 11/7)

A stress tree like (4) can represent relative prominence relations within the verses above. Alliteration is obligatory on the strongest (leftmost) S position of every verse and optional on the weak S of the strong verse (the rightmost S of the a-verse). Comparable verses in *Beowulf* obey the same constraint, though alliteration on the second S of the a-verse occurs significantly more often, as predicted. Verses with the Sx/Sx pattern of example (5) appear about 2,050 times in *Beowulf* and about 1,050 times in the Eddic poems. Double alliteration occurs in 59 per cent of the Old English a-verses with this pattern and in 45 per cent of the comparable Norse a-verses. The difference is greater than these figures suggest because fewer of the Norse examples appear in the first half of the line. In the Norse corpus, only 16 per cent of total Sx/Sx verses have double alliteration, as compared with 30 per cent in *Beowulf*.

The more complex pattern Sxx/Sx has a much lower frequency, with seventy-nine Old English examples and forty Old Norse examples.[15]

---

[10] 'you could not stop the battle ...'   [11] 'destroyer of the sun ...'
[12] 'eat more eagerly...' Cf. 25/6.   [13] 'they named [him] Karl ...'
[14] 'Þræll and Þír ...'
[15] Sxx/Sx verses include two-word paradigms like *þrēatedon / þearle* (*Beo* 560a) and variants like *wēox under / wolcnum* (*Beo* 8a). Note that if *under* were excluded from its first foot as extrametrical, *Beo* 8a would be too short by Old English standards. Once *under* is included within the foot, each of its syllables must be assigned to a distinct x position (see R1–2). Verse 2728a seems a clear case of Sxx/Sx despite the lack of double alliteration (see Fulk, *History of Old English Meter*, pp. 72–3). For further discussion of the Sxx/Sx pattern see below, p. 168. Examples in *Beowulf* are 8a, 48a, 52a, 119a, 140a, 211a, 231a, 240a, 342a, 404a, 534a, 560a, 580a, 617a, 651a, 685a, 714a, 995a, 1008a, 1037a, 1118a, 1169a, 1216a, 1255a, 1289a, 1361a, 1404a, 1631a, 1720a, 1770a, 1775a, 1848a, 1859a, 1964a, 2070a, 2073a, 2096a, 2179a, 2268a, 2411a, 2415a, 2461a, 2539a, 2559a, 2702a, 2728a, 2768a, 2883a, 2908a, 2967a, 3019a, 3025a, 3145a; 57b, 105b, 142b, 279b, 548b, 649b, 788b, 1049b, 1137b, 1177b,

About 70 per cent of the Old English examples (55/79) appear in the first half of the line. The only Sxx/Sx a-verse with single alliteration (2728a) consists of a large compound with a non-alliterating secondary constituent. The corresponding Norse examples also favour the first half of the line, with twenty-seven a-verses (68 per cent), but only thirteen of these are like (6), with double alliteration.[16]

Old English light Da verses of the form S/Sxx tend to appear in the second half of the line because they usually end with Sxx verbs. Such verbs bear a relatively light stress, especially in their finite forms, and are strongly attracted to line-final position, partly perhaps for syntactic reasons.[17] In *Beowulf*, only 8 of the 102 S/Sxx variants appear as a-verses. Four of these have double alliteration.[18] In the Norse corpus, nine of the twenty-six S/Sxx variants are a-verses, and six have double alliteration, like (7).[19] The higher frequency of double alliteration among the Norse

1224b, 1286b, 1364b, 1487b, 1699b, 1768b, 1907b, 1909b, 2049b, 2517b, 2528b, 2903b, 2959b and 3097b. Cf. also 6a (as emended) and 3103a (disregarding the epenthetic vowel in *wundur*). Norse a-verses: *Vsp* 20/5, 26/5, 30/9, 34/3, 45/1; *HH* 36/1; *HHv* 40/1; *HH II* 2/1, 18/7, 28/5, 34/1, 37/3, 47/1; *Bdr* 8/1, 10/1, 12/1; *Rþ* 34/7; *Hdl* 6/1, 7/1, 10/7, 11/1, 13/7, 18/1; *Grt* 5/1, 17/1, 18/1, 24/3; Norse b-verses: *Vsp* 12/6, 20/8, 51/2 (possibly Sxx/Ss); *Hym* 39/6; *HH* 6/8, 25/6, 52/4; *HHv* 31/2, 33/2, 40/2; *HH II* 25/6; *Rþ* 34/4; and *Hdl* 12/8.

[16] *Vsp* 20/5, 26/5, 34/3, 45/1; *HH* 36/1; *HH II* 28/5, 47/1; *Rþ* 34/7; *Hdl* 6/1, 10/7, 13/7; *Grt* 17/1 and 18/1.

[17] See below, p. 126.

[18] S/Sxx with double alliteration: *Beo* 2409a, 2758a, 2805a and 3133a. Other S/Sxx a-verses: *Beo* 253a, 286a, 2668a and 2744a. S/Sxx b-verses: *Beo* 81b, 132b, 156b, 166b, 172b, 188b, 204b, 227b, 258b, 320b, 340b, 370b, 423b, 432b, 451b, 470b, 508b, 570b, 611b, 625b, 639b, 720b, 725b, 770b, 787b, 796b, 808b, 840b, 843b, 901b, 951b, 971b, 983b, 1090b, 1102b, 1117b, 1204b, 1206b, 1212b, 1222b, 1237b, 1380b, 1391b, 1397b, 1407b, 1413b, 1426b, 1440b, 1444b, 1500b, 1566b, 1573b, 1589b, 1626b, 1630b, 1662b, 1687b, 1721b, 1795b, 1799b, 1843b, 1898b, 1916b, 2045b, 2075b, 2084b, 2085b, 2098b, 2102b, 2164b, 2168b, 2211b, 2285b, 2336b, 2352b, 2383b, 2402b, 2589b, 2594b, 2605b, 2652b, 2655b, 2658b, 2748b, 2773b, 2793b, 2897b, 3008b, 3025b, 3027b, 3032b, 3050b, 3056b and 3104b. Scansions of 840b, 1573b and 3032b disregard an epenthetic vowel in the first foot. Some uncertain examples are 402b, 724b and 1455b.

[19] Old Norse S/Sxx with double alliteration: *Vsp* 40/7; *Hym* 32/7; *Þrk* 21/5; *Rþ* 29/5, 29/7; and *Hdl* 43/7. Other S/Sxx a-verses: *Hym* 33/5, *HH* 37/7 and *Hdl* 49/5. S/Sxx b-verses: *Vsp* 7/4, 7/6; *Hym* 12/8, 31/8; *Þrk* 6/6; *HH* 31/8, 41/8, 43/4; *HHv* 41/2; *Rþ* 1/4, 29/6; *Hdl* 28/10, 44/2; *Grt* 4/4, 15/2, 20/6 and 23/2. For putative examples with enclitics in the second foot, see below, p. 135.

71

examples can be attributed entirely to increased use of nominal and adjectival Sxx words (e.g. *tiúgari*), which have a higher probability of alliteration than Sxx verbs. The *Beowulf* poet uses the light expanded Da pattern Sx/Sxx twenty-six times in the a-verse, but this type is even less productive than the bare numbers would suggest. All of the a-verses have the ancient formulaic structure X *maþelode* 'X spoke', where X is a personal name.[20] No name begins with *m*, so double alliteration does not occur. The Old English poem contains only two b-verses of the form Sx/Sxx (*Beo* 1125b, 1663b). In the Norse corpus, we find two Sx/Sxx b-verses but no corresponding a-verses. There is one apparent case of double alliteration (*Þrk* 25/6), but since it stands in the second half of the line, where double alliteration is forbidden, it should be excluded from consideration as an error. Verse (8) seems to be the only legitimate Norse example of its kind. The light Da variants, then, provide very little evidence for comparison of alliterative frequencies. The fact that the Old English examples almost always end in finite verbs makes it especially difficult to compare them with the Norse examples. Double alliteration seems to be the exception rather than the rule among Norse Sxx/S verses and short patterns. There are few verses like (9) and (10).[21]

If we set aside the variants with an Sxx foot in second position, the contrast between the two traditions seems clear. In native Eddic fornyrðislag, the second S alliterates significantly less often than in *Beowulf*. As predicted, the more forceful stress of the Old Norse language is reflected as a stronger metrical stress. Assignment of alliteration to the first arsis in Norse type A1 causes deep subordination of the second arsis, inhibiting optional alliteration.

[20] *Beo* 348a, 360a, 371a, 405a, 456a, 499a, 529a, 631a, 925a, 957a, 1215a, 1321a, 1383a, 1473a, 1651a, 1687a, 1817a, 1840a, 1999a, 2425a, 2510a, 2631a, 2724a, 2862a, 3045a, 3076a; 1125b and 1663b.

[21] Other Norse Sxx/S verses with double alliteration: *HH II* 32/1, 36/1; *Rþ* 6/1, 20/1, 21/3, 33/5; *Hdl* 14/1; and *Grt* 17/3. Other Sxx/S a-verses: *Vsp* 20/3; *Hym* 10/5, 19/5, 31/1; *Þrk* 9/7; *HH* 2/1; *HHv* 33/1, 42/1; *HH II* 18/1, 32/5, 33/1, 36/3, 50/1; *Rþ* 27/1; *Hdl* 20/5, 40/5, 44/5; and *Grt* 7/3. Sxx/S b-verses: *Vsp* 29/2, 38/4; *Hym* 3/4, 6/4, 34/4, 38/2; *Þrk* 8/8, 11/8, 22/6; *HH* 26/8, 33/2, 50/2; *HHv* 33/12; *Rþ* 4/8, 26/4 and 32/4. The remaining short patterns with double alliteration are *Þrk* 18/3 (Sx/S), ?*HHv* 7/7 (possibly Sx/S), *Rþ* 41/7 (Sx/S) and *Rþ* 24/5 (S/Sx).

NON-REVERSED HEAVY PATTERNS

Several patterns with an S position in the first foot have an s position as well as an S position in the second foot. These patterns have a tree structure like that below:

(11)

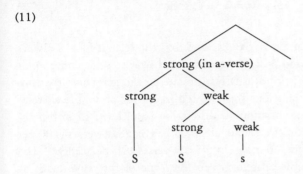

This tree represents the hierarchical structure of a-verses, which are dominated by a strong node.[22] In such a-verses, the second S lies within the weak constituent of a strong constituent, and may alliterate optionally. The rightward S and s positions will always undergo metrical subordination to the first S, which alliterates obligatorily, like the first S of any verse pattern. When the second S alliterates as well, the following s position is doubly subordinated (see R7b) and becomes too weak for optional alliteration (see R8b). Because the S position of a compound foot has priority for alliteration (see R8d), verses with the structure of (11) never have alliterating s. The tree for the corresponding b-verses is like (11) except for its highest labelled node, which is weak. In such b-verses, the second S lies within the weak constituent of a weak constituent, and must not alliterate (see R8b). The a-verses below illustrate the maximum extent of alliteration for this hierarchical structure:

(12) briótr / berg-Dana[23]   (*Hym* 17/7)
      [S/Ssx]

---

[22] A node is said to *dominate* every node into which it branches downwards. A node *immediately dominates* the first pair of nodes into which it branches (those immediately below it on the tree).

[23] 'destroyer of giants ...'

(13) Renni / raucn bitluð[24]   (*HH* 51/1)
[Sx/Ssx]

(14) Haraldr / hilditǫnn[25]   (*Hdl* 28/1)
[S/Sxs, first S resolved]

(15) brotinn var / borðveggr[26]   (*Vsp* 24/5)
[Sx/Ss, first S resolved]

(16) svort verða / sólscin[27]   (*Vsp* 41/5)
[Sxx/Ss]

In a-verses of the form Sx/Ss, Sxx/Ss, or S/Sxs, the second foot is always occupied by a compound or a group of stressed words. Since compounds and word groups of this kind usually alliterate on the first constituent in Germanic poetry, all traditions show a high frequency of double alliteration.[28] The *Beowulf* poet has double alliteration in all but four of ninety-eight Sx/Ss a-verses (96 per cent), in all seventeen Sxx/Ss a-verses (100 per cent) and in all but one of sixty-six S/Sxs a-verses (98 per cent).[29] The Norse poets have double alliteration in forty-one of forty-five Sx/Ss a-verses (91 per cent), in two of four Sxx/Ss a-verses (50 per cent) and in ten of seventeen S/Sxs a-verses (59 per cent).[30] There is 100 per cent double

---

[24] 'Let the bitted steeds run ...'   [25] 'Harald War-tooth ...'
[26] 'The plank-wall was broken ...'   [27] 'the sun's light will be dimmed ...'
[28] See *OEM*, ch. 8.
[29] My analysis differs little from that of Pope, *Rhythm*, which lists examples of the patterns Sx/Ss and Sxx/Ss under the heading A2b in the catalogue of scansions. As Pope notes (p. 258), there is a compound proper name in all four Sx/Ss a-verses with single alliteration (*Beo* 417a, 863a, 1181a and 2663a). The Sxx/Ss verses are 515a, 641a, 693a, 922a, 1161a, 1426a, 2085a, 2132a, 2173a, 2893a, 2957a, 2980a, 2991a, 3090a, 3118a, 3132a and 3173a. Verse 2119a, which also has double alliteration, might be Sxx/Ss or Sxx/Sx. Very uncertain are 2420b, 2721b and 2728b (see *OEM*, examples 99b, 100). The S/Sxs a-verse with single alliteration is *Flōd / blōde wēol* (1422a). Other examples are listed by Pope under subtype D4. This list includes four a-verse examples of the pattern S/Sxxs with double alliteration: 387a, 729a, 848a and 2367a. Cf. 2527a and 2774a, also with double alliteration.
[30] Norse Sx/Ss a-verses with single alliteration: *Vsp* 12/1; *Þrk* 15/5, 19/1; and *Hdl* 13/1. With double alliteration: *Vsp* 1/5, 12/5, 12/7, 24/5, 31/7, 41/7, 46/5, 49/1, 58/1; *Hym* 34/5; *Þrk* 15/3; *HH* 14/3; *HHv* 1/1; *HH II* 14/1, ?20/1 (probably xx/Ss); *Rþ* 13/5, 41/5; *Hdl* 14/7, 15/1, 15/5, 16/9 (plus 9 repetitions), 17/7, 18/3, 18/7, 18/9, 20/1, 23/5, 31/3, 32/5, 34/3, 36/3, 39/3; and *Grt* 23/5. Sxx/Ss a-verses with single alliteration: *HH* 41/1 and *Bdr* 13/1. Another with double alliteration: *Hdl* 14/5. S/Sxs a-verses with single alliteration: *Hym* 32/5; *Rþ* 2/7, 14/7, 15/1, 23/1, 25/1 and 31/5. In some of these, there is a weakly stressed word on the s position of the Sxs foot, and R1a would

alliteration in long Old English variants of type Db with no Old Norse equivalents (including thirty-one of the form Sx/Sxs and one of the form Sx/Sxxs).[31]

Da variants with the pattern S/Ssx or Sx/Ssx often have a compound or word group in the second foot (cf. examples (12) and (13)). In a significant number of cases, however, the second foot contains an Ssx simplex with a long medial syllable:

$$(17) \quad \text{Rígr / gangandi}^{32} \qquad\qquad (R\flat\ 36/3)$$
$$\qquad\quad \text{[S/Ssx]}$$
$$(18) \quad \text{goð- / málugra}^{33} \qquad\qquad (Hym\ 38/3)$$
$$\qquad\quad \text{[S/Ssx]}$$

Ssx forms like *gangandi* and *málugra* have a lower probability of alliteration than Ssx compounds. The Norse corpus contains six other S/Ssx a-verses like (17), three with double alliteration, and one other S/Ssx a-verse like (18), which has single alliteration.[34] A-verses of this kind occur significantly more often in *Beowulf*. I counted twenty-five like (17), eight with double alliteration, and forty-eight like (18), six with double alliteration.[35] The Norse poet prefers to place Da verses with Ssx

not mandate alliteration on the preceding S. Others with double alliteration: *Vsp* 41/3, 47/3; *Þrk* 13/3, 21/7; *HH* 1/3; *Rþ* 42/1; *Hdl* 11/11, 16/7 and 46/3.

[31] The Sx/Sxxs a-verse is *oncýð / eorla gehwǽm* (*Beo* 1420a). Sx/Sxs a-verses: *Beo* 358a, 400a, 402a, 421a, 625a, 726a, 938a, 1023a, 1274a, 1312a, 1359a, 1447a, 1450a, 1452a, 1617a, 1627a, 1679a, 1729a, 1757a, 1837a, 1854a, 2044a, 2286a, 2422a, 2451a, 2478a, 2687a, 2731a, 2964a, 3115a and 3123a. If epenthetic vowels were disregarded, 1023a would scan as Sx/Ss and 2687a as S/Sxs. Uncertain cases are 2107a (possibly xx/ Sxs) and 2205a (which may well originally have had *hild-* rather than *hilde-*; see Terasawa, *Nominal Compounds*, pp. 20–2).

[32] 'Rígr walking ...'   [33] 'of those who know divine lore ...'

[34] Like (17) are *HH* 40/1; *HH II* 20/7 and 51/3. With double alliteration: *Vsp* 3/7, *Hym* 29/5 and *HH* 47/5. Like (18) is *HH* 26/9. *HH* 29/7, an S/Ssx verse consisting of a triple compound, has alliterating constituents on both S positions.

[35] S/Ssx a-verses with an Ssx simplex: *Beo* 148a, 291a, 351a, 412a, 428a, 663a, 1021a, 1083a, 1183a, 1203a, 1418a, 1601a, 1653a, 2093a, 2159a, 2350a and 2424a. With double alliteration: 473a, 546a, 581a, 612a, 1690a, 1919a, 2062a and 3142a. S/Ssx a-verses wholly occupied by a compound: 2a, 63a, 245a, 246a, 255a, 295a, 299a, 744a, 861a, 919a, 952a, 1006a, 1016a, 1019a, 1346a, 1355a, 1389a, 1402a, 1586a, 1625a, 1637a, 1788a, 1798a, 1811a, 1945a, 2004a, 2125a, 2235a, 2504a, 2548a, 2565a, 2708a, 2734a, 2814a, 2837a, 2868a, 2895a, 2921a, 2955a, 3112a and 3158a. Cf. 2795a (disregarding epenthetic vowel). With double alliteration: 176a, 394a, 799a, 1438a, 2106a and 2338a.

75

simplexes in the second half of the line. I counted twenty-seven b-verses corresponding to the seven a-verses like (17) and (18).[36] In *Beowulf*, the distribution of variants like (17) and (18) is more nearly even, with about eighty-six b-verses and seventy-three a-verses.[37] A higher percentage of a-verses containing Ssx simplexes naturally brings down the percentage of double alliteration for total S/Ssx verses in the Old English poem. S/Ssx verses with an Ssx compound occupying the second foot, however, alliterate with a frequency of about 80 per cent in both traditions. Norse Da variants with the appropriate structure for single alliteration may have been shifted to the b-verse to make room for B and E variants, which had become more complex and were therefore shifted to the a-verse.[38]

REVERSED HEAVY PATTERNS

Reversal of the patterns S/Ssx and Sx/Ss yields Ssx/S (type E) and Ss/Sx (an A2 subtype). The metrical tree for these reversed patterns corresponds to the purely linguistic tree (3), which represents relative prominence relations in Norse triple compounds with a heavy first constituent:

---

[36] S/Ssx b-verses comparable to (17): *Vsp* 17/6, 20/2, 47/2, 66/2; *Hym* 36/2; *Þrk* 10/4, 13/6, 15/8, 19/4; *HH* 9/6, 16/4, 27/4, 49/8; *HH II* 8/2; *Rþ* 1/6, 36/2; *Hdl* 14/4, 22/4, 47/2; and *Grt* 12/4. Comparable to (18): *Hym* 7/6; *Þrk* 13/8; *HH II* 27/6; *Rþ* 39/6; *Hdl* 43/6; and *Grt* 3/2.

[37] OE S/Ssx b-verses with an Ssx simplex in the second foot: *Beo* 30b, 47b, 58b, 170b, 216b, 229b, 270b, 294b, 312b, 345b, 371b, 456b, 500b, 521b, 620b, 652b, 778b, 847b, 1069b, 1096b, 1210b, 1321b, 1563b, 1851b, 1860b, 2026b, 2052b, 2101b, 2381b, 2484b, 2537b, 2603b, 2809b, 2889b, 2912b, 2985b, 3002b, 3017b, 3080b and 3107b. Cf. 306b, 1803b (possibly with Ssx verbs); 1724b (disregarding an epenthetic vowel); 1871b (reading *betestan*); and 2259b (reading *ïrenna*). Wholly occupied by a compound: 9b, 51b, 95b, 237b, 309b, 372b, 377b, 449b, 464b, 468b, 535b, 568b, 597b, 746b, 962b, 1004b, 1013b, 1039b, 1108b, 1142b, 1155b, 1227b, 1308b, 1518b, 1684b, 1710b, 1780b, 1888b, 2015b, 2022b, 2089b, 2205b, 2382b, 2503b, 2607b, 2694b, 2716b, 2720b, 2778b, 2781b, 2908b, 2927b, 3017b, 3091b, 3113b and 3138b. Cf. 3017b (disregarding an epenthetic vowel) and 3180b (as emended).

[38] See above, pp. 39, 41 and 42.

(19)

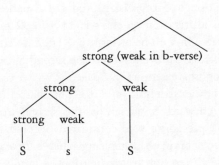

As noted above, a-verses of the form Sx/Ss and S/Ssx tend to have double alliteration because compound feet tend to alliterate. Reversal displaces the compound foot to the left, where its S position will alliterate in accord with R8a, like any other verse-initial S position. One effect of reversal, then, is to cancel out the influence of compound feet on alliterative patterns. When the second foot contains a simplex word, the frequency of double alliteration in the a-verse should provide a straight-forward indication of metrical strength.

The following a-verses illustrate the maximal extent of alliteration in fornyrðislag patterns with the hierarchical structure (19):

(20) harðráðr / Hymir[39]   (*Hym* 10/3)
      [Ss/Sx]

(21) Sigrlinnar / sonr[40]   (*HHv* 35/7)
      [Ssx/S]

Only about 52 per cent of Norse Ss/Sx a-verses are like example (20), which has alliteration on the second S position (34/65).[41] Deep subordi-

---

[39] 'cruel Hymir . . .'   [40] 'son of Sigrlinn . . .'

[41] Norse Ss/Sx a-verses with single alliteration: *Vsp* 19/3, 37/7, 42/7, 43/7; *Hym* 4/7, 19/3, 22/7, 30/3, 30/7; *Þrk* ?26/5; *HH* 6/3, 11/7, 16/7, 25/5, 27/7, 30/7, 37/3, 38/7; *HHv* 33/3; *HH II* 10/3, 25/3, 39/3; *Bdr* 6/1; *Rþ* 25/3; *Hdl* 9/7, 14/3, 22/3, 24/3, 30/9, 40/1; and *Grt* 16/3 (triple compound incorporating Ss compound). With double alliteration: *Vsp* 1/7, 2/7, 13/7, 28/3, 30/7, 32/3, 35/3, 48/7, 52/5, 63/5, 65/3, 66/3, 66/7; *Hym* 2/3, 5/3, 8/7, 9/1, 10/3, 20/3, 23/7, 24/1, 25/1, 35/7; *HH* 1/7, 5/7, 8/7, 49/7, 55/3; *HH II* 25/7, 42/7, 45/7; *Rþ* 25/3; *Grt* 8/3 and 19/3. Some of these examples have heavy derivative suffixes like -*ungr* on the s position. I interpret -*ungr* as stressed because it is so often followed by unresolved S in the second foot, which is characteristic of the pattern Ss/Sx but rare in the pattern Sx/Sx.

nation of this position in fornyrðislag produces a marked contrast with *Beowulf*, which has alliteration on the second S in 92 per cent of about 170 Ss/Sx a-verses.[42] Only eight of forty-one Ssx/S a-verses in the Norse corpus (20 per cent) have alliteration on the second S, but the figure for about 130 corresponding examples in *Beowulf* is 78 per cent.[43]

In a-verses with the structure of (19), optional alliteration usually appears on the rightward S, which is the second-strongest metrical position. Since the preceding s is dominated by only one weak node, however, it may also contain an alliterating syllable. *Beowulf* provides four examples of double alliteration in the first foot, a number that turns out not to be suspiciously small.[44] Three corresponding verses occur in our Norse corpus:

(22)	Baldrs bróðir / var[45]	(*Vsp* 32/5)
	[Ssx/S]	
(23)	Reis Rígr at / þat[46]	(*Rþ* 33/3)
	[Ssx/S]	
(24)	Ól úlf / Loki[47]	(*Hdl* 40/1)
	[Ss/Sx]	

In heavy verses, rule R2b mandates assignment of stressed words to feet in accord with syntactic constituency. The major syntactic break of (22) obviously falls between the subject noun phrase and the verb. In (23), the subject *Rígr* stands in closer constituency with the preceding verb *reis*

---

[42] See Sievers, 'Rhythmik', pp. 275–8.

[43] Norse Ssx/S a-verses with single alliteration: *Vsp* 8/7, 14/7, 16/7, 26/1, 38/3; *Hym* 5/7, 7/3, 9/3, 28/3, 39/1; *HH* 16/3, 24/5, 27/5, 30/3, 33/1, 35/3, 42/3, 53/1; *HHv* 4/3, 8/7, 34/3, ?35/3, 39/3, 43/3; *HH II* 30/7, 36/9, 47/3, 50/3; *Rþ* 25/5; *Hdl* 18/5, 35/3; *Grt* 1/3 and 13/3. *Hdl* 49/7 would be added to these if emended to *eitrblandinn mioc*. With alliteration in each foot: *Vsp* 6/3, 9/3, 23/3, 25/3; *HH* 41/3; *HHv* 35/7; *Rþ* 10/5; and *Hdl* 38/3. I exclude doubtful variants of type E with finite verbs in medial position, which generally have single alliteration (see below, p. 134). The 130 Old English examples include *Beo* 2150a (read *liss ā gelong*) but exclude 1889a and 3179a, which are Ssx/S with double alliteration as printed by Klaeber. Verse 2673a could be type Db or type E with double alliteration in the first foot, depending on interpretation of the syntax. The count is only slightly different in Pope, *Rhythm*, pp. 314–18. Alternative methods of counting E verses are imaginable, but any reasonable method, if applied consistently, would show the same dramatic difference between Old English and Old Norse practice.

[44] See *OEM*, §7.5.3. [45] 'Baldr's brother was ...'

[46] 'Then Rígr rose up ...' [47] 'Loki gave birth to a wolf ...'

than with the following pronoun *þat*. In (24), the major syntactic break falls between the verb phrase and the subject. Sievers made an *ad-hoc* attempt to explain away Old English verses analogous to (22) and (23), classifying them against the syntax as Db variants of the form S/Sxs.[48] This approach is even less plausible when applied to the Norse verses, since type Db is quite rare in Eddic poetry. If (22) and (23) are type E verses, as they seem to be, they constitute a significant share of the examples with double alliteration. Rules R8a–d apply in their full generality here, permitting optional alliteration on any arsis not dominated by two weak nodes, whether in the first foot or the second. Note that in (23) and (24) the s position is occupied by a noun with more prominent linguistic stress than the preceding finite verb. Double alliteration in the first foot may have occurred most frequently under these conditions.[49]

ULTRA-HEAVY VERSES

A small number of A2 variants have an S position and an s position in each foot, with the hierarchical structure below:

(25)

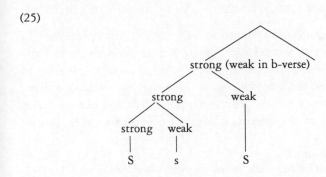

---

[48] See *OEM*, §7.5.3. The Old Saxon *Heliand* also contains some heavy verses with double alliteration in the first foot, for example the Ss/Sx variant *fagar folc / godes* 412a (cf. *grôt craft / godes* 2870a, another Ss/Sx verse with optional alliteration on the stronger primary arsis of the second foot, the more usual location). A clear case in type E is *uuorduuîse / man* 1433a. A third example, *berht bôcan / godes* 661a, with an epenthetic *-a-* in *bôcan*, could be type E or type A2.

[49] See *OEM*, §9.12.

Like reversed patterns, ultra-heavy patterns must have no more than the usual number of metrical positions, four. Only the pattern Ss/Ss, in which every metrical position is an arsis, can have the hierarchical structure represented above. Since it is dominated by only one weak node, the first s position of an Ss/Ss verse is theoretically eligible for alliteration, but the handful of relevant English and Norse examples have the second alliterating syllable in the usual place, on the second S, which is metrically stronger than the first s. The Norse example below illustrates this type:

(26)   vindǫld, / vargǫld[50]   (*Vsp* 45/9)
       [Ss/Ss]

As in the pattern Sx/Ss, the verse-final Ss foot often contains a compound or word group with a high probability of alliteration. In the Norse corpus, eight of the nine other verses like (26) appear in the first half of the line with double alliteration.[51] In *Beowulf*, twenty-six of twenty-seven a-verses have double alliteration, and there seem to be only two examples in the b-verse.[52]

VERSES WITH A LIGHT FOOT AND A COMPOUND FOOT

The verse types considered so far have at least one arsis in the first foot. In such types, the feet are bound together by a metrical equivalent of the compound stress rule, which subordinates the second foot to the first. In the remaining types, the first foot consists of one or more weak positions, and is inherently weaker than the following foot. The feet of such verses are bound together by the metrical equivalent of proclisis rather than by

---

[50] 'an age of storm and crime ...'

[51] Ss/Ss in the b-verse: *Rþ* 8/8 (possibly Ss/Sx). Others with double alliteration: *Vsp* 26/7, 45/7; *HH* 8/3, 8/5, 14/5, 50/7; *HH II* 45/11; and *Hdl* 21/1.

[52] Ss/Ss a-verse with single alliteration: *Beo* 653a. With double alliteration: 61a, 193a, 215a, 251a, 287a, 308a, 330a, 485a, 608a, 653a, 690a, 1017a, 1189a, 1246a, 1267a, 1424a, 1489a, 1650a, 1698a, 1719a, 1881a, 2154a, 2339a, 2624a, 2618a, 3135a. Cf. 780a, 1424a and 3041a (as emended). The only comparable cases in the b-verse are 367b and 1148b. Verses 457b, 530b and 1704b might scan as Ss/Ss, however, if *mīn* had significant stress in post-nominal position. A lexicalized, non-alliterating Ss compound might have the metrical value Sx in some variants listed above (see *OEM*, §3.4), but the strong preference of such variants for the a-verse suggests that Ss was the default value.

R7. Most verses with a light first foot have a heavy second foot that contains an s position as well as an S position. These have the hierarchical structure below:

(27)

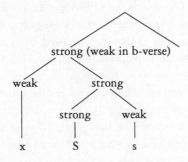

Representation (27) has no nodes for the x positions that correspond to non-radical syllables, since these do not participate in compound or phrasal stress rules. The x foot attaches to a node, however, since it corresponds to the root syllable of a word that has become proclitic through stress subordination at the level of the phrase. Alliteration is assigned obligatorily to the S position (see R8d) and the following s position then undergoes subordination (see R7b). In the a-verse, the s position is a weak constituent of a strong constituent, and may contain an alliterating syllable.

The following examples illustrate the maximum extent of alliteration in the a-verse:

(28) Þat vann / næst nýs[53]   (*HH II* 8/1)
      [xx/Ss, double alliteration]

(29) óx / geira gnýr[54]   (*HH* 54/3)
      [x/Sxs, double alliteration]

(30) enn / iofur annan[55]   (*HH II* 16/3)
      [x/Ssx, S resolved, double alliteration]

In general, Norse poets make freer use of A3 variants than does the *Beowulf* poet, for whom this type can present the appearance of an incomplete a-verse with anacrusis or an incomplete hypermetrical

---

[53] 'Accomplished that most recently . . .' Cf. *Hdl* 5/7, also with double alliteration.
[54] 'the battle became more intense . . .'   [55] 'but to another prince . . .'

b-verse.[56] The heavy A3 pattern xx/Ss appears less than thirty times in the Old English epic.[57] In the smaller Norse corpus, there are sixty-six heavy A3 verses, including one b-verse, two unambiguous examples of the Norse variant xxx/Ss and twenty-seven examples with a word group in the second foot.[58] The greater complexity of heavy A3 for Old English poets seems to preclude employment of a word group in the Ss foot.[59] In *Beowulf*, where the Ss foot is always occupied by a compound, double alliteration is unlikely, perhaps even infelicitous, since the subordinated word-final syllable on the s position may have especially low prominence.[60] In the Norse corpus, where an independent word may occupy the second arsis, there are two examples like (28) with double alliteration.

As we have often observed, the foot pattern Sxs corresponds to a low-frequency compound pattern, serving most often as a convenient site for word groups. Because an unsubordinated constituent often fills the s position, a significant frequency of double alliteration is expected. Of 168 Norse type B variants appearing in the first half of the line, 155 (92 per cent) have a word group rather than a compound in the Sxs foot, and forty-one of these are like (29), with double alliteration (24 per cent of total a-verses).[61] Of 232 corresponding a-verses in *Beowulf*, 191 (82 per

---

[56] See above, pp. 48–9.

[57] OE xx/Ss verses: *Beo* 168a, 219a, 484a, 506a, 1059a, 1496a, 1504a, 1599a, 1652a, 1836a, 1877a, 1995a, 2101a, 2258a, 2376a, 2389a, 2437a, 2466a, 2699a, 2770a and 3147a. *Beo* 9a would belong here if *æghwylc* had significant stress on the secondary constituent. Verse 2892a is probably xx/Ss, since *Heht* functions as an auxiliary and probably does not count as an alliterating syllable. Cf. 1794a and 2172a, where alliteration in the first foot seems more likely, though perhaps not certain.

[58] The xx/Ss b-verse is *Bdr* 6/2. Two-word xxx/Ss: *HHv* 3/1 and 10/1. ON xx/Ss a-verses: *Vsp* 4/3, 21/1, 24/3, 29/1, 39/7, 48/3; *Þrk* 1/1, 15/1, 26/7, 27/5, 28/7; *HH* 12/1, 33/5, 35/1, 41/5, 48/5, 48/7, 50/1, 54/5, 56/1, 56/5; *HHv* 2/5, 4/5; *HH II* 19/1, 20/1, 21/5, 22/1, 25/1, 38/5, 39/1, 42/1, 45/1, 45/9; *Hdl* 4/5, 27/5 and 37/5. With a word group in the second foot: *Vsp* 6/1, 9/1, 19/7, 23/1, 23/7, 25/1, 25/5; *Þrk* 4/1, 12/7, 20/5; *HH* 50/3; *HHv* 33/9; *HH II* 2/3, 8/1, 9/1, 9/3, 18/5, 40/1, 41/1; *Rþ* 45/1, 47/3; *Hdl* 5/1, 5/ 5, 5/7, 6/5, 7/3 and 10/3. Some of these examples would scan as xx/Sx if the verse-final function word was enclitic. Heavy derivative syllables such as *-ungr* are assigned to a secondary arsis here as in the pattern Ss/Sx.

[59] *OEM*, §5.4.2.

[60] According to *OEG*, §§88–9, Ss forms had a weaker subordinate stress than corresponding Ssx forms (in which s would be strong relative to x).

[61] ON type B with double alliteration in a word group: *Vsp* 3/3, 7/3, 26/3, 33/3, 44/7, 49/7, 58/7; *Hym* 3/7, 10/7, 39/3; *Þrk* 25/7; *HH* 3/3, 6/7, 9/5, 13/5, 17/3, 20/3, 27/1,

cent) have a word group in the Sxs foot, and there are seventy-three instances of double alliteration (31 per cent of total a-verses).[62] The Norse type C pattern x/Ssx presents us with a surprisingly high frequency of double alliteration, which occurs in 26 per cent of total a-verses (72/279) as compared with 10 per cent (50/500) for the corresponding Old English a-verses.[63] The difference can be attributed entirely to the character of the alliterating constituent occupying the s position. Of the 279 Norse a-verses, 51 per cent (143) have an Ssx foot filled by a word group, as in example (30), where the s position is occupied by the root syllable of an independent word. The corresponding frequency for the Old English poem is only 16 per cent (81/500). The *Beowulf* poet obtains a single word more often for the second foot of type C through the technique of poetic compounding, which is not used systematically in Eddic metres.

27/3, 28/5, 31/7, 47/7, 50/9, 54/3; *HHv* 6/7; *HH II* 8/3, 10/7, 27/7, 35/5, 39/7, 40/3; *Bdr* 11/7, 14/7; *Rþ* 48/1; *Hdl* 2/3, 15/3; *Grt* 10/7 and 19/7. Three doubtful examples of long type B, which may originally have been ordinary type B, are *Vsp* 29/5, *HH* 21/3 and *Hdl* 24/7. With double alliteration in a compound: *HH II* 35/3.

[62] OE type B with double alliteration in a word group: *Beo* 30a, 102a, 182a, 185a, 264a, 267a, 337a, 384a, 403a, 407a, 414a, 432a, 478a, 507a, 511a, 518a, 576a, 578a, 611a, 642a, 674a, 686a, 725a, 821a, 980a, 983a, 991a, 997a, 1030a, 1057a, 1063a, 1115a, 1148a, 1173a, 1199a, 1210a, 1228a, 1300a, 1335a, 1393a, 1394a, 1405a, 1448a, 1551a, 1693a, 1726a, 1764a, 1787a, 1950a, 2008a, 2013a, 2015a, 2052a, 2060a, 2105a, 2208a, 2255a, 2287a, 2312a, 2316a, 2348a, 2431a, 2472a, 2619a, 2633a, 2645a, 2879a, 2989a, 3005a, 3069a and 3117a. With double alliteration in a compound: 2935a and 3150a. Long type B variants with double alliteration having no certain Old Norse equivalents: 79a, 362a, 504a, 639a, 756a, 760a, 800a, 1360a, 1484a, 1696a, 1763a, 1864a, 2045a, 2259a, 2353a, 2441a, 2505a and 2767a.

[63] ON type C with double alliteration in an Ssx word group: *Vsp* 4/7, 9/7, 20/9, 21/5, 24/7, 25/7, 27/7, 28/11, 28/13, 29/3, 39/9, 50/7, 51/3, 52/7, 53/5, 57/7, 63/3; *Hym* 6/3, 11/1, 11/5, 26/3, 30/5, 35/5, 37/5, 38/1; *Þrk* 31/7, 32/7; *HH* 4/5, 36/9, 44/7, 46/7; *HHv* 10/5, 31/1, 41/7, 43/5; *HH II* 1/7, 4/13, 8/7, 10/5, 16/3, 24/7, 35/1, 36/5, 40/5, 41/5, 43/5, 50/9; *Bdr* 5/5, 5/7, 10/5, 10/7, 14/5; *Rþ* 3/5, 5/5, 15/3, 19/7, 26/5, 30/5; *Hdl* 1/1, 1/5, 3/1, 7/5; *Grt* 2/3, 3/1, 5/3, 6/3, 6/7, 12/3 and 21/3. With double alliteration in an Ssx compound: *Hym* 1/3, 2/1, 36/5; *Þrk* 31/3; and *HH* 17/7. Comparable OE verses with double alliteration in an Ssx word group: *Beo* 4a, 20a, 60a, 188a, 212a, 319a, 424a, 604a, 659a, 735a, 765a, 855a, 865a, 974a, 1024a, 1034a, 1073a, 1167a, 1202a, 1233a, 1280a, 1352a, 1703a, 1737a, 1766a, 1842a, 1930a, 2160a, 2264a, 2380a, 2394a, 2473a, 2477a, 2533a and 2570a. Possible additions to this list are 164a (if *fela* has significant stress), 2212a (as emended) and 3171a (as emended). With double alliteration in an Ssx compound: 178a, 187a, 324a, 707a, 792a, 840a, 851a, 885a, 921a, 1146a, 1149a, 1704a, 2560a, 2652a and 2946a.

ULTRA-LIGHT VERSES

The simplest hierarchical structure represents verse types with only one arsis:

(31)

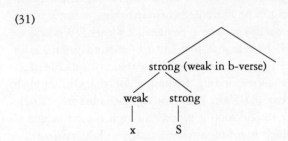

R8a mandates alliteration on the strongest two S positions of the line, that is, on the strongest S position of the a-verse and the strongest S position of the b-verse. In either half of the line, obviously, the isolated S of a structure like (31) must contain an alliterating syllable. All verses with this structure therefore have the same alliterative pattern:

$$(32) \quad \text{verða / flestir}^{64} \qquad \text{(Hdl 49/3)}$$
$$\text{[xx/Sx]}$$
$$(33) \quad \text{um / sacnaði}^{65} \qquad (\textit{Þrk} \ 1/4)$$
$$\text{[x/Sxx]}$$
$$(34) \quad \text{Þá qvað þat / Þrymr}^{66} \qquad (\textit{Þrk} \ 22/1)$$
$$\text{[xxx/S]}$$

Since the poet has no alliterative choices to make in verses with the structure of (31), there is nothing more to say about them here.[67]

SUMMARY

In fornyrðislag, a rightward arsis underwent particularly deep subordination to a preceding arsis within its metrical domain. Norse metrical subordination imitated the forceful subordination of the natural language, which reduced many syllables to the point of extinction and incorporated

---

[64] 'most are destined ...'
[65] 'realized that he had lost ...' [66] 'Then Þrymr spoke ...'
[67] On the restricted frequency of type A3 in the second half of the line, see above, p. 49.

many unstressed function words into larger words.[68] Old English had a less forceful primary stress, as evidenced by the greater number of unstressed syllables that survived and the more restricted scope of clitic incorporation.[69] In *Beowulf*, therefore, metrical subordination was less deep, and an alliterating syllable was more likely to occupy a rightward arsis. We can be quite sure that the lower frequency of double alliteration in the Norse corpus reflects genuine stylistic preference rather than accidental limitation. Although the Eddic poems are anonymous, our corpus unquestionably contains the work of several authors, and its traditional subject matter would have allowed for employment of traditional style. We also have the testimony of *Háttatal*, which states that the a-verse should have single alliteration in fornyrðislag.[70]

Norse metres showing a preference for double alliteration in the a-verse do not employ the technique of metrical compounding. In málaháttr, there is no word-foot structure on which metrical compounding could operate. The negligible frequency of two-word verses in *Atlamál*, for example, can be seen at a glance.[71] In dróttkvætt and related skaldic metres, foot structure may be present, but the link between relative prominence and alliteration has been broken. The skalds assign alliteration to a fixed position at the beginning of the b-verse, allowing function words to alliterate if necessary. At the beginning of the skaldic a-verse, monosyllabic nouns and adjectives sometimes fail to alliterate.[72] Without metrical compounding, the only way to emphasize the structural integrity of the line is to exaggerate the asymmetry between its subcomponents. In dróttkvætt, the number of alliterating syllables is fixed at two in the a-verse and at one in the b-verse. The a-verse normally has double alliteration in *Atlamál*, and Snorri's paradigmatic example of málaháttr has double alliteration in every a-verse.[73]

---

[68] See above, p. 26.

[69] A few OE forms like *næs* (< *ne wæs*) show absorption of a negative proclitic by a following auxiliary. There are no OE enclitic forms comparable to the Norse ones.

[70] See Faulkes, *Háttatal*, p. 38.

[71] There are only seventeen two-word b-verses in this poem of 105 stanzas: 2/2, 4/6, 13/6, 37/6, 54/6, 65/6, 67/4, 70/6, 72/8, 73/2, 80/4, 88/2, 89/2, 91/2, 94/2, 98/2 and 98/4. In *HH*, there are seventeen two-word b-verses in the first seven stanzas: 1/4, 1/6, 1/8, 2/2, 2/6, 2/8, 3/4, 3/6, 3/8, 4/2, 4/6, 5/2, 6/2, 6/4, 7/2, 7/6 and 7/8.

[72] See Frank, *Old Norse Court Poetry*, pp. 35–6.

[73] See Faulkes, *Háttatal*, p. 37.

Since the skalds alliterate according to new principles, their technical terms are not reliable guides to Eddic versecraft. The term *hǫfuðstafr*, for example, is defined in *Háttatal* as the first syllable of the dróttkvætt b-verse.[74] It was probably considered the 'chief stave' by skalds because of its fixed, central position in the line, not because it had the highest relative prominence as that concept is understood here. The two alliterating syllables of the dróttkvætt a-verse, called *stuðlar* by the skalds, seem to have been conceived as buttresses supporting a central pillar, but this metaphor can hardly be interpreted as evidence for subordination of the Eddic a-verse to the Eddic b-verse. According to *Háttatal*, the position of the chief stave in fornyrðislag is fixed *í miðju orði* 'in the middle of the verse'.[75] This obviously misrepresents Eddic practice, which assigns alliteration to the first prominent syllable of the b-verse, irrespective of position. The value of *Háttatal* for students of Eddic metres is to show what variants were regarded as typical by skalds with a strong impulse toward regularization and access to material now lost. Skaldic fornyrðislag may have been regularized to some extent in direct contrast to dróttkvætt, which always has two alliterating syllables in the a-verse and always has alliteration on the first syllable of the b-verse.

[74] Ibid., p. 4.   [75] Ibid., p. 38.

7

Metrical subordination within the foot

Printed editions of the Eddic poems represent verse and line boundaries by visual means for an audience of readers. The original audience had to recover these boundaries from the acoustic signal at the speed of recitation. Studies of Old English metre have emphasized the importance of alliteration as an acoustic boundary marker for the verse and the line.[1] Alliteration sometimes provided a useful marker for the boundary of the foot as well. Rule R2a provides one important cue to the location of the foot boundary by requiring that it coincide with a word boundary. When a verse contains extrametrical words, however, or when a word group occupies the foot, the audience must determine which of two or more word boundaries corresponds to the verse-medial foot boundary. In such cases, Old English poets used optional alliteration to make the leftward boundary of the second foot more conspicuous. Old Norse poets also used this technique to some extent:

(1)	grœnom / lauki[2]	(Vsp 4/8)
	[Sx/Sx, two words]	
(2)	meiri / (oc) minni[3]	(Vsp 1/3)
	[Sx/(x)Sx, with extrametrical word]	
(3)	Ár var / alda[4]	(Vsp 3/1)
	[Sx/Sx, word group in first foot]	
(4)	gær á / morgon[5]	(HH II 12/3)
	[Sx/Sx, word group in first foot]	

In the Norse corpus, two-word realizations of type A1 tend to appear in

---

[1] Kuryłowicz, *Metrik und Sprachgeschichte*, p. 151; Creed, *Reconstructing*, p. 22.
[2] 'with green plants'.   [3] 'more and less important ...'
[4] 'It was the beginning of time ...'   [5] 'yesterday morning ...'

the second half of the line, comprising 61 per cent of Sx/Sx b-verses (416/ 679) but only 32 per cent of Sx/Sx a-verses (118/364). Of the 118 two-word a-verses, seventy-nine (67 per cent) have single alliteration, like (1). The remaining A1 verses have extrametrical words, like (2), or word groups in the first foot, like (3). These have a relatively high frequency in the a-verse (49 per cent, as opposed to 32 per cent for the two-word verses) and 137 of the 246 a-verses have double alliteration (56 per cent, as opposed to 33 per cent for the two-word verses). Although double alliteration obviously helps to mark boundaries obscured by the syntax in fornyrðislag, deep subordination of the rightward arsis restricts employment of this strategy. In *Beowulf*, where subordination is less forceful, 93 per cent of the variants comparable to (2) and (3) have double alliteration. The contrast shows up most clearly in a-verses of the kind represented by (4), with a preposition before the final Sx word. Of sixty-four such Norse variants, twenty-four (38 per cent) have single alliteration.[6] Kendall finds 181 comparable a-verses in *Beowulf*. Single alliteration occurs in only two of these, and one of the two is an editorial emendation.[7]

DOUBLE ALLITERATION AND HEAVY FEET

Heavy word groups occupying the second foot of an a-verse usually have alliteration on the first constituent. In such cases the word group resembles a short verse with two S positions:

$$(5) \quad \text{miór oc / mioc fagr}^8 \qquad\qquad (Vsp\ 31/7)$$
$$[\text{Sx//S/S, equivalent to Sx/Ss}]$$

[6] Additional examples with single alliteration: *Vsp* 8/4, 10/7, 37/3, 42/1, 42/5, 43/1, 55H/7; *Hym* 22/5; *Þrk* 6/1; *HH* 34/1; *HHv* 35/1, 39/1; *HH II* 26/5, 30/5, 37/7; *Rþ* 4/7, 11/3, 16/5, 16/7, 19/3, 32/7; *Hdl* 41/1; and *Grt* 5/5. With double alliteration: *Vsp* 8/1, 20/7, 45/5, 55/7, 56/11, 57/3, 59/3; *Hym* 3/3, 7/7, 9/7, 15/7, 17/5, 18/3, 21/3, 21/7, 22/1, 27/5, 27/7, 33/3, 36/1, 39/7; *Þrk* 21/3, 23/1, 27/1; *HH* 5/1, 5/5, 42/7, 49/1, 53/ 7, 53/9; *HHv* 9/1, 9/3; *HH II* 22/5, 48/7; *Rþ* 10/3, 31/3, 31/7; *Hdl* 8/1; *Grt* 5/7, 13/7 and 15/7.

[7] *Metrical Grammar*, p. 119. Some of the Norse A1 verses listed in the previous note resemble Old English verses analysed by Kendall as type A3 with an alliterating verb in the thesis. As Kendall points out (ibid.), these always have double alliteration in *Beowulf*, but in our Norse corpus they are no less likely to have single alliteration than variants classified by Kendall as type A1 (cf. *Vsp* 42/1, 42/5, 43/1; *Hym* 22/5; *Þrk* 22/3; *HH* 34/1; *HHv* 35/1, 39/1; *HH II* 26/5; *Rþ* 11/3, 19/3; *Grt* 5/5).

[8] 'slender and very fair . . . '

(6) drǫgom / dólgs siotul[9]   (*Grt* 16/7)
     [S//S/Sx, equivalent to S/Ssx]

(7) Renni / raucn bitluð[10]   (*HH* 51/1)
     [Sx//S/Sx, equivalent to Sx/Ssx]

(8) óc / Óðins sonr[11]   (*Þrk* 21/7)
     [S//Sx/S, equivalent to S/Sxs]

These variants have a significant mismatch on the last arsis of the heavy foot, which is occupied by a syllable of primary stress in a noun or adjective, the kind of syllable that usually occupies an S position. The second foot of (8), for example, looks much like a short Sx/S verse. Let us assume that the heavy feet in (5)–(8) do contain two S positions, as indicated in the scansions to the left. On this hypothesis, the heavy feet are domains for application of the metrical compounding rule (R7), which will assign alliteration to the first S and subordinate the second S, making it equivalent to an s position.[12] Application of R7 yields a verse with two feet, as indicated in the scansions to the right, so (5)–(8) have the binary structure required by principle P2. The posited effect of R7 is quite consistent with its basis in the natural language. Since linguistic compounding makes a larger word out of two smaller words, it seems reasonable to suppose that metrical compounding can create a larger word foot out of two smaller word feet.

Consider the following verses, which are like (5)–(8) except that the root syllable of a finite verb or function word occupies the final arsis:

(9) Bindo / (vér) Þór þá[13]   (*Þrk* 15/5)
     [Sx/(x)Ss]

(10) flýgr / vǫll yfir[14]   (*Vsp* 66/6)
     [S/Ssx]

(11) Snúðu / burt heðan![15]   (*Hdl* 46/1)
     [Sx/Ssx]

(12) brúðr / orð um qvað[16]   (*Grt* 24/2)
     [S/Sxs]

(13) líðr / lǫnd yfir[17]   (*Hdl* 42/3)
     [S/Ssx]

---

[9] 'we are turning the stiller of strife (i.e., the millstone of peace) ... '
[10] 'Let the bitted steeds run ... '   [11] 'Óðinn's son drove ... '
[12] See *OEM*, §8.3.   [13] 'Let us bind Þórr then ... '
[14] 'it flies over the ground ... '   [15] 'Go away from here!'
[16] 'The woman uttered words ... '   [17] 'it overwhelms the land ... '

The root syllables of the verse-final words, which have a linguistically subordinated stress, are most naturally assigned to s positions in underlying patterns.[18] Because metrical subordination applies only within a domain containing two S positions, it will not apply in the second foot of (9)–(13). R7 will not assign alliteration to the S position of the second foot, though this S may alliterate optionally, as in (13).

Old English verses comparable to (9)–(13) can appear with or without double alliteration, like their Old Norse counterparts. Old English verses comparable to (5)–(8) must have double alliteration, however, and are confined to the first half of the line accordingly. The observed distribution of these verses suggests that there was a categorical rule requiring strongly stressed constituents to occupy S positions.[19] Although Norse a-verses like (5)–(8) always have double alliteration, we find a few corresponding b-verses:

(14)	gorr / illz hugar[20]	(*Hym* 9/8)
	[S/Ssx]	
(15)	hver / Sifiar verr[21]	(*Hym* 34/6)
	[S/Sxs]	
(16)	hrís / gerstan dag[22]	(*Rþ* 9/6)
	[S/Sxs]	

The bracketed scansions for (14)–(16) presuppose that the verse-final words may occupy s positions. In fornyrðislag, apparently, the root syllable in nouns and adjectives, though normally assigned to an S position, could occupy an s position at a cost in complexity. The syntax often indicates the proper verse division in such cases. Observe the very sharp syntactic boundary between the feet in (15) and (16), for example, where the nouns *hver* and *hrís*, as direct objects of immediately preceding verbs, stand closer syntactically to the last word in the previous verse than to the following heavy word group. Isolated syntactically in this way, the heavy word group must have had sufficient integrity to be recognizable as a foot without metrical compounding. The absence of anything comparable to (15) and (16) in *Beowulf* may be due in part to stricter constraints on enjambment.

The probability of alliteration for a word with two stressed syllables

---

[18] See *OEM*, §8.2. [19] Ibid., §8.3, rule 66. [20] 'inclined to ill temper...'
[21] 'Sif's husband (placed) the cauldron ...'
[22] '(gathered) brushwood the weary day long'.

depends on the extent to which it is *lexicalized*, that is, perceived by the native speaker as a single constituent.[23] Consider the following:

(17)	margs / vitandi[24]	(*Vsp* 20/2)
	[S/Ssx]	
(18)	arf / Fiorsunga[25]	(*HH II* 20/7)
	[S/Ssx]	
(19)	Hróðrs / andscoti[26]	(*Hym* 11/8)
	[S/Ssx]	
(20)	vel / fullmikill[27]	(*Hym* 16/4)
	[S/Ssx]	
(21)	Veigr oc / Gandálfr[28]	(*Vsp* 12/1)
	[Sx/Ss]	
(22)	mǫgr / Sigfǫður[29]	(*Vsp* 55/2)
	[S/Ssx]	

The uncompounded Ssx forms in (17) and (18) have a long medial syllable that normally counts as stressed but bears no resemblance to a root syllable. Ssx forms with this type of medial syllable may stand without alliteration in the b-verse (see 17) or, less often, in the a-verse (see 18).[30] Comparable forms in *Beowulf* have the same type of distribution.[31] The Ssx word in (19) is a lexicalized form with a stressed prepositional adverb as the first constituent. Norse words of this kind appear several times in the b-verse without alliteration.[32] The *Beowulf* poet uses comparable

---

[23] *OEM*, §§1.1.2, 8.4, 8.6 and 9.2; Kendall, *Metrical Grammar*, pp. 159–91.

[24] 'knowing many things ... '   [25] 'inheritance of the Fiorsungs ... '

[26] 'Hróðr's adversary ... '   [27] 'very great indeed'.

[28] 'Veigr and Gandálfr ... '   [29] 'son of Óðinn ... '

[30] Other Norse Ssx simplexes without alliteration in the b-verse: *Vsp* 17/6, 20/2, 20/6, 47/2, 66/2; *Hym* 36/2; *Þrk* 10/4, 13/6, 15/8, 19/4; *HH* 9/6, 16/4, 27/4, 49/8; *HH II* 8/ 2; *Rþ* 1/6, 36/2; *Hdl* 2/4, 14/4, 22/4, 47/2; and *Grt* 12/4. Others without alliteration in the a-verse: *HH* 40/1, *HH II* 51/3 and *Rþ* 36/3. Simplexes with closed medial syllables have a distribution quite unlike those I represent as Sxx, which are frequently followed by a trochaic word when they appear verse-initially. In *Beowulf*, where the pattern Sxx/S is forbidden, words like *murnende* 'mourning' are almost always followed by a monosyllable or resolvable disyllable. Lexicalized words with long medial syllables do sometimes count as Sxx, but very infrequently. There are few verses like *wrǣtlicne / wundur-māððum* (*Beo* 2173a), which must be an instance of the pattern Sxx/Ss, with two pre-epenthetic forms in the Ss foot. See further *OEM*, §3.4.

[31] See Kendall, *Metrical Grammar*, p. 191.

[32] Cf. *Vsp* 2/6, 33/4, 35/4, 39/8; *Hym* 13/8; *HH II* 34/4; and *Bdr* 11/8. The only comparable a-verses are *HH* 38/3 and *HH II* 33/9, both with double alliteration.

words in the same way.[33] Clear subordination of the secondary constituent in forms like ON *andscoti* and OE *andsaca* evidently rendered their medial stressed syllables appropriate for placement on the weak line-final s position.[34] Subordination may have been equally clear in productive forms with an intensifier as the first constituent, if we may judge from (20), the only pertinent example.[35] In compound proper names, the second element is often obscured by lexicalization. Such names may appear without alliteration in the a-verse, as in (21), or in the b-verse, as in (22).[36] Old English compound names have the same type of distribution.[37]

English and Norse traditions diverge with regard to treatment of compounds in which each constituent has a distinct nominal or adjectival form. Except for proper names, compounds with this structure almost always alliterate in *Beowulf*. The only other exceptions occur in three b-verses:

(23)	fēond / mancynnes[38]	(*Beo* 164b)
	[S/Ssx]	
(24)	Fæder / alwalda[39]	(*Beo* 316b)
	[S/Ssx]	
(25)	hider / wilcuman[40]	(*Beo* 394b)
	[S/Ssx]	

The compounds in (23), (24) and (25) had a high frequency in the natural language and probably qualified as sufficiently foot-like for that reason. Given such a small sample of b-verses, we cannot assign much weight to the absence of comparable a-verses. Such a-verses do appear in the work of

---

[33] E.g. *Godes / andsaca* (*Beo* 1682b). Cf. 406b, 502b, 786b, 1311b, 1840b, 1932b, 2076b, 2123b, 2483b, 2860b and 2942b. There are no S/Ssx a-verses of this kind in *Beowulf*, but I found similar Ssx words in four Sx/Ssx a-verses, all with double alliteration (689a, 1002a, 1351a and 1886a). The comparative significance of these examples is uncertain, since expanded D verses are rare in Eddic poetry.

[34] See Fulk, *History of Old English Meter*, §234.

[35] Four possible analogues appear in *Beowulf* (1111b, 1230b, 2241b and 2767b), but their scansion is disputed (see Fulk, *History of Old English Meter*, p. 157).

[36] Other examples with non-alliterating compounds in the b-verse: *Vsp* 1/4, 11/8, 56/2; *Hym* 4/6; *HH* 6/2, 8/8; and *Hdl* 12/6. In the a-verse: *Vsp* 13/5; *Hym* 16/3, 27/1; *Þrk* 31/1; *HH* 41/1; and *Bdr* 13/1.

[37] *OEM*, §8.6.   [38] 'enemy of mankind ... '   [39] 'the all-ruling father ... '

[40] 'welcome here'.

other Old English poets whose metrical practice is generally regarded as strict. Cynewulf, for example, uses the epithet *fēond mancynnes* twice in the first half of the line.[41]

Norse compounds analogous to OE *mancynnes* alliterate significantly less often in fornyrðislag:

(26)	þurs / ráðbani[42]		(*Hym* 19/2)
	[S/Ssx]		
(27)	hendr / úrsvalar[43]		(*HH II* 44/9)
	[S/Ssx]		
(28)	rǫmm, / sigtýva[44]		(*Vsp* 44/8)
	[S/Ssx]		
(29)	briótr / berg-Dana[45]		(*Hym* 17/7)
	[S//S/Sx]		

The Ssx words in examples (26) and (27) are ordinary compounds like OE *mancynnes*. Eddic poets used such words without alliteration in a significant number of cases.[46] A strictly Norse type of variant is represented by the thrice-repeated (28), in which the poetic compound *sigtýva* fails to alliterate.[47] Poetic compounds appear very frequently in *Beowulf*, but never without alliteration.[48] The two traditions are more similar in their handling of a-verses with a poetic compound preceded by another stressed word. Double alliteration usually occurs in Norse examples like (29), which has a compound kenning for 'giant' in the second foot.[49] Like other poetic compounds, kennings have a secondary

---

[41] *Jul* 523a and 630a.   [42] 'the one who conspires in the giant's death ... '

[43] 'hands (are) wet and cold ... '

[44] 'great (destiny) of the victory-gods'. Repeated as 49/8 and 58/8.

[45] 'destroyer of giants ... '

[46] B-verses like (26): *Vsp* 22/6, 30/12; *Hym* 6/2, 10/2, 39/8; *HH* 9/8, 29/4, 38/2; *HHv* 9/6; *HH II* 12/2, 12/4; *Rþ* 3/6, 5/6, 10/4, 19/8, 29/4, 30/6, 38/6; *Hdl* 19/2, 22/2, 24/6, 29/8, 30/2; and *Grt* 10/6. A-verses like (27): *HHv* 10/3, *Rþ* 28/1 and *Hdl* 28/5.

[47] Cf. *Vsp* 52/4, 62/6; *Hym* 23/8, 27/4; *HH* 14/8 and 53/12. Poetic compounds can be identified not only by their absence from prose but also by their peculiar semantic structure. Most poetic compounds in *Beowulf* are comparable to *sigtýva*, with a semantically inessential first constituent. The distinction between ordinary compounds and poetic compounds is less clear in our Norse corpus because the latter are used less systematically by Eddic poets.

[48] *OEM*, §8.5.

[49] Beside the four verses with single alliteration can be set (29) and nineteen others with double alliteration: *Vsp* 39/3, 62/7; *Hym* 11/9, 13/3, 22/3, 23/3; *Þrk* 23/3; *HH* 9/3, 22/

---

constituent that resembles an unsubordinated word. In *Beowulf*, such compounds were made more cohesive by obligatory assignment of alliteration to the first constituent, with metrical subordination of the second constituent.

In general, then, poetic compounds and heavy word groups appear more often as non-alliterating feet in fornyrðislag than in Old English poetry. This is an expected consequence of the more forceful Norse subordination. Since reduction of stress was more pronounced in Norse compounds, including neologisms, there would be less need to handle the secondary constituent like a fully stressed word. Note that the poetic compound is isolated by enjambment in (28), just like the heavy word groups in (15) and (16). The same sort of isolation occurs in two of the other six examples with non-alliterating poetic compounds.[50] Evidently, strong syntactic cues to the proper grouping of stressed constituents mitigated the complexity of any verse in which a syllable assigned to an s position was not firmly subordinated. Preferential assignment of the unusual Norse verses to the second half of the line must have kept confusion to a minimum. In the a-verse, the audience could expect poetic compounds and heavy word groups to alliterate, and this expectation would seldom be thwarted. In the b-verse, the anomalous constituents would occur only after the alliteration had been completed, at which point no further alliteration would be expected.[51]

DOUBLE ALLITERATION AND ULTRA-HEAVY FEET

Our Norse corpus contains a few type C verses in which a stressed root syllable occupies the final x position:

    (30)   troða / halir helveg[52]   (*Vsp* 52/7)
             [xx//S/Ss, first S resolved, equivalent to xx/Ssx}
    (31)   oc / drífr drótt ǫll[53]   (*HH II* 50/9)
             [x//S/Ss, equivalent to x/Ssx]

7, 31/3; *HHv* 2/3, 6/3, 7/3; *HH II* 5/3, 11/3, 19/3, 35/7; *Grt* 9/7 and 18/3. On the semantic structure of kennings, see *OEM*, §8.5.

[50] *Vsp* 52/4 and *Hym* 27/4.

[51] For discussion of a similar issue in Old English verse see Kendall, *Metrical Grammar*, p. 55.

[52] 'men tread the road to hell ...'   [53] 'and the whole troop flocks ...'

The three other verses like (30) come from the same poem.[54] All have double alliteration. In *Vǫlospá*, at least, heavy type C variants were acceptable. The only heavy C verse with three independent stressed words is (31). This has double alliteration as well. *Beowulf* contains nothing like (30) or (31), but such verses could be derived by a slight generalization of the metrical compounding rule (R7). If the pattern of (30) was xx//S/Ss, the first alliterating S of the foot would reduce the second S to the status of an s position, as in verses like (5). It seems reasonable to suppose that the verse-final s of (30), immediately preceded within the same foot by two alliterating constituents, would be reduced to the status of an x position. The result would then be equivalent to xx/Ssx. Such a reduction of s to x would parallel the linguistic reduction undergone by the most deeply embedded root syllable in an Ssx triple compound, which has less than secondary stress.[55] The same analysis could apply to (31), with assignment of the function word *ǫll* to the verse-final s position. In such verses the Norse metrical stress reveals its special power to incorporate words into the x positions of the foot, even stressed words.[56]

SUMMARY

The overlap constraint (U2) exists to ensure that feet are readily enumerated. The well-marked binary structure required by P2 could hardly be achieved if feet were easily confused with verses. Fundamental principles of the metre exert pressure against U2, however. Since P1 and P2 are natural principles, they will apply in the most general form consistent with metrical coherence. Any compound, no matter how large, has some claim to be regarded as a foot. Any pair of word feet, no matter how small, has some claim to be regarded as a verse. Both traditions reconcile a high degree of generality with coherence. The Old English poet grants foot status to large compounds in hypermetrical patterns, which are set aside in clusters to prevent confusion. Old Norse poets grant the status of a short verse to small foot pairs, matching stresses to metrical positions with special care to indicate the proper scansion.

The idea that heavy feet of the sort investigated in this chapter are verse-like structures receives support from each tradition. Sievers pointed

---

[54] *Vsp* 24/7, 27/7 and 50/7.   [55] *OEM*, §7.4, example 46b
[56] See above, p. 26.

95

out long ago that Old English hypermetrical verses have normal verses as subconstituents.[57] This suggests that a two-foot structure may play the role of a compound foot. Norse short verses provide us with analogues for the smaller two-foot structures embedded as subconstituents of Old English normal verses.[58] The differing alliterative behaviour of heavy feet in the two traditions can be attributed to the generally deeper subordination of rightward constituents in fornyrðislag.

---

[57] *AGM*, §94.   [58] *OEM*, §8.8.

8

Resolution

The metrical positions of word feet correspond to the positions employed in metrical phonology, which contain a single syllable in the unmarked (simplest) case. Because full stress is associated with length in Germanic languages, however, a resolvable sequence under full stress is most naturally assigned to a single arsis.[1] Like alliteration, resolution shows sensitivity to metrical as well as linguistic prominence, occurring most often on the strongest S position of the verse (see R8). Stress reduction often shortens syllables in Germanic languages. When a resolvable sequence undergoes linguistic subordination or occupies a metrically subordinated position, the expectation of length is weakened and an unmarked, one-to-one assignment of syllables to metrical positions becomes more natural. Within the word-foot theory, rules for resolution do not have to be stipulated, since they derive from more general principles as corollaries.[2] The only assumption required is that the poet prefers the most natural matching of syllables with metrical positions.

The principle of natural matching has a number of entailments, which can be expressed in the following detail rules:

R9a Within the word, resolution is most natural under primary stress, less natural under subordinate stress and forbidden under zero stress.

---

[1] For the definition of *resolvable sequence*, see above, p. 16.

[2] Sievers had to stipulate that resolution is obligatory except when the resolvable sequence is immediately preceded by a stressed syllable. For objections to this rule, which leaves much unexplained, see Árnason, *Rhythms of Dróttkvætt*, §2.5; Hoover, *New Theory*, ch. 4; Russom, 'Constraints on Resolution'.

R9b Within the foot, resolution is most natural on an S position, less natural on an s position and forbidden on an x position.

R9c Alliteration on the most prominent S position makes resolution less natural on a subordinate S or s position within the same metrical domain.

R9d Resolution of a short syllable is less natural when the following syllable is long and the resolved sequence would therefore be equivalent to an 'ultra-long' closed syllable containing a long vowel.[3]

R9e On the most deeply subordinated s positions, both resolved sequences and long syllables are unnatural. Such s positions are most naturally occupied by a short stressed syllable (unresolved).

The effect of R9d is clearly evident in subordinate constituents of Old English Ssx compounds.[4] In Eddic poetry, however, R9d has little work to do because a more general rule blocks resolution on the secondary arsis, as we shall see shortly.

When one constraint on naturalness is violated, the poet is less likely to violate another such constraint in the same verse, keeping total verse complexity within reasonable limits. Many Germanic verses violate one of the detail rules in (R9), but simultaneous violations may be rare or unattested. The mutually inhibiting effect of rule violations can be attributed to a poetic universal, which I now state explicitly for convenience:

U4 Metrical complexity is additive.

SOME CLEAR CASES OF RESOLUTION

In *Beowulf*, Sxs compounds like *middan-geard* 'middle earth' appear only at the end of the verse (see R5a), but Ss compounds like *frum-sceaft* 'first creation' appear most often verse-initially. If resolvable sequences like *fela* always counted as bisyllabic, compounds like *fela-hrōr* 'very vigorous' would behave like Sxs words. In fact, such compounds behave like Ss words, and are found most often at the beginning of the verse.[5] Eddic

---

[3] See Kaluza, 'Betonungs- und Verslehre'.

[4] See Bliss, *Metre*, p. 35. For detailed discussion of Kaluza's law as it bears on a variety of metrical issues, see Fulk, *History of Old English Meter*.

[5] Compounds like *fela-hrōr* appear verse-initially in *Beo* 27a, 61a, 67a, 69a, 381a, 401a, 406a, 438a, 490a, 522a, 552a, 608a, 776a, 786a, 1015a, 1176a, 1180a, 1267a, 1435a,

poetry provides little evidence for this sort of demonstration because it contains relatively few Sxs compounds. Because anacrusis plays no role in fornyrðislag, however, resolution shows up clearly in type C:

(1) í / iotunheima?[6]   (*Þrk* 7/4)
      [x/Ssx, not x//Sx/Sx]
(2) oc / mǫrom sínom[7]   (*Þrk* 6/5)
      [x/Ssx, not x//Sx/Sx]
(3) er Gunnarr átti[8]   (*Am* 6/6)
      [unambiguously xSxSx]
(4) oc / qvennváðir[9]   (*Þrk* 16/3)
      [unambiguously x/Ssx]

If the resolvable sequence *iotun-* occupies a single S position in (1), the verse is a two-word paradigm of type C. In (2), assignment of *mǫrom* to a single S position yields a common type C variant with a word group in the second foot. Without resolution, (1) and (2) would have to be analysed as xSxSx. In an Old Saxon poem, such a pattern might qualify as type A1 with non-prefixal anacrusis.[10] Unambiguous Norse examples of this pattern occur with significant frequency only in málaháttr, however. One such example is (3), from *Atlamál*, a poem based on South Germanic legendary material. The native fornyrðislag corpus contains only a few doubtful verses resembling (3), most in a single poem, *Hyndlolióð*. These can hardly serve as paradigms for analysis of the more than 270 verses like (1) and (2). If we claimed that verses of the form xSxSx were permitted in fornyrðislag, it would be very difficult to explain why their first stressed syllable had to be short (the handful of apparent exceptions remaining doubtful under this analysis as well). Any such explanation would be *ad hoc* in that it would not generalize to other verse patterns. In the type E pattern Ssx/S, for example, the first stressed syllable must always be long. Ssx compound forms like *iotun-heima* never appear at the beginning of the

1519a, 1553a, 1590a, 1649a, 1650a, 1698a, 1820a, 1923a, 2016a, 2017a, 2191a, 2404a, 2434a, 2474a, 2553a, 2757a, 2959a; 64b, 303b, 619b, 1202b, 1925b, 2158b, 2265b and 3065b. Such compounds appear verse-finally in *Beo* 380a, 408a, 484a, 558a, 594a, 619a, 688a, 1060a, 1444a, 1545a, 1562a, 1563a, 1564a, 1758a, 1794a, 2085a, 2175a, 2196a, 2252a, 2258a, 2370a, 2376a, 2389a, 2466a, 2660a, 2691a, 2704a, 2892a, 2929a and 2000b. Cf. 3041a (as printed).

[6] 'into the land of the giants?'   [7] 'and for his horses ...'
[8] 'whom Gunnarr had (as wife) ...'   [9] 'and women's clothes ...'
[10] See below, p. 152.

verse, for reasons we shall consider shortly. Resolution in (1) and (2) yields a pattern that is not only acceptable but very common. Our corpus contains about 450 type C verses like (4) with a single long syllable on the S position. It seems clear that (1) and (2) were realizations of the x/Ssx pattern represented by (4).

RESOLUTION IN NATIVE EDDIC FORNYRÐISLAG

Early syncopation eliminated Old Norse nouns and adjectives comparable to Old English *werodes* 'of the troop' (gen. sg.). The only resolvable sequences that survived were those of bisyllabic constituents like *gamall* 'old' and *dreki* 'dragon'. Our Norse corpus contains a handful of trisyllabic words with short root syllables like *konunga* (gen. pl.), but these seem to resist resolution, perhaps due to the inhibiting effect of the long medial syllable (see R9d). Such an effect is evident in comparable Old English forms.[11] There are a few weak class II forms like ON *riðoðo*, with a short root syllable and an open medial syllable, but the low frequency of such forms makes it difficult to determine their range of metrical values. The major difference between the Old Norse and Old English corpora with respect to resolution can be stated very briefly: in native Eddic fornyrðislag, resolution occurs only on S positions. The categorical Norse rule against resolved sequences on s positions can be viewed as a strict implementation of R9b, which defines such resolution as 'less natural'.

RESOLUTION ON THE STRONGEST ARSIS

In any verse with more than one arsis, the first S position has the highest relative prominence. This S always contains the root syllable of an independent word or primary compound constituent because the principle of syntactic integrity (U1) would reject any verse beginning with the subordinated constituent of a compound. The first S is therefore a 'most natural' site for resolution according to both R9a and R9b. As we have seen, resolution takes place on the first S of many fornyrðislag type C verses like (1) and (2). Resolved syllables also appear on the first S in Norse type A1 (Sx/Sx) and type Da (S/Ssx):

[11] See Fulk, *History of Old English Meter*, §275; Kuhn, 'Westgermanisches', p. 189.

Resolution

(5)	hamar um / fólginn?[12]	(Þrk 7/8)
	[Sx/Sx]	
(6)	dreki / fliúgandi[13]	(Vsp 66/2)
	[S/Ssx]	

Resolution seems quite certain in a number of variants like (5) with a filler word in verse-medial position.[14] If the first word in (5) counted as Sx, it is hard to see why the poet would add *um* to produce the pattern Sxx/Sx, which is much less common than Sx/Sx. I assume that the poet used a filler word because (5) would otherwise constitute a doubtful short pattern S/Sx. Resolution seems equally certain on the first S of example (6), which I have analysed as S/Ssx. There are about 200 clear cases of the pattern S/Ssx, but only seven clear cases of the expanded Da pattern Sx/Ssx. Since there are twenty-four variants like (6), it seems best to associate them with the higher-frequency pattern.[15]

Resolution also occurs on the first S of some less common patterns:

(7)	brotinn var / borðveggr[16]	(Vsp 24/5)
	[Sx/Ss]	
(8)	Malit hǫfom, / Fróði[17]	(Grt 24/3)
	[Sxx/Sx]	
(9)	Haraldr / hilditǫnn[18]	(Hdl 28/1)
	[S/Sxs]	
(10)	Þá gengo / regin ǫll[19]	(Vsp 6/1)
	[(x)xx/Ss]	

The number of resolved variants like (7)–(10) is small, but not suspiciously small, since the other variants of these patterns have a low frequency as well.[20] Here as elsewhere resolution seems to have been

[12] 'concealed the hammer?' [13] 'the dragon flying ... '
[14] See Vsp 4/2, 47/8; Þrk 7/8, 8/2, 10/6, 10/8, 14/8, 31/4; and Bdr 2/4.
[15] Clear cases of Sx/Ssx: Vsp 20/6; Þrk 21/4; HH 16/4, 51/1; Hdl 13/5, 32/2 and 46/1. A possible case is Þrk 30/7, vígit / ocr saman, assuming that the major syntactic break comes after the first word. Other verses analogous to (6): Vsp 1/4, 11/8, 35/4, 39/8, 51/5; Þrk 19/4; HH 18/7, 22/7, 23/8, 27/4, 38/3, 40/1, 42/8, 47/5, 49/8; HHv 42/7; HH II 15/3, 44/2; Rþ 38/6; Hdl 19/1, 24/5, 43/8; and Grt 16/7. Vsp 22/3 belongs here if decontracted.
[16] 'The plank-wall was broken ... ' [17] 'We have ground, Fróði ... '
[18] 'Harald War-Tooth ... ' [19] 'Then all the gods went ... '
[20] Like (7) are Vsp 12/7 and Hdl 31/3 (repeated as 34/3, 36/3 and 39/3). Examples of this pattern without resolution are Vsp 1/5, 12/1, 12/5, 31/7, 41/7, 46/5, 49/1, 58/1; Þrk

101

obligatory on the arsis with the greatest relative prominence, due to the combined influence of R9a–b (see U4).

In fornyrðislag, as in Old English poetry, we find apparent instances of type A3 with an unresolved short syllable:

(11) Nú em ek svá / fegin[21] (HH II 43/1)
      [(xx)xx/Sx]

(12) þone þín / fæder[22] (Beo 2048a)
      [xx(x)/Sx]

The single S position of type A3 cannot of course have prominence relative to any other arsis in the verse. It is not surprising to find that occasional instances of an unresolved first S occur in this type.[23] Scansion is straightforward in (12) because Old English poets do not use a verse type of the form xxx/S. Verses like (11), however, are putative instances of xxx/S with resolved S. Though possible, this scansion seems quite implausible, since there are no more than fifteen unambiguous examples of xxx/S in our Norse corpus, as compared with over 300 unambiguous examples of type A3.

The Beowulf poet employs resolution on the first S in type B and also in the complex reversed patterns. Norse poets impose much stricter constraints. Consider the following examples:

15/3, 15/5, 19/1; HH 14/3; HHv 1/1; HH II 14/1; Rþ 13/5, 41/5; Hdl 15/1, 15/5, 16/9 (repeated as 17/5, 20/9, 21/7, 23/7, 24/9, 26/7, 27/9, 28/11 and 29/9); 18/3, 20/1, 23/ 5, 32/5; and Grt 23/5. Like (8) are Rþ 34/7, Hdl 7/1 and possibly Vsp 51/2, though this is probably Sxx/Ss with the first S resolved. Sxx/Sx without resolution: Vsp 12/6, 20/5, 20/8, 26/5, 30/9, 34/3, 45/1; Hym 39/6; Þrk 11/3; HH 6/8, 25/6, 36/1, 52/4; HHv 31/2, 33/2, 40/1, 40/2; HH II 2/1, 18/7, 25/6, 28/5, 34/1, 37/3, 47/1; Bdr 8/1, 10/1, 12/1; Rþ 34/4; Hdl 6/1, 10/7, 11/1, 12/8, 13/7, 18/1; Grt 5/1, 17/1 and 18/1. Like (9) is HH 1/3. Without resolution: Vsp 41/3, 47/3; Hym 32/2, 32/5, 34/6, 36/6, 38/6; Þrk 13/3, 21/7; Bdr 4/8; Rþ 9/6; Hdl 11/11, 16/7, 46/3; Grt 17/2 and 24/2. Like (10) are Vsp 9/1 (a repeat of 6/1 further repeated as 9/1, 23/1 and 25/1), 19/7, 23/7, 51/3; Þrk 4/1, 12/7, 20/5; and HH II 9/3. Without resolution: Vsp 4/3, 21/1, 24/3, 25/ 5, 29/1, 39/7; Þrk 1/1, 15/1, 26/7, 27/5, 28/7; HH 12/1, 33/5, 35/1, 41/5, 48/5, 48/7, 50/1, 50/3, 54/5, 56/1, 56/5; HHv 2/5, 4/5, 33/9; HH II 2/3, 8/1, 9/1, 18/5, 19/1, 20/ 1, 21/5, 22/1, 25/1, 38/5, 39/1, 40/1, 41/1, 42/1, 45/1, 45/9; Bdr 6/2; Rþ 45/1, 47/3; Hdl 4/5, 5/1, 5/5, 5/7, 6/5, 7/3, 10/3, 27/5 and 37/5.

[21] 'Now I am so pleased ...' [22] 'which your father (bore) ...'
[23] With (11) cf. Þrk 18/1, 20/1; HH II 43/1; Hdl 30/7; and Grt 9/3. With (12) cf. Beo 262a, 459a, 779a, 1514a and 1728a.

Resolution

(13)	lagucræftig / mon[24] [Ssx/S, first S resolved]	(*Beo* 209a)
(14)	heaðoreaf / heoldon[25] [Ss/Sx]	(*Beo* 401a)
(15)	gǫfuct lið / gylfa[26] [Ss/Sx]	(*HH* 49/7)
(16)	oðð þæt seo / geogoð geweox[27] [x(xx)/Sxs]	(*Beo* 66b)

The Old English poem contains more than 110 verses like (13), with resolved S in an initial Ssx foot, and more than fifty like (14), with resolved S in an initial Ss foot.[28] The Norse corpus contains no analogues to (13), and (15) is the only analogue to (14). Since resolution has a more restricted linguistic basis in Old Norse, as compared with Old English, an Eddic verse with resolution is more complex than the corresponding verse from *Beowulf*. To keep average verse complexity within tolerable limits, Eddic poets avoided resolution in reversed patterns, which are inherently complex (see U4). As we have frequently observed, the complexity of the Eddic Sxs foot increased due to elimination of many Sxs compounds from the language. The Norse poets never assign resolvable sequences to the S position of an Sxs foot. There is nothing in native Eddic fornyrðislag comparable to the Old English (16).[29]

RESOLUTION ON THE SECOND PRIMARY ARSIS

In a verse with two S positions, the rightward S position undergoes subordination by R7b, the metrical compounding rule. According to R9c, metrical subordination makes this S position less natural as a site for a resolvable sequence. Because rightward constituents are deeply subordi-

---

[24] 'skilled sailor ... '   [25] 'they guarded the war-gear ... '
[26] 'the prince's splendid troop ... '   [27] 'until the young warriors matured ... '
[28] There is considerable agreement about resolution in the Old English cases. For detailed discussion see the catalogue of scansions in Pope, *Rhythm*, under type A2 (a-verse subtypes 29–31, 54, 57, 61–2; b-verse subtypes 29 and 54) and type E (a-verse subtypes 5–7, 10, 15–16; b-verse subtypes 5–7 and 14).
[29] Like (16) are *Beo* 713b, 915b, 919b, 1016b, 1681b, 1984b, 2364b and 2429b. The first S is also resolved in many Old English type B verses like *heo fore þæm / werede spræc* (*Beo* 1215b). Absence of such variants from our Norse corpus is attributable to the loss of nominal and adjectival forms comparable to *werede*.

nated in Old Norse, Eddic poets seldom assign a resolvable sequence to the rightward S of a verse. The following variants from *Beowulf* have no analogues in the Norse corpus:

(17)	Scyldes / eafera[30]	(*Beo* 19a)
	[Sx/Sx, second S resolved]	
(18)	wlanc / Wedera lēod[31]	(*Beo* 341a)
	[S/Sxs, second S resolved]	
(19)	heall / heorudrēore[32]	(*Beo* 487a)
	[S/Ssx, second S resolved]	
(20)	healðegnes / hete[33]	(*Beo* 142a)
	[Ssx/S, second S resolved]	

Absence of Norse analogues to (17) and (18) has limited significance. There are no analogues to (17) because syncopation eliminated the resolvable sequence in early Norse forms comparable to *eafera*. S/Sxs variants like (18) are rare even in *Beowulf*, which has only two other putative examples of this complex pattern with resolution on the second S.[34] No such variants would be expected among the twelve type Db verses in the Norse corpus. Variants like (19) and (20), on the other hand, have significant frequency in *Beowulf* and would have been quite easy for Eddic poets to construct, since comparable word patterns existed in Old Norse.[35] No such Eddic variants occur, however. Old Norse words like *iotun-heima* never appear in type E verses or in heavy type Da verses like (19), only in type C verses like example (1), which has the normal number of stresses. Old Norse words like *dreki* never undergo resolution on the second S of the reversed type E pattern, only on the first S of the simpler type Da pattern, as in example (6). We can generalize over these

---

[30] 'Scyld's heir...'   [31] 'splendid prince of the Weders...'
[32] 'the hall [was stained] with blood...'   [33] 'the hall-thane's hatred...'
[34] *Beo* 423a and 2705a (see 2367a, the sole example with the S/Sxxs pattern, and 421a, the sole example with the expanded Db pattern Sx/Sxs).
[35] With (19) cf. *Beo* 501a, 723a, 737a, 914a, 1109a, 1454a, 1485a, 1847a, 1897a, 2161a, 2239a, 2408a, 2756a, 2769a, 2950a; 495b, 758b, 813b, 1530b (which appears non-resolvable due to spelling variation), 2206b, 2386b and 2958b. Variants with resolvable Ssx simplexes are excluded, since there are no such resolvable forms in Old Norse. Like (20) are *Beo* 154a, 329a, 476a, 477a, 650a, 667a, 697a, 775a, 1136a, 1271a, 1416a, 2182a, 2748a, 2761a; 876b, 995b, 1009b, 1028b, 1089b, 1199b, 1411b, 1425b, 1577b, 2140b, 2602b, 2631b, 2757b, 2763b, 2765b, 2862b and 3076b. Cf. 343b, which seems to be an Ssx/S variant, though an unusual one.

cases by saying that resolution to S or Ssx is restricted to the most prominent arsis of relatively simple patterns. Because resolution never occurs on the secondary arsis in fornyrðislag, this restriction has the effect of excluding resolved sequences from type E altogether.

Our Norse corpus contains ten examples of resolution to Ss in verses with the pattern xx/Ss (see example 11). Resolution occurs once on the first S of the heavy reversed pattern Ss/Sx (see 15). Among the Sx/Ss verses, which are heavy but not reversed, there are perhaps ten examples like the following with resolution on the second S:

> (21) Ámr oc / Iosurmarr[36]   (*Hdl* 18/7)
> [Sx/Ss, second S resolved]

Hyndlolióð alone accounts for eight of these examples.[37] For other Norse poets, resolution on the second primary arsis may have been unacceptable.

NON-RESOLUTION ON THE SECOND PRIMARY ARSIS

An arsis that undergoes metrical subordination, becoming a less natural site for a resolved sequence, becomes a more natural site for an unresolved short syllable. As expected, the deeper metrical subordination characteristic of fornyrðislag leads to an increase in the frequency of verses with an unresolved syllable on the second S. Consider the following examples with resolvable Sx words standing unresolved in second position:

> (22) fiárnám / mikit[38]   (*HH* 11/7)
> [Ss/Sx]
> (23) dagsbrún / siá[39]   (*HH* 26/6)
> [Ss/Sx]
> (24) vígbǫnd / snúa[40]   (*Vsp* 34/2)
> [Ss/Sx]

Reversal serves an obvious metrical purpose in these verses. If the unresolved Sx words appeared verse-initially, they would have to undergo resolution, creating short Ss/S verses of doubtful status. Example (23)

---

[36] 'Ámr and Iosurmarr...'
[37] Cf. *Hdl* 13/1, 17/7, 18/9, 31/3, 34/3, 36/3 and 39/3. The others are *Hym* 34/5 and *Vsp* 26/7 (probably Ss/Ss).
[38] 'great plunder...'   [39] 'to see the brow of day (i.e., the dawn)...'
[40] 'to make war-fetters...'

illustrates the use of *siá* with the archaic value equivalent to a resolvable sequence. In example (24), *snúa* counts as a resolvable sequence because of the rule that shortens a long vowel when another vowel follows.[41] The heavy, reversed Ss/Sx pattern is quite complex, and we might expect most examples to appear as a-verses, in accord with the principle of closure (U3). The *Beowulf* poet locates variants comparable to (22)–(24) most often in the b-verse, however.[42] The apparent anomaly is due to the metrical subordination rule (R7), which subordinates the b-verse to the a-verse within the domain of the line, making resolution less desirable in the b-verse and unresolved S more tolerable there. R7 has an even stronger effect on the distribution of Eddic variants like (22)–(24), as expected, since rightward constituents are more forcefully subordinated in Norse tradition. Our Norse corpus contains 141 Ss/Sx variants with an unresolved second S, and of these 103 are b-verses.[43] In Ss/Sx variants with an ordinary long syllable on the second S, R7 cannot interfere with the principle of closure. Such variants occur most often in the a-verse, as expected.[44]

[41] See ch. 5.

[42] Old English Ss/Sx variants with short second S in the a-verse: *Beo* 67a, 69a, 90a, 120a, 252a, 284a, 406a, 570a, 629a, 643a, 657a, 776a, 817a, 973a, 1015a, 1256a, 1432a, 1672a, 1682a, 2035a, 2191a, 2588a, 2947a, 2959a, 3000a and 3172a. In the b-verse: *Beo* 64b, 303b, 619b, 838b, 908b, 994b, 1278b, 1287b, 1288b, 1289b, 1510b, 1731b, 1834b, 1896b, 1914b, 1925b, 1964b, 2007b, 2060b, 2110b, 2158b, 2174b, 2256b, 2265b, 2334b, 2417b, 2460b, 2613b, 2754b, 2906b, 2969b, 2972b, 3019b and 3081b. Uncertain examples are 2663b and 3131b. Examples with putative Ss simplexes have been excluded for comparative purposes because they might count as Sx/Sx in fornyrðislag, which is fairly tolerant of unresolved S in the second foot of type A1 verses (see example 27).

[43] Other Norse Ss/Sx variants with short second S in the a-verse: *Vsp* 1/7, 13/7, 37/7, 42/7, 43/7, 52/5, 66/3, 66/7; *Hym* 2/3, 4/7, 5/3, 8/7, 10/3, 19/3, 20/3, 22/7, 23/7, 25/1, 30/3, 30/7, 35/7; *HH* 1/7, 6/3, 8/7, 16/7, 25/5, 30/7, 37/3, 38/7; *HHv* 33/3; *HH II* 25/3, 39/3; *Hdl* 9/7, 24/3, 30/9, 40/1; and *Grt* 19/3. In the b-verse: *Vsp* 11/4, 12/2, 15/4, 15/6, 32/8, 34/2, 45/6, 50/2, 56/6, 59/6; *Hym* 1/8, 2/2, 8/4, 8/8, 10/8, 15/8, 16/8, 18/4, 18/8, 23/6, 27/8, 29/4, 31/6, 33/4, 37/4, 38/8; *Þrk* 3/6, 6/4, 18/6, 20/4, 21/6, 24/10, 26/2, 28/2; *HH* 7/4, 7/8, 11/7, 12/4, 18/4, 18/6, 21/2, 29/2, 30/2, 36/12, 42/6, 43/2, 46/2, 50/12, 52/8, 53/10, 54/2, 54/6; *HHv* 1/6, 5/6, 9/8, 10/2, 38/2, 40/4, 43/6; *HH II* 2/6, 3/4, 7/8, 9/4, 12/8, 16/8, 24/2, 25/8, 26/2, 27/2, 27/4, 36/8, 40/8, 41/8, 43/8, 44/8, 45/4, 46/6, 48/2, 49/4, 49/6, 49/8; *Bdr* 4/6, 9/2, 11/4; *Rþ* 6/2, 20/2, 33/6, 38/2; *Hdl* 5/6, 21/2, 28/8, 32/4, 40/8, 41/4, 41/8, 46/8, 47/8, 49/4, 50/8; *Grt* 1/6, 7/6 and 23/6. Variants with putative Ss simplexes are excluded as in the previous note.

[44] Ss/Sx variants with long second S in the a-verse: *Vsp* 2/7, 19/3, 28/3, 30/7, 32/3, 35/3,

A short syllable sometimes appears on the second S in type A1, causing problems of overlap in *Beowulf*:

(25) Hrēðel / cyning[45]   (*Beo* 2430b)
     [Sx/Sx, not *Sx/S]
(26) syððan / Gēata cyning[46]   (*Beo* 2356a)
     [xx/Sxs]
(27) sáttir / saman[47]   (*HH II* 21/3)
     [Sx/Sx, second S unresolved]

The *Beowulf* poet employs no more than five verses like (25).[48] This kind of verse has a rather unclear two-foot structure because it resembles an Sxs foot occupied by a word group (see the second foot of 26). In fornyrðislag, which introduced a constraint against resolved s, word groups comparable to *Gēata cyning* could no longer occupy an Sxs foot, and there was no possibility of overlap with Sx/Sx verses like (27). Freed from concern about metrical ambiguity in such verses, Norse poets could employ them more often, and seem in fact to have done so. Beside the five examples from *Beowulf* can be set eighteen like (27) from the smaller Norse corpus.[49] An Sx/S analysis is barely imaginable for the Eddic examples, but quite unlikely, since the Norse poets rarely place a resolved sequence on the second S position of any verse type (see example 21 and accompanying discussion). Attainment of significant frequency by variants like (27) suggests that the corresponding Old English variants, though rare, were nevertheless legitimate.

Among the Da verses of the Norse corpus are three examples of unresolved S. Such examples are uncommon because relatively few trisyllables have the relevant phonological pattern:

(28) lítt / megandi[50]   (*Vsp* 17/6)
     [S/Ssx, second S unresolved]

48/7, 63/5; *Hym* 9/1, 24/1; *HH* 5/7, 49/7, 55/3; *HH II* 25/7, 42/7, 45/7; *Bdr* 6/1; *Rþ* 25/3; *Hdl* 14/3, 22/3; and *Grt* 8/3. In the b-verse: *Vsp* 23/6, 25/8, 50/8, 56/8, 63/2; *Þrk* 5/2, 9/2; *HH* 10/4; *Bdr* 3/6; *Hdl* 4/4 and 13/4. In *Beowulf* I counted 143 corresponding a-verses and 25 corresponding b-verses.
[45] 'King Hrethel ...'   [46] 'after the king of the Geats ...'
[47] 'having come to a meeting ...'   [48] See *Beo* 845a, 881a, 954a and 1828b.
[49] The others are *Vsp* 11/1, 12/3, 13/4, 55/3, 62/4; *Hym* 28/7, 34/2; *Þrk* 5/1, 9/1, 30/3; *Rþ* 8/5, 16/1, 27/2, 41/3; *Hdl* 1/6, 8/2 and 19/8.
[50] 'having little power ...' Cf. *Vsp* 20/2.

(29)   feorh / cyninges[51]   (*Beo* 1210b)
       [S/Ssx, second S unresolved]
(30)   Faðir / varattu[52]   (*HH* 40/1)
       [S/Sxx, first S resolved, second S unresolved]

In (28) and one other Da variant from the same poem, the trisyllabic form
occupying the second foot has an unresolved root syllable followed by a
closed medial syllable with a short vowel. Both Da variants are b-verses,
with the unresolved syllable on the weakest S position of the line.
Comparable variants appear in *Beowulf*, e.g. (29). The Sxx word in (30)
consists of a monosyllabic verbal stem followed by an enclitic negative
and an enclitic pronoun.[53] Resolution of the second S in (28)–(30) would
yield the short pattern S/Sx, which would be doubtful in fornyrðislag and
unmetrical in *Beowulf*.

SYLLABLE LENGTH ON THE SECONDARY ARSIS

Under certain conditions, Old English poets could assign a resolved
sequence to an s position, and Old Saxon poets had even more freedom in
this respect.[54] The more deeply subordinated s position of fornyrðislag
seems to have been totally unsuitable for resolution, however. With
resolution forbidden on s positions, the Norse poets could not assign a
short stressed syllable to the final arsis in a foot with the pattern Ss or
Sxs.[55] In feet with the Ssx pattern, however, a short stressed syllable could
stand unresolved on the medial s position while the following unstressed
syllable occupied the foot-final x position.

The effect of metrical subordination on syllable length shows up most
clearly in type Da. Consider first some two-word examples from the
Norse corpus with a single alliterating syllable:

(31)   burr / Sigmundar[56]   (*HH* 6/2)
       [S/Ssx, long s]

---

[51] 'the king's life ... ' Cf. 2912b.   [52] 'you were not the father ... '
[53] With regard to scansion of such enclitic forms, see above, p. 19.
[54] See below, p. 160.
[55] The bracketing rules (R2a–b) require that any syllable assigned to a foot-final arsis
must be word-final, and Germanic languages have no short stressed syllables word-
finally. A short stressed syllable can occupy a foot-final arsis only as part of a resolved
sequence assigned to that arsis.
[56] 'Sigmund's child ... '

Resolution

(32)   Baldrs / andscota[57]   (*Vsp* 33/4)
       [S/Ssx, short s]

The Old English poet assigns a long syllable to the s position in most Da
verses with single alliteration, employing at least twenty-five two-word
variants with long s (comparable to Norse example 31) but only seven
with short s (comparable to 32).[58] This bias is understandable, especially
in a complex heavy pattern, because a long syllable provides an unambiguous occupant for the s position. No such bias is evident in the Eddic
poems. I found twenty-two variants like (31), with long s, and twenty-
nine variants like (32), with short s.[59] In fornyrðislag, the ban on resolved
s makes assignment of short syllables to s positions totally automatic,
eliminating the problems of metrical ambiguity that arise in *Beowulf.*

---

[57] 'the one who threw a dart at Baldr ... '

[58] OE S/Ssx with single alliteration and long s: *Beo* 235a, 613a, 795a, 872a, 1971a; 164b,
529b, 621b, 631b, 957b, 1111b, 1383b, 1473b, 1498b, 1651b, 1769b, 1817b,
1999b, 2123b, 2177b, 2425b, 2483b, 2538b, 2681b and 2767b. Examples with the
prefix *un-* in verse-medial position are 833a, 2120a, 3012a; 120b, 727b, 741b, 885b,
2413b, 2578b and 2881b. These might scan as Sx/Sx (see Kendall, *Metrical Grammar*,
p. 192), though that analysis is not forced within the theory proposed here. Uncertain
examples are 1020b (as emended), 2076b (as emended) and 2223b (as emended). With
single alliteration and short s: 469a, 1319a, 2604a; 1020b, 1230b, 2241b and 2860b.
Unless the reader is notified otherwise, the statistics given in this section are for two-
word variants free of extrametrical syllables with no resolved sequences on S positions.
Such variants provide clean contrasts with respect to the features of interest here,
which include the order of feet and the length of the syllable on the s position. Variants
containing Ssx simplexes with long medial syllables are excluded from the count
because there are no corresponding variants with short syllables (see discussion of the
Sxx foot below, p. 114).

[59] Like (31) are *Vsp* 30/12, 44/8, 49/8, 52/4, 56/12, 58/8, 62/6; *Hym* 6/2, 23/8, 27/4, 39/
8; *HH* 8/8, 14/8, 38/2; *Bdr* 5/2; *Rþ* 3/6, 5/6, 10/4, 19/8, 30/6; *Hdl* 28/5. Like (32) are
Vsp 13/5, 55/2; *Hym* 4/6, 10/2, 11/8, 13/8, 16/3, 16/4, 19/2; *HH* 9/8, 29/4, 53/12;
HHv 9/6, 10/3; *HH II* 12/2, 12/4, 34/4, 44/9; *Bdr* 11/8; *Rþ* 28/1, 29/4; *Hdl* 12/6, 19/
2, 22/2, 24/6, 30/2; *Grt* 10/6 and 21/2. In Ssx compounds employed by skaldic poets,
an unresolved short syllable in the secondary constituent is usually preceded by an
ultra-long root syllable (a closed syllable containing a long vowel), whereas a long
syllable in the secondary constituent is normally preceded by an ordinary long root
syllable (Craigie, 'Points of Skaldic Metre', p. 366). This is no more than a tendency, as
noted by Kuhn (*Dróttkvætt*, §17). Example (35) is an Eddic exception. Craigie's law
does not of course explain the positional and alliterative constraints of interest here,
which depend entirely on the length of the secondary constituent.

109

Since the Norse s positions are more deeply subordinated, moreover, they provide more appropriate locations for unresolved syllables.

When preceded by two alliterating S positions, an s position undergoes double subordination by provision R7b of the metrical compounding rule. In both traditions, rule R9e defines an unresolved stressed syllable as the preferred occupant for a deeply subordinated s position of this type. Consider the following:

(33)	vá / Valhallar[60]	(*Vsp* 33/7)
	{S/Ssx, long s}	
(34)	Hár, / Haugspori[61]	(*Vsp* 15/3)
	{S/Ssx, short s}	
(35)	ginnheilog / goð[62]	(*Vsp* 6/3)
	{Ssx/S, long s}	
(36)	Sūð-Dena / folc[63]	(*Beo* 463b)
	{Ssx/S, short s}	

Our Norse corpus contains seven verses like (33) and twenty-four like (34).[64] The *Beowulf* poet adheres even more strictly to sub-rule R9e, employing only three verses comparable to (33) but twenty-three comparable to (34).[65] Rather than producing variants like (33), the *Beowulf* poet often reverses the order of constituents to produce type E variants of the form Ssx/S, with a less deeply subordinated s position. There are thirty-five Old English examples comparable to the Norse example (35), in which the long medial syllable of the compound occupies the subordinate arsis of the dominant foot rather than the subordinate arsis of the subordinate foot.[66] In fornyrðislag, the complexity of type E had

[60] 'The woe of Valhalla ... '   [61] 'Har and Haugspori ... '
[62] 'the very holy gods ... '   [63] 'the people of the South-Danes ... '
[64] Like (33) are *Vsp* 21/9, 35/7, 62/7; *Þrk* 23/3; *Rþ* 12/7; and *Grt* 18/3. Like (34) are *Vsp* 39/3; *Hym* 11/9, 13/3, 17/7, 18/5, 22/3, 23/1, 23/3, 37/3; *Þrk* 31/1; *HH* 9/3, 31/3; *HHv* 2/3, 6/3, 7/3, 36/5; *HH II* 5/3, 11/3, 19/7, 33/9, 35/7; *Bdr* 6/7; and *Grt* 9/7.
[65] Comparable to (33) are *Beo* 1927a, 2582a and 2965a. Comparable to (34) are 31a, 54a, 57a, 160a, 288a, 322a, 551a, 554a, 692a, 742a, 936a, 1409a, 1845a, 1954a, 2025a, 2042a, 2090a, 2226a, 2271a, 2315a, 2368a, 2563a and 2827a. Cf. 3152a (as printed).
[66] OE Ssx/S with long s: *Beo* 105a, 167a, 190a, 512a, 542a, 573a, 636a, 722a, 734a, 850a, 891a, 908a, 1042a, 1128a, 1160a, 1276a, 1278a, 1299a, 1429a, 1500a, 1536a, 1567a, 1613a, 1991a, 1993a, 2068a, 2393a, 2543a, 2650a, 2671a, 2695a, 2807a, 2843a, 2890a, 2904a, 3052a and 3154a. In 743a and 1538a, reversal is forced by the presence of two alliterating constituents inside the Ssx foot. This may also be the motivation for reversal in *lāðlicu lāc* 1584a (so in Klaeber's edition), where the vowel of

increased, making reversal less advantageous.[67] I found only six other variants like (35).[68] The problematic character of reversal in fornyrðislag explains why the percentage of Da variants with double alliteration and long s remains about the same in both traditions. This seems surprising at first because the deeper subordination of the s position in fornyrðislag should produce a stronger bias against long syllables. The bias may in fact have been stronger, but it seems to have encountered a contrary bias that was also stronger in the Norse tradition. Germanic poets do not usually pay the cost in complexity associated with reversal except to obtain some metrical benefit. We would not expect to find many reversals of felicitous Da variants like (34), with short s. Only four reversals like (36) appear in *Beowulf*, and there is nothing comparable in the Norse corpus.[69]

Non-alliterating compounds in verses like (31) and (32) are usually lexicalized forms such as proper names. Unlexicalized compounds usually alliterate. For an alliterating Ssx compound with a long medial syllable, the most suitable verse types are C and E. In these types the s position, preceded by only one alliterating S position, provides a fairly natural site for long syllables:

$$(37) \quad \text{á / rǫcstóla}^{70} \qquad\qquad\qquad (Vsp\ 6/2)$$
$$[\text{x/Ssx}]$$
$$(38) \quad \text{Nástrǫndo / á}^{71} \qquad\qquad\quad (Vsp\ 38/3)$$
$$[\text{Ssx/S}]$$

Germanic poets sometimes use an archaic word order for reversal of type C variants like (37), which yields type E variants like (38). In such cases the reversal transforms an inconspicuous one-syllable x foot into a much more conspicuous S foot. The *Beowulf* poet employs only one variant

---

-*lic*- is etymologically long, though metrists usually disregard the alliterative matching on this constituent and assume that its vowel has been shortened.

[67] See above, p. 41.

[68] *Vsp* 9/3, 23/3, 25/3 (all repeats of 6/3); *HH* 41/3; *HHv* 35/7; and *Hdl* 38/3.

[69] Like (36) are *Beo* 623b, 783b and 2779b. The only other clear case with short s is 1009b, with resolved second S. In 1681a, the short secondary constituent might be resolved. Observe that example (36) has unmarked word order, with the genitive modifier preceding its governed noun. Reversal may have a syntactic motivation in such cases. Compounds in the verses like (36) were unambiguously Ssx for the *Beowulf* poet, since they all had the type of ending subject to Kaluza's law, which precluded resolution to Ss (Fulk, *History of Old English Meter*, §237).

[70] 'at the seat of judgement . . . '   [71] 'at Nástrandr . . . '

analogous to (37) in the second half of the line, as compared with five reversals analogous to (38).[72] Reversal occurs in eight Norse b-verses like (38), but there are at least seventeen b-verses like (37).[73] As we have observed (ch. 4), weak x feet cause less complexity in fornyrðislag because there is no danger of confusion with anacrusis. For Norse poets, reversal of type C yielded a smaller benefit and incurred a greater cost, adding to the weight of the verse in a characteristically light metre. The *Beowulf* poet prefers double alliteration in a-verses of type E. Reversal of Old English type C, which would usually yield type E with single alliteration, does not occur in the first half of the line, and there are five a-verses comparable to (37).[74] In the Norse corpus, two reversals like (38) appear as a-verses, and there is only one a-verse with the structure of (37).[75] Reversals with single alliteration and variants with inconspicuous feet seem to have been about equally acceptable to Norse poets in the first half of the line, if we may judge from available evidence.

In type C, an unresolved short syllable may occupy the s position:

(39)	né / upphiminn[76]	(*Vsp* 3/6)
	[x/Ssx, short s]	
(40)	um / himinioður[77]	(*Vsp* 5/4)
	[x/Ssx, resolved S, short s]	

The Norse corpus contains sixty-five two-word verses like (39), with short s, and forty-four with long s (e.g. 37).[78] *Beowulf* has forty-six comparable

---

[72] With (37) cf. *Beo* 1429b, *on / seglrāde.* With (38) cf. 110b, *mancynne / fram.* The others analogous to (38) are 564b, 1715b, 1924b and 2357b. Cf. 2411b and 2831b, with *nēah,* which should probably be analysed as an adjective rather than a preposition. Prepositional phrases that undergo reversal all seem to represent spatial movement or location, and I restrict attention to such phrases here.

[73] The other reversals in the b-verse are *HH* 13/2, 19/4, 26/2, 47/4; *HH II* 50/10, 51/4; and *Bdr* 2/6. Closely similar to (37) are *Vsp* 9/2, 23/2, 25/2 (all repeats of 6/2), 30/4, 37/6; *HH* 1/8, 3/4, 42/2; *HH II* 6/4, 24/6; *Bdr* 11/2; *Hdl* 6/6, 7/4, 11/12, 16/8; and *Grt* 13/2.

[74] E.g. *on / wælbedde* 964a. Cf. 461a, 566a, 1026a and 1952a.

[75] Like (60b) is *Hym* 7/3. The a-verse allowed to stand as type C is *Hdl* 1/7.

[76] 'nor heaven above ... '   [77] 'over the horizon ... ' Cf. *Hdl* 40/4.

[78] The other x/Ssx variants with short s are *Vsp* 15/2, 30/8, 33/6, 36/2, 40/2, 42/6, 47/1, 47/6, 48/6, 57/6; *Hym* 1/3, 2/1, 4/3, 10/1, 20/1, 27/9, 29/1, 31/4, 31/7, 36/5; *Þrk* 2/7, 16/7, 19/11, 31/3; *HH* 4/6, 7/6, 8/2, 16/1, 16/2, 23/2, 32/1, 38/4, 40/8, 45/7, 48/2, 51/6, 56/8; *HHv* 1/5, 31/4, 37/7; *HH II* 11/7, 13/2, 13/5, 19/3, 22/3, 34/2, 35/4, 38/ 3, 43/3; *Bdr* 7/5, 11/2; *Rþ* 28/5; *Hdl* 12/7, 17/4, ?24/4, ?26/5, 30/6, 33/5, 35/2, 37/4,

verses with short s and seventeen with long s.[79] As expected, short s occurs less frequently in type C than in type Da with double alliteration (see (33)–(34)). I found only two verses like (40), in which the first of two adjacent resolvable sequences must undergo resolution, while the second must stand unresolved. Terasawa suggests that contrary operations in immediately adjacent sequences were cognitively dissonant, and were avoided for that reason alone.[80]

The s position of type C is less suitable for long syllables, and therefore evidently weaker, than the s position of type Da with a single alliterating S position. In both traditions, Da variants with long s (e.g. (31)) have a higher relative frequency than C variants with long s (e.g. (37)). Alliteration on a preceding S within the same foot, then, seems to have a more forceful subordinating effect than alliteration on an S in a preceding foot. It is worth recalling here the extreme case of metrical subordination that arises inside the second foot of heavy Norse type C, where two alliterating S positions reduce a following s position to the status of an x position.[81] In general, we would expect metrical subordination to grow

40/2; *Grt* 17/7, 22/3 and 24/1. The other variants with long s are *Vsp* 9/2, 10/5, 21/3, 23/2, 25/2, 29/4, 30/4, 37/6, 39/4, 55/4; *Hym* 1/1, 28/2; *Þrk* 16/3, 19/7; *HH* 1/8, 3/4, 42/2, 51/3; *HHv* 4/7, 11/7; *HH II* 6/4, 23/5, 49/7; *Bdr* 7/6, 8/3, 10/3, 12/3; *Rþ* 43/4; *Hdl* 1/7, 2/7, 6/6, 7/4, 11/12, 16/8, 21/3, 33/2, 33/4, 33/6, 37/6, 37/8, 48/2; *Grt* 13/2 and 20/8. As before, these are two-word variants with no resolvable sequences on S positions, and variants with Ssx simplexes are excluded.

[79] OE two-word x/Ssx with short s: *Beo* 37a, 68a, 174a, 180a, 285a, 317a, 382a, 383a, 486a, 492a, 601a, 707a, 851a, 971a, 976a, 1070a, 1094a, 1262a, 1325a, 1433a, 1695a, 1704a, 1862a, 2438a, 2479a, 2502a, 2515a, 2635a, 2798a, 3010a, 3097a, 3177a; 1b, 126b, 175b, 460b, 1192b, 1279b, 1330b, 1578b, 1856b, 2079b, 2437b, 2884b, 2896b and 2932b. Verses 1105a and 906b should probably be added to this list (disregarding epenthetic vowels), as they would otherwise constitute B variants ruled out by Terasawa. With long s: *Beo* 173a, 243a, 493a, 566a, 585a, 921a, 964a, 981a, 1046a, 1708a, 1734a, 1952a, 2202a; 334b, 1429b, 3181b and 3182b. A doubtful example with long s is 436a (assuming unstressed *mīn*). I exclude from consideration 178a, 112b and 629b, which contain unusual decontracted forms possibly subject to vowel shortening. The more complex examples of type C with short s might appear at first glance to be analysable as xx/Ss with resolved s. Kaluza's law forces scansion of these as type C when the second foot contains a compound, however; and in the remaining cases, the poet indicates scansion as type C by avoiding variants of xx/Ss with two independent monosyllables in the second foot (see *OEM*, §5.4.2.).

[80] 'Metrical Constraints', p. 13. See Terasawa, *Nominal Compounds*, for verse lists and full discussion of putative Old English exceptions.

[81] See above, p. 95.

weaker with distance, since linguistic subordination does so, for example when a clitic is distanced from its associated stress-word. A fairly close linguistic analogue to (31), in which an intervening arsis inhibits metrical subordination, is provided by the kind of triple compound in which the tertiary constituent comes immediately after the primary constituent and seems to inhibit subordination of the secondary constituent. The crucial case is a type B verse with a triple compound *in-wit-searo* in the Sxs foot.[82] Subordination of *-searo* must have been inhibited significantly, since resolution of a subordinate constituent on a secondary arsis is otherwise avoided in type B.[83]

Rule R8d requires alliteration on the S position of any foot with an alliterating s position. This makes it impossible to construct a type D verse with the kind of optional alliteration found in type C, that is, with an optionally alliterating s preceded by an obligatorily alliterating S. By R8d, any type D verse with an alliterating s position would have to have alliteration on the S of the second foot, and this could not be the only alliterating S, since R8a would require the S of the first foot to alliterate as well, like the first S of any other verse. Preceded by two alliterating S positions, the alliterating s would be a fully subordinated constituent of a weak constituent, in violation of R8b. The s position in type C can alliterate only because it stands in the same foot with the first S of the verse, which can satisfy both R8a and R8d.

NON-RESOLVABLE SEQUENCES IN SXX WORDS

According to the five-types theory, the metrical constant of the verse is its number of significant stresses, supposedly two. In order to eliminate some apparent exceptions with a single stress, Sievers posited a second stress in certain forms of weak class II verbs. Norse forms of this type appear in the following verses:

(41) um / sacnaði[84]   (*Þrk* 1/4)
      [x/Sxx]

(42) mǫn / iafnaði[85]   (*Þrk* 6/6)
      [S/Sxx]

---

[82] *Beo* 1101a, *nē þurh / inwitsearo.*
[83] This observation is made in Terasawa, 'Metrical Constraints', p. 7.
[84] 'he missed ...'   [85] 'he trimmed the mane'.

Resolution

The bracketed scansions in (41) and (42) presuppose that *sacnaði* and *iafnaði* have no medial stress, contra Sievers. These scansions are consistent with the account of Fulk, who finds no independent linguistic evidence for medial stress in comparable Old English forms such as *tryddode*.[86] The claim that some degree of stress survived on medial vowels after they underwent shortening seems to stand or fall with the two-stress hypothesis.[87] Since the word-foot theory makes it unnecessary to posit a second stress in the problematic class II forms, they are scanned as Sxx. The xx segment of an Sxx form cannot of course undergo resolution (see R9a–b).

In our Norse corpus, there are about five ordinary type C verses for every ordinary verse of type Da. If the problematic class II forms had the value Ssx, as Sievers claimed, verses like (41) should outnumber those like (42). In fact, there are thirteen verses like (42) but only six like (41).[88] These figures make perfect sense if (41) has a single arsis, like the relatively complex type A3, while (42) has standard weight, like type A1. The frequency of verses like (41) is probably somewhat elevated by the Norse bias towards the lighter patterns. The *Beowulf* poet favours the variant with standard weight more conspicuously, using 100 verses comparable to (42) but only nineteen comparable to (41).[89]

[86] *History of Old English Meter*, §261.
[87] See Luick, *Historische Grammatik*, §314.
[88] Like (41) are *Þrk* 1/2, 13/2; *HH* 23/7; *HH II* 4/5; and *Rþ* 45/5. Like (42) are *Vsp* 7/4, 7/6; *Hym* 12/8, 31/8, 33/5; *Þrk* 21/5; *HH* 31/8, 41/8, 43/4; *Hdl* 28/10; *Grt* 4/4 and 23/2.
[89] OE S/Sxx: 286a, 2409a, 2668a, 2744a, 2758a, 2805a, 3133a; 81b, 132b, 156b, 172b, 188b, 204b, 208b, 227b, 320b, 370b, 402b, 423b, 432b, 451b, 470b, 508b, 570b, 611b, 625b, 639b, 720b, 725b, 770b, 787b, 796b, 808b, 840b, 843b, 901b, 951b, 971b, 983b, 1090b, 1102b, 1117b, 1204b, 1206b, 1212b, 1222b, 1237b, 1380b, 1391b, 1397b, 1407b, 1413b, 1426b, 1440b, 1444b, 1500b, 1566b, 1573b, 1589b, 1626b, 1630b, 1662b, 1687b, 1721b, 1795b, 1799b, 1843b, 1898b, 1916b, 2045b, 2075b, 2084b, 2085b, 2098b, 2102b, 2164b, 2168b, 2211b, 2285b, 2336b, 2352b, 2383b, 2402b, 2589b, 2594b, 2605b, 2652b, 2655b, 2658b, 2748b, 2773b, 2793b, 2897b, 3008b, 3025b, 3027b, 3032b, 3050b, 3056b and 3104b. Verses 1125b and 2671b scan as Sx/Sxx if the verb is *nēosian* rather than *nēosan*. For the purposes of this argument, there is no reason to exclude examples with resolved S in the first foot, but the disproportion is equally evident when they are excluded. The S/Sxx verses 258a, 340b and 724b are excluded as irrelevant. Old English x/Sxx and xx/Sxx: 96a, 115a, 144a, 480a, 536a, 630a, 1363a, 1944a, 2177a, 2766a, 2933a, 2985a, 3159a, 3178a; 292b, 560b, 1819b, 2619b and 3103b.

115

The Norse corpus contains only two verses with a weak class II form in the first foot. Consider the following:

(43) kǫlloðo / Karl[90]   (*Rþ* 21/3)
      [Sxx/S]
(44) setti á / bióð[91]   (*Rþ* 4/8)
      [Sxx/S]
(45) riðoðo / augo[92]   (*Rþ* 21/6)
      [Sx/Sx or ?Sxx/Sx]

Example (43) would scan as Ssx/S, type E, if the short medial syllable of the verb had stress. On this hypothesis, however, (43) would be our only example of Norse type E with a short stressed syllable. If Norse poets allowed short medial s in E verses, we would expect a few clear cases analogous to the Old English *Sūð-Dena / folc* (example 36), with an Ssx compound in the first foot; but these are not to be found. Consider, too, how odd it would be if the only resolvable sequence in Norse type E stood unresolved on the sx portion of the verse. In *Beowulf*, resolvable sequences appear far more often on the verse-initial or verse-final S position of this type. It seems best to suppose that (43) has the pattern Sxx/S, like (44) and other verses in the same poem.[93] Even in (43), then, the evidence points toward scansion of the weak class II form as Sxx, with no metrically significant stress on the short medial syllable.[94] Example (45) is the only verse in the corpus that contains a trisyllabic weak class II form with a short root syllable. The medial syllable in this form is also short, so resolution probably occurred.

RESOLUTION: SUMMARY

Placement of resolvable sequences is consistent with the hypothesis that the poet assigns syllables to metrical positions in the most natural way. Constraints on resolution are predictable from linguistic properties and

---

[90] 'they named him Karl ... '   [91] 'she set it on the table ... '
[92] 'he darted his eyes'.   [93] See *Rþ* 6/1, 14/7, 20/1, 26/4, 27/1, 32/4 and 33/5.
[94] It is worth emphasizing that Sxx words behave quite differently from words like *eisandi* 'rushing forward'. Trisyllabic simplexes with long initial and medial syllables have a distribution similar to that of Ssx compounds and are rarely followed within the verse by a non-resolvable trochaic word such as *dróttinn* 'lord'. Words like *murnende* 'mourning' have the same type of distribution in *Beowulf*.

Resolution

P1–4, the independently necessary principles of verse construction. Detail rules R9a–e are corollaries, and have been stated for expository convenience only. In a strict sense, there are no rules for resolution.

In Old English and Old Norse, syllable length is directly related to the degree of stress. Metrical subordination mimics this feature of the natural language, making a subordinated arsis less suitable for resolved sequences or long syllables and more suitable for unresolved short syllables. As expected, the deeper linguistic subordination characteristic of Old Norse is reflected as a deeper metrical subordination. Resolution on a subordinate arsis, though not uncommon in *Beowulf*, hardly ever occurs in fornyrðislag, and resolvable sequences stand unresolved significantly more often in the Norse metre. The evidence of resolution thus converges with the evidence of alliteration discussed in ch. 6.

9

Word order and stress within the clause

The Light Foot Rule (R6) incorporates Kuhn's observations about clustering of unstressed Satzpartikeln at the level of the verse. We must now consider why unstressed Satzpartikeln tend to occupy the first verse of the clause, in Old Norse as well as Old English poems.[1] It is worth emphasizing that Kuhn's laws do not mandate word orders unattested in the early Germanic prose that survives to us. K1–2 simply declare certain word orders attested in prose to be unacceptable in verse.[2] Since rules of poetic metre perform a similar function, we have no aprioristic basis for attributing the Kuhn's-law effects to archaic syntax. There is nothing archaic about the way in which Kuhn's laws operate. General linguistic principles suffice to explain why Satzpartikeln often appear as proclitics to the Germanic clause or to the verb phrase, the major subconstituent of the clause.[3] Research on Old English by theoretical linguists indicates that the Kuhn's-law effects are simply exaggerations of ordinary-language tendencies. Traugott, for example, observes that movement of unstressed words toward the beginning of the clause is a familiar feature of prose syntax and is supported by a tendency to move heavy constituents in the

---

[1] This tendency is strong in Old English poems widely divergent as to date, authorship and style, as Momma has shown (*Composition of Old English Poetry*, ch. 6). The fact that the tendency shows up with comparable strength in our Norse corpus underscores its generality.

[2] Contrast the use of genuinely archaic syntax in Old English verses like *grund-wong þone* (*Beo* 2588a), with the demonstrative-article *þone* placed after its governed noun to avoid the unacceptable two-word variant of type A3. Here employment of archaic syntax produces a word order unattested, so far as I know, in Old English prose and is motivated by purely metrical considerations (cf. *OEM*, §5.4.2).

[3] See Cowper, *Introduction to Syntactic Theory*, §8.3.2.

opposite direction.[4] Our primary task, then, is to explain why a familiar type of optional movement became obligatory for Germanic poets, or very nearly so.[5] We will also need to deal with exceptions to Kuhn's second law in verses with finite verbs.

A TEST CASE FOR KUHN'S LAWS

According to Kuhn, his laws were well observed in native Eddic fornyrðislag.[6] Let us consider what K1–2 have to tell us about word order in a poem of manageable size. A look at *Þrymsqviða* will show that the poet does have regular procedures for placement of Satzpartikeln, but these are often explained by fundamental principles of the word-foot theory or by universal constraints on syntactic form.

When a clause consists of a single verse, that verse will of course contain all the unstressed function words of the clause. Any Satzpartikeln in a one-verse clause will be assigned to metrical positions by the light foot rule (R6). One-verse clauses appear frequently in all of the early Germanic traditions. In the first stanza of *Þrymsqviða*, four of the eight verses are complete clauses.[7]

---

[4] *CHEL I*, §4.6.1.

[5] Pintzuk and Kroch, 'Rightward Movement', captures effects of Kuhn's first law with a rule of 'floating'. This simply requires movable unstressed particles to move as far as possible from their underlying positions, usually assumed to lie toward the end of the clause in recent syntactic research. The authors also assume that stressed words may undergo optional movement to a pre-clausal position before the particles (called an 'XP' position within the X-bar theoretic framework). When topicalization does not occur, the particles will cluster before the first stressed word; otherwise, after it. Coinage of the term 'floating' is motivated by the fact that unstressed particles move 'upward' on a syntactic tree diagram of the kind employed by the authors, into 'higher-level' constituents. Pintzuk and Kroch also posit an optional rule of verb fronting, which may group a finite verb with the particles (ibid., p. 127). The authors assume that floating was obligatory in ordinary speech during the period when *Beowulf* was composed. This assumption would be difficult to substantiate, however, given the scarcity of relevant prose texts. All evidence for floating cited by the authors comes from verse. Campbell, 'Epic Style', does observe fairly regular conformity to K1–2 in some early Old English prose texts, attributing this to the influence of poetic tradition. It seems simpler to suppose that any stylistic features common to poetry and prose reflect ordinary-language tendencies.

[6] 'Wortstellung', pp. 26 and 46.   [7] *Þrk* 1/1, 1/2, 1/5 and 1/6.

Sievers pointed out that Eddic poetry is characteristically stichic.[8] In this tradition, the clause is usually initiated at the beginning of the line and seldom extends beyond the end of the line. The only clauses in *Þrymsqviða* that begin in the middle of the line are one-verse clauses (e.g. 1/6). Six clauses in the poem seem to extend beyond the line boundary, but all of them are derived from shorter clauses by the 'adding style' of formulaic composition. Consider the following:

(1)	Þrymr sat á haugi, þursa dróttinn[9]	(6/1–2)
(2)	nú fœrið mér Freyio at qván,	
	Niarðar dóttur, ór Nóatúnom[10]	(22/5–8)

Epithets of chieftains are among the most common formulas employed by early Germanic poets. The epithet *þursa dróttinn*, for example, used in (1) as an apposition to *Þrymr*, has obvious parallels in Old English verse.[11] This phrase appears six times in *Þrymsqviða*, always in the second half of the line following an a-verse that would be syntactically complete without it.[12] Since epithets contain no movable *Satzpartikeln* of their own, any *Satzpartikeln* in such a line will occupy the syntactically complete a-verse.[13] Example (2) begins with a one-line clause, the poet's other type of stylistic building block. The two-word verses that make up the second line of (2) are adjoined in the manner of *þursa dróttinn*. Patronymics like *Niarðar dóttur* appear frequently as appositions, with many parallels in cognate traditions.[14] Prepositional phrases like *ór Nóatúnom* are also widely used in the poem as b-verses following a-verses that would be syntactically complete without them.[15] The five other

---

[8] *AGM*, §4. See Stanley, *Foreground*, p. 112.

[9] 'Þrymr sat on a mound, the lord of the giants … '

[10] 'now bring me Freyia as a wife, the daughter of Njǫrð, from Nóatún.'

[11] E.g. *eorla drihten* 'lord of men' (*Beo* 1050b and 2338b); *gumena dryhten* 'lord of men' (*Beo* 1824a); *Gēata dryhten* 'lord of the Geats' (*Beo* 2560b, 2576a and 2996b).

[12] See *Þrk* 11/4, 22/2, 25/2, 30/2 and 31/6.

[13] Additional examples like (1) that reduce to one-verse clauses are *Þrk* 15/1–2, 17/1–2, 18/1–2 and 24/5–7.

[14] E.g. *Wēoxstānes sunu*, used appositionally at *Beo* 2602b, 2862b and 3076b.

[15] Cf. *Þrk* 7/4, 12/8, 13/10, 20/6, 21/8, 23/4, 26/4, 26/8, 27/4, 28/4, 28/8, 30/6, 32/6 and 32/8. In a closely related type of b-verse, the prepositional function is performed by case endings alone (cf. 9/8, 12/6, 15/6, 17/6, 18/4, 19/2, 26/6, 28/6, 27/4 and 30/8). Some of these b-verses are in fairly close construction with the main verb of the a-verse, and might be regarded as complements rather than adjuncts. The distinction

multi-line clauses in *Þrymsqviða* are constructed in a similar way, by adjunction of independent constituents that contain no movable unstressed Satzpartikeln of their own.[16] General linguistic principles explain why poets never move unstressed Satzpartikeln from a syntactically complete a-verse into a following adjunct or complement. This is blocked by the universal requirement that particle movement must be 'upward'. A particle can move only to a higher-level syntactic constituent that contains the lower-level constituent in which the particle originated. A b-verse adjunct or complement obviously does not contain a preceding a-verse that consists of a main clause. Adjuncts and complements cannot therefore accept particles from such an a-verse.[17] By its very nature, the 'adding style' will tend to produce rightward extensions of the clause that are free of movable function words.

Þrymsqviða has a total of 129 lines. In many of these, Kuhn's prediction that unstressed Satzpartikeln will occupy the first verse of the clause has no meaningful work to perform, and the claim that the poem conforms well to K1–2 has correspondingly limited significance. In thirty lines, the a-verse is syntactically complete and the b-verse is a one-verse clause or an adjunct with no movable particles of its own. In an additional six lines, the a-verse is an adjunct to a clause in a previous line and the b-verse is a one-verse clause or another adjunct. No special laws of poetic grammar are required to explain why Satzpartikeln occupy the first verse of the clause in these cases.[18] In seventeen lines, the a-verse could stand alone as a complete clause and the b-verse is either an adjunct or the complement of some element in the a-verse.[19] Satzpartikeln are confined to the a-verse by universal syntactic constraints in these lines as well, since neither adjuncts nor complements could provide landing sites for them. The fact that adjuncts and complements usually occupy the b-verse

has little importance for our purposes, since none of these phrases have movable particles of their own and none could provide a landing site for Satzpartikeln.

[16] *Þrk* 2/5–7, 8/1–4, 23/1–4, 24/5–7 and 29/7–10.

[17] See Chomsky, *Barriers*, p. 4.

[18] Lines with a-verse clauses: *Þrk* 1/1–2, 1/5–6, 2/3–4, 4/1–2, 4/3–4, 5/1–2, 6/1–2, 7/1–2, 7/5–6, 9/1–2, 9/7–8, 10/1–2, 11/1–2, 11/3–4, 13/1–2, 15/1–2, 15/3–4, 17/1–2, 18/1–2, 20/1–2, 21/3–4, 21/5–6, 22/1–2, 22/3–4, 23/5–6, 24/5–6, 25/1–2, 27/1–2, 30/1–2 and 31/5–6. Lines with a-verse adjuncts: 2/7–8, 8/3–4, 22/7–8, 23/3–4, 24/7–8 and 29/9–10.

[19] *Þrk* 7/3–4, 12/7–8, 13/9–10, 18/3–4, 20/5–6, 21/7–8, 26/3–4, 26/5–6, 26/7–8, 27/3–4, 28/3–4, 28/5–6, 28/7–8, 30/3–4, 30/7–8, 32/5–6 and 32/7–8.

is attributable to the stichic character of fornyrðislag and the general tendency to shift heavy elements rightward. When the clause normally terminates at the end of the line, the b-verse will provide the most natural location for constituents like prepositional phrases. It is interesting to note that thirty of the adjuncts and complements employed as b-verses in the poem consist of exactly two words.[20] Such expressions achieved formulaic status not only because they filled out the line but also because they provided the most desirable type of closure (see U3). Finally, we can set aside the twenty-eight one-line clauses that contain no movable unstressed Satzpartikeln.[21] Our task reduces to analysis of the forty-eight remaining one-line clauses.

The poet handles one-line clauses so consistently that the most important syntactic tendencies can be illustrated with a single example:

(3)   Mic muno æsir   argan kalla[22]   (17/3–4)

Concepts already introduced suffice to explain the word order of (3). The principle of closure restricts deviation from underlying patterns in the second half of the line, favouring employment of two-word b-verses like *argan kalla*. Of the forty-eight one-line clauses that contain movable unstressed Satzpartikeln, twenty-five have two-word b-verses.[23] The movable Satzpartikeln *mic* and *muno* in (3) occupy the thesis of a type A3 pattern. As we have observed, this pattern is most appropriate in the a-verse, and the poet prefers to support its first foot with an extrametrical syllable.[24] Of the forty-eight relevant one-line clauses, twenty-six have

---

[20] *Þrk* 2/6, 6/2, 7/4, 9/8, 10/2, 11/2, 11/4, 12/8, 13/10, 15/2, 17/2, 18/2, 18/4, 20/2, 20/6, 21/8, 22/2, 22/8, 24/6, 25/2, 26/6, 26/8, 27/4, 28/6, 28/8, 29/10, 30/2, 30/8, 31/6 and 32/6.

[21] These include lines like *Þrk* 6/3–4, which contains no unstressed Satzpartikel, and others like 1/3–4, where the only unstressed Satzpartikel, a conjunction, is confined to clause-initial position by a rule of ordinary grammar that applies in prose as well as poetry. The other examples are *Þrk* 2/5–6, 5/3–4, 5/5–6, 6/5–6, 8/7–8, 9/3–4, 9/5–6, 10/7–8, 13/3–4, 14/3–4, 16/3–4, 16/5–6, 16/7–8, 19/3–4, 19/7–8, 19/9–10, 19/11–12, 22/5–6, 24/3–4, 25/7–8, 29/3–4, 30/5–6, 31/1–2, 31/3–4, 31/7–8 and 32/3–4.

[22] 'The gods will call me a degenerate ... '

[23] Cf. *Þrk* 3/2, 3/6, 3/8, 10/4, 12/6, 13/6, 14/6, 15/6, 15/8, 16/2, 17/6, 18/6, 19/2, 20/4, 23/2, 23/8, 25/4, 26/2, 27/6, 28/2, 29/2, 29/6, 29/8 and 32/2. The only two-word a-verse is 10/5.

[24] See above, p. 52.

their Satzpartikeln in an a-verse of type A3.[25] Assignment of movable Satzpartikeln to a b-verse tends to interfere with metrical closure, but such words can actually improve the metre in an a-verse.

Two-word b-verses of types A1, A2, D and E necessarily exclude unstressed Satzpartikeln. Types A3 and B seldom appear in the second half of the line due to their inherent complexity. Type C favours the second half of the line, however, and it is pertinent to ask why b-verses of this type seldom have movable Satzpartikeln on verse-initial x positions. Consider the following examples:

> (4) oc síns hamars   um sacnaði[26]   (1/3–4)
> (5) svá var hon óðfús   í iotunheima[27]   (26/7–8)
> (6) Hefir þú erindi   sem erfiði?[28]   (10/1–2)

In example (4), the only Satzpartikel present is *oc*, a conjunction restricted to the beginning of the clause in prose as well as poetry. All other lines in the poem that close with two-word type C have syntactically complete a-verses or a-verse adjuncts. The b-verse is a prepositional phrase in nine lines like (5) and an abbreviated clause in two lines like (6).[29] Most often, then, a two-word b-verse of type C will be an adjunct or complement that contains no movable Satzpartikeln of its own and cannot accept Satzpartikeln from the preceding a-verse. The large number of adjuncts among two-word type C verses can be attributed in part to the principle of syntactic integrity (U1). Since a verse is most readily identifiable as such if it forms a natural syntactic constituent, the variants most highly

---

[25] Cf. *Þrk* 2/1–2, 3/1–2, 3/3–4, 3/5–6, 9/9–10, 10/3–4, 11/7–8, 12/1–2, 12/3–4, 13/5–6, 13/7–8, 14/1–2, 14/5–6, 15/7–8, 16/1–2, 18/5–6, 19/5–6, 21/1–2, 24/1–2, 25/3–4, 25/5–6, 27/5–6, 27/7–8, 29/5–6 and 32/1–2. One-line clauses with a-verses of type B: 1/7–8, 8/5–6, 11/5–6, 17/5–6, 20/3–4, 24/9–10, 29/7–8 and the last line of the poem (not included in a stanza); of type C: 3/7–8, 7/7–8, 8/1–2, 10/5–6, 14/7–8, 18/7–8, 26/1–2 and 28/1–2; of type A: 12/5–6, 15/5–6, 19/1–2, 23/1–2, 23/7–8 and 29/1–2.

[26] 'and looked for his hammer ... '

[27] 'she was that eager to go to the land of the giants'.

[28] 'Have you received tidings as well as troubles?'

[29] Other lines with a prepositional phrase in the b-verse following a syntactically complete a-verse: *Þrk* 7/3–4, 12/7–8, 13/9–10, 20/5–6, 21/7–8, 28/7–8 and 32/5–6. Line 22/7–8 has a prepositional phrase in the b-verse following an a-verse adjunct. The other line with an abbreviated clause following a syntactically complete a-verse is 11/1–2.

123

favoured in the b-verse will consist of two words in close syntactic composition. Prepositional phrases like *í iotunheima* are ideal in this respect. The only movable Satzpartikeln likely to form a natural constituent with an Ssx compound are finite main verbs. Kuhn's laws would receive significant empirical support if finite main verbs frequently occupied the initial thesis of a two-word type C verse placed at the beginning of the clause, but in fact this seldom happens in our Norse corpus, and never in *Þrymsqviða*. The absence of such verses later in the clause therefore has limited theoretical significance. *Þrymsqviða* contains only one two-word a-verse of type C with a movable particle occupying the initial x position.[30]

As we observed above, the b-verse is the most natural location for heavy elements such as prepositional phrases when the poet terminates the clause at the end of the line. In *Þrymsqviða*, the more complex b-verse variants of types B and C often contain a prepositional phrase, which is sometimes followed by another late-placed element such as a clause-final verb:

(7)	um / kné falla[31]		(16/4)
	[x/Ssx]		
(8)	of / beðit hafði[32]		(32/4)
	[x/Ssx]		
(9)	í / meyiar kné[33]		(30/6)
	[x/Sxs]		

Six one-line clauses in *Þrymsqviða* have a b-verse of type C that contains more than two words. Four of the six have a b-verse like (7), with a preposition occupying the light foot.[34] The two others have a b-verse like (8), with the light foot occupied by a prefixal filler word derived from a

---

[30] Verse 10/5, *opt sitianda.*
[31] 'to fall about his knees ... ' Repeated as 19/8.
[32] 'had requested ... ' Cf. 24/2.
[33] 'onto the maid's knees ... ' Cf. 32/8.
[34] Cf. *Þrk* 16/8 and 19/12. Four other complex variants of type C appear as adjuncts in the b-verse. Three of them are prepositional phrases (8/4, 26/4 and 28/4). The exception is 15/4, probably best regarded as a reduced one-verse clause. Among the three light type C b-verses with a second foot of the form Sxx, one is a complete clause (1/2), one is the verb of a one-line clause accompanied by a filler word (1/4) and one is a reduced one-verse clause (10/2).

prepositional adverb.[35] The complexity of Norse type B restricts it for the most part to the a-verse. Among the one-line clauses in our test poem, only two have type B verses in the second half of the line, and both of these type B verses are prepositional phrases like (9).

Let us now consider one-line clauses that end with relatively complex variants of type A1:

    (10)   hann engi maðr   aptr um heimtir[36]   (8/5–6)

    (11)   Ganga þeir fagra   Freyio at hitta[37]   (12/1–2)

The first foot of the Sx/Sx b-verse in (10) is occupied by the word group *aptr um* rather than by a trochaic word. The b-verse in (11) has the form Sx/(x)Sx, with an extrametrical syllable before the second foot. *Þrymsqviða* provides fourteen other b-verses like *aptr um heimtir* and two others like *Freyio at hitta*.[38] Two additional b-verses of the form Sx/(x)Sx have both types of complexity, with a word group in the first foot and extrametrical material as well.[39] These are one-verse clauses, however, and their complexity is mitigated by close adherence to the principle of syntactic integrity (U1). Because it is the standard pattern, with no inherent complexity of its own, type A1 is the most tolerant of deviation from the two-word norm (see U4). As we would expect, the most common pattern among complex b-verses in one-line clauses is Sx/Sx.[40] Moreover, complex variants of Sx/Sx seem to be used primarily for a single purpose: to place a trochaic verb in line-final position. Of the twenty complex A1 variants appearing in the second half of the line, all but five end with such a

[35] The natural constituent formed by a prefixed non-finite verb and its associated auxiliary is frequently employed as a b-verse by the *Beowulf* poet. A close parallel to (8) is *Beo* 1928b, *gebiden hæbbe*.

[36] 'no man is ever going to recover it ... ' Repeated as 11/5–6.

[37] 'They go to see fair Freyia ... '

[38] Like *aptr um heimtir* are Þrk 1/8, 7/8, 8/2, 10/6, 10/8, 11/5–6, 14/8, 18/8, 21/2, 25/8, 27/8, 31/2, 31/4 and the unnumbered last line. Like *Freyio at hitta* are 14/2 and 14/4.

[39] Þrk 1/6, 23/6.

[40] The remaining complex b-verses in *Þrymsqviða* are represented by one example of type A2 (24/10); two of type Da (13/8 and 24/4); four of type E, all identical (2/2, 3/4, 9/10 and 12/4); and three with the Sxx/S pattern, all identical (8/8, 11/8 and 22/8). One possibly relevant example of Sx/(x)Sxx is 25/6. This makes weak stylistic evidence, however, since it is clearly unmetrical, exceeding the allowable number of alliterating syllables in the b-verse.

verb.[41] In type C, a trochaic verb can occupy the sx portion of the Ssx foot. Of the six complex b-verses like (7) and (8), all but one end with such a verb.[42] Since the only complex variants to occur very often in the b-verse have the two simplest patterns (A1 and C), we can generalize as follows: deviation from two-word paradigms in the b-verse serves primarily to allow for one-line clauses with the verb in final position.[43] The constraints on verb placement within the poetic clause seem, then, to be stricter than, and different from, those imposed by Kuhn's laws. Kuhn's laws predict that a finite verb will alliterate if it stands first in the b-verse of a one-line clause, but such verbs appear so seldom in this position that supporting evidence is as hard to find as counter-evidence. What stands out is the tendency to place any sort of verb occupying the b-verse at the end of the line. If this tendency is a syntactic archaism, it might reflect the clause-final placement of verbs in common Germanic, now widely regarded as an SOV language.[44] The poet also has a purely metrical incentive for line-final placement of finite verbs. The root syllable in these constituents, with its subordinate but perceptible stress, makes an ideal occupant for the weakest arsis in the line.[45]

GROUPING IN OLD ENGLISH POETRY

Beowulf raises problems we have not yet considered, since the poet more often initiates clauses in the b-verse and more often extends clauses beyond the end of the line. Analysis of Kuhn's-law effects in Old English verse at the level of fine detail would obviously constitute too long a digression here, but I would like to suggest that important principles operative in *Þrymsqviða* are operative in *Beowulf* as well. Consider the following passage, in which Wulfgar agrees to pass on Beowulf's request for an interview with King Hrothgar:

[41] *Þrk* 14/2, 14/4, 23/6, 31/2 and 31/4.

[42] *Þrk* 24/2, where the line-final word is an adverb that modifies a preceding verb.

[43] Among the complex heavy b-verses is one verb-final example of type Da (24/4). The verb is also final in the four identical examples of complex type E (2/2, 3/4, 9/10 and 12/4). For systematic discussion of verb-final patterns employed by Old English poets, see Donoghue, *Style*.

[44] Robinson, *Old English and its Closest Relatives*, p. 165; *CHEL I*, 60–3; Kuhn, 'Wortstellung', p. 59.

[45] The rules given in ch. 6 will always subordinate the line-final arsis most deeply.

(12)   *Ic þæs* wine Deniga,
frēan Scildinga   frīnan wille
bēaga bryttan,   *swā þū* bēna eart,
þēoden mærne   ymb þīnne sīð,
ond þē þā andsware   ædre gecȳðan,
ðē mē se gōda   āgifan þenceð.[46]   (350b–55)

Word order in the passage above follows from fundamental principles of verse construction and from the defining characteristic of Satzpartikeln, which are not closely bound to any lexical subconstituent of the clause. In general, grouping of Satzpartikeln within one verse will free all remaining verses of syntactically extraneous function words, bringing them into better conformity with the principle of syntactic integrity (U1). Such grouping can result in significant metrical improvement as the number of verses in the clause increases and will be particularly effective if the Satzpartikeln are placed in a verse with a pattern that is tolerant of extrametrical words. Note that in the representative passage above, the italicized Satzpartikeln support the light foot in a clause-initial verse of type A3 (355a), B (352b) or C (350b and 354a). In these types, as we have frequently observed, additional unstressed words add little to metrical complexity. Variants like *Ic þæs wine Deniga* and *swā þū bēna eart* may initiate clauses in the b-verse with no undue offence to the principle of closure (U3). The metre of *ðē mē se gōda* (the A3 variant) is actually improved by addition of the Satzpartikel *mē*, as in Norse example (3) above. If the poet wants to establish a regular site for grouping, moreover, the first verse of the clause is the obvious choice. Many Satzpartikeln are conjunctions or relative pronouns confined to clause-initial position by the rules of ordinary prose syntax (e.g. *swā, ond* and *ðē* in the example above). When a poetic clause contains a Satzpartikel of this kind, its fixed position restricts possibilities of grouping to the first verse. In *Þrymsqviða*, as we have seen, grouping of movable function words in a clause-initial a-verse often improves the metre of a following b-verse subject to the principle of closure. In *Beowulf*, grouping can improve the metre of following a-verses as well as b-verses in addition to providing a useful marker for clause boundaries, which are not predictably associated with

---

[46] 'I shall ask the friend of the Danes, lord of the Scyldings, distributor of rings, illustrious ruler, about this mission of yours, as you request, and quickly make known to you the answer that the great man decides to give me.'

the a-verse in West Germanic poetry.[47] In ch. 11 we will consider why a West Germanic poet might have wished to initiate clauses in the b-verse and continue them beyond the end of the line. Whatever the explanation for this important stylistic feature, it seems clear that grouping of Satzpartikeln would have reduced average verse complexity in West Germanic as well as North Germanic poetry.

METRICAL INTERPRETATION OF FINITE VERBS

In *Beowulf*, the constituent most likely to appear as an anacrusis is the isolated unstressed prefix of an alliterating verb placed at the beginning of a clause. Kuhn analysed such an isolated prefix as an unaccompanied Satzteilpartikel placed before the first stressed constituent, in violation of K2.[48] Some researchers interpret the verb as unstressed and assign it to the thesis in such cases, despite the alliteration.[49] On this hypothesis, the verbal root counts as a Satzpartikel in the same thesis with the prefix, and the violation disappears. The unstressed-verb hypothesis has been challenged on strictly internal grounds.[50] It is also worth emphasizing that alliteration provides much of the evidence for phrasal stress in early Germanic languages. Setting aside alliterative evidence in a study of Germanic stress and syntax is an inherently doubtful procedure requiring the most careful justification. In some cases, consonant matching clearly does not count as alliteration. Consonant matching that involves unstressed function words may safely be disregarded, since words of this type do not obey constraints on the number of alliterating syllables.[51]

---

[47] On the usefulness of grouping for resolution of syntactic ambiguity, see Stanley, '*Beowulf*', p. 120; Blockley and Cable, 'Kuhn's Laws', pp. 268–9; and Momma, *Composition of Old English Poetry*, p. 193.

[48] Kuhn acknowledges the violation when he assigns the root syllable of the prefixed verb to a *Hebung* or arsis ('Wortstellung', p. 11), though he refers to this necessity as *gelegentlich* ('occasional' or 'incidental') and represents syntactically similar verses with non-alliterating verbs as the norm (ibid., p. 12).

[49] Bliss, *Metre*, §§12–21; Lucas, 'Verse Grammar and Metre', p. 152; Kendall, 'Displacement', p. 8.

[50] See Hutcheson, 'Kuhn's Law, Finite Verb Stress, and the Critics'; Blockley and Cable, 'Kuhn's Laws', pp. 270–1; and Russom, Review.

[51] If, for example, the conjunction *oc* counted as an alliterating syllable in *oc / grindi* (Þrk 11/2), this b-verse would have double alliteration, violating the most widely observed rule of Old Germanic metre.

When a finite main verb alliterates, on the other hand, it must not be followed by another alliterating word in the b-verse or by more than one alliterating word in the a-verse.[52]

If we restricted our attention to *Beowulf*, it might not seem too implausible to disregard the stress on alliterating main verbs placed at the beginning of the clause. Such verbs usually appear in the a-verse, where they are usually followed by a second alliterating word.[53] In most cases, therefore, the unstressed-verb hypothesis allows for acceptable scansion:

(13)	(Ā-)rās þā se rīca[54]	(*Beo* 399a)
(14)	stonc ðā æfter stāne[55]	(*Beo* 2288a)
(15)	fundode wrecca[56]	(*Beo* 1137b)
	[alliteration on f-]	
(16)	Gemunde þā se gōda[57]	(*Beo* 758a)
	[alliteration on m-]	

Example (13) violates K2 if the alliterating verb has stress, since the prefix then constitutes a clause-initial thesis without a Satzpartikel. With the verb redefined as an unstressed Satzpartikel, K2 is satisfied and the verse scans as a type A3 variant of the form xx/(xx)Sx. Bliss also posits an unstressed verb in variants like (14), where there is no apparent violation of K2, citing the predominance of examples that scan as type A3.[58] Alliteration on the verb is said to be 'non-functional' in such cases. Bliss does acknowledge stress on the finite main verb of variants like (15), where no other element alliterates. These variants arise, he thinks, primarily under special syntactic conditions, e.g. when there is no other major-category word in the verse or when the verb is the last Satzpartikel before a major-category word.[59] Such an approach to apparent exceptions seems *ad hoc*, and does not explain (16), which is syntactically very much

---

[52] See *OEM*, §§9.3 and 9.5. Unusual verses like *einn át oxa* (*Þrk* 24/5) can be analysed as Ss/Sx, with a kind of triple alliteration sanctioned by the word-foot theory (*OEM*, §7.5.3). There is no need to disregard alliteration on the finite main verb *át*.

[53] Double alliteration is preferred for reasons discussed in *OEM*, §9.12.

[54] 'The powerful man arose then ...'   [55] 'then it sniffed along the stones ...'

[56] 'the adventurer desired to go ...'

[57] 'The good one remembered then ...'   [58] *Metre*, §17.

[59] Ibid., §26. In *Metrical Grammar*, Kendall argues that the root syllable of a clause-initial verb never occupies an arsis, but the theoretical manoeuvres used to support this claim are open to question (Russom, Review).

like (13). Verses like (16) have a rather low frequency in Old English poems, however. Bliss deals with them by emendation or simply acknowledges them as inconsistencies.[60]

As we saw in ch. 6, deep subordination of rightward constituents in native Eddic fornyrðislag restricts the frequency of double alliteration in the a-verse. If the unstressed-verb hypothesis were correct, we would expect Norse poets simply to avoid alliteration on clause-initial verbs. As it turns out, examples of such alliteration occur in all of the major verse types:

(17) seið hon, hvars hon kunni[61] (*Vsp* 22/5)
      {alliteration on s-}

(18) þeir kunno vel[62] (*Rþ* 48/5)
      {alliteration on k-}

(19) oc stráið becci![63] (*Þrk* 22/4)
      {alliteration on st-}

(20) reis hann upp þaðan[64] (*Rþ* 4/11)
      {alliteration on r-}

(21) sígr fold í mar[65] (*Vsp* 57/2)
      {alliteration on s-}

Example (17) has single alliteration on the verse-initial finite verb and a clause boundary after the following function word. This Old Norse variant resembles *Beo* 603b and 658a, a problematic residue of Bliss's group (9) in which the alliterating verb counts as stressed because 'the metre of the verse absolutely requires it'.[66] Variants in which a finite verb takes the sole alliteration and is followed by a non-alliterating stressed word occur with considerable frequency in the Norse corpus.[67] Some of

---

[60] *Metre*, §20.   [61] 'she cast spells wherever she could ... '
[62] 'they knew well ... '   [63] 'and strew the benches!'
[64] 'he rose up from there ... '
[65] 'the earth sinks into the sea ... '   [66] *Metre*, p. 20.
[67] The most numerous of these are a-verses of type A1 with the sole alliteration on the finite verb. In addition to (17), these include *Vsp* 24/1, ?42/1, 42/5, 43/1, 46/7, 47/5, 48/5; *Hym* 1/5, 22/5; *Þrk* 5/1, 9/1, 12/5, 22/3, 26/5, 30/3; *HH* 34/1; *HHv* 35/1, 36/1, 39/1, 41/1, 43/1; *HH II* 26/5, 30/5; *Rþ* 11/3, 15/5, 16/1, 19/3, 28/7, 40/3; and *Grt* 18/5. Such variants are not much less common than the corresponding variants with double alliteration: *Vsp* 8/1, 20/7, 41/1, 57/3, 59/5; *Hym* 3/3, 7/5, 7/7, 8/3, 12/1, 17/5, 22/1, 24/3, 24/5, 27/7, 36/1; *Þrk* 23/1, 27/1; *HH* 49/1; *HH II* 6/5, 14/5, ?22/5; *Rþ* 11/5, 12/3, 23/9, 32/9, 39/1; *Hdl* 8/1, 13/3, 15/7; *Grt* 3/3, 4/1, 5/7, 13/5, 13/7, 14/1, 21/5 and 23/1. Verses like (18) appearing in the first half of the line are *Vsp* 28/5, 40/3,

these might qualify as 'legitimate exceptions' within Bliss's framework, but their sheer numbers seem incompatible with the unstressed-verb hypothesis, which depends for its initial plausibility on the near-absence of comparable variants in *Beowulf*. Within the word-foot framework, the rarity of such Old English variants is attributable to weaker metrical subordination, which allows for more regular use of optional alliteration as a boundary marker for the second foot in complex verses.[68] It is worth emphasizing that complex verses are usually eligible for double alliteration, since the principle of closure promotes their assignment to the a-verse. Here again Kuhn's-law effects can be traced to purely metrical differences between the a-verse and the b-verse.

The unstressed-verb hypothesis might be sustained for Old English poetry if finite verbs had a more prominent stress in Old Norse, in which case they would be expected to behave more like nouns and adjectives. Consider the following, however:

(22)	Heim ríð þú, Óðinn[69]	(*Bdr* 14/1)
	[alliteration on H-]	
(23)	Valði henni Herfǫðr[70]	(*Vsp* 29/1)
	[alliteration on H-]	
(24)	brast rǫnd við rǫnd[71]	(*HH* 27/3)
	[alliteration on r-]	
(25)	kaupom vel saman![72]	(*HHv* 3/7)
	[alliteration on v-]	

If the Norse verb had an especially prominent stress, we would not expect to find many variants like examples (22)–(25), which have non-alliterating main verbs in the thesis. As it turns out, Norse poets assign a finite

---

60/5, 62/5; *Þrk* 8/7, 13/9, 17/5, 22/5; *Grt* 10/5, 12/5 and 15/5. Comparable examples with double alliteration: *Hym* 39/3; *HH* 9/5; *HH II* 10/7, 27/7; *Hdl* 2/3; *Grt* 10/7. There are no verses like (19) in the first half of the line. *HH II* 35/1 and *Vsp* 35/5 are comparable a-verses with double alliteration. Two other S/Ssx variants like (20) appear in the a-verse: *Hym* 27/1 and *Rþ* 28/1. Ten comparable examples have double alliteration: *Vsp* 51/5; *Hym* 23/1, 29/5; *Þrk* 31/1; *HHv* 36/5; *HH II* 19/7, 45/5; *Hdl* 24/5, 42/3; and *Grt* 16/7. Examples with double alliteration preponderate here because compounds normally alliterate. Only one other Ssx/S variant has an alliterating verb on the first S, like (21): *Rþ* 33/3, an a-verse with double alliteration in the first foot.

[68] See above, p. 88.   [69] 'Ride home, Óðinn ... '
[70] 'The father of hosts endowed her ... '
[71] 'shield clashed against shield ... '   [72] 'let us bargain fairly!'

main verb to the thesis even more readily than their Old English counterparts. There is nothing in *Beowulf* comparable to (22), a type A1 verse with a finite main verb in the thesis after the first stress.[73] Finite main verbs sometimes appear as light x or xx feet in *Beowulf*, but these tend to be high-frequency constituents with low information content, notably verbs of motion or perception. In the Norse corpus, we find a significantly wider variety of verbs in unstressed usage.[74] The comparative evidence, then, makes it impossibly awkward to sustain the defence of K2 initiated by Bliss. The view of finite main verbs designed to explain away anacrusis does not generalize to the Norse corpus, where such verbs often supply the only alliteration but are also often found in the thesis without alliteration.[75]

Finite main verbs alliterate significantly less often than nouns and adjectives but significantly more often than auxiliary verbs.[76] In addition, as we have observed, consonant matching in finite main verbs is always constrained by the alliterative rules, unlike consonant matching in auxiliaries. Since our theoretical framework allows full weight to this evidence, we may conclude without hesitation that finite main verbs placed near the beginning of the clause had a subordinate but perceptible

---

[73] See *OEM*, §9.6. Verses like (22) are by no means rare in the Norse corpus. Cf. *Vsp* 1/1, 2/5, 3/5, 4/5, 5/1, 18/5, 18/6, 18/7, 19/1, 27/5, 28/1, 28/7, 30/5, 35/1, 36/1, 38/1, 40/1, 50/1, 50/5, 51/1, 52/1, 64/1; *Hym* 3/1, 12/5, 17/1, 32/1; *Þrk* 6/1, 23/5, 23/6, 29/1, 31/5; *HH* 4/8, 5/5, 5/8, 12/5, 22/5; *HHv* 5/3, 6/5; *HH II* 17/3, 34/5; *Bdr* 2/1, 3/5, 9/1; *Rþ* 21/4, 34/1, 36/5, 36/6, 38/3; *Hdl* 3/5, 41/1, 42/1, 49/1; and *Grt* 19/1. In *Beowulf*, some main verbs are employed as light x or xx feet, which should be fairly conspicuous, but never on a subordinate x position of a foot with an S position – i.e., on the kind of x position that should be inconspicuous. The Old English poet also avoids use of main verbs as extrametrical syllables, which should be as inconspicuous as possible. The one exception occurs in a hypermetrical verse, *Beo* 1166a.

[74] The following seem significantly more vivid than any verb used as a light foot by the *Beowulf* poet: *slítr* 'rends' (*Vsp* 50/7), *troða* 'they tread' (*Vsp* 52/7), *drap* 'he killed' (*Þrk* 31/5), *ríð* 'ride' (*Bdr* 14/1), and *mǫlom* 'we grind' (*Grt* 5/1). According to Momma, 'Most verbal lexemes never occur as unstressed finite verbs in the extant Old English poetry, and most verbal lexemes that can occur as unstressed finite verbs still have a tendency to be stressed prosodically' (*Composition of Old English Poetry*, p. 174). Within the present framework, 'never occur as unstressed finite verbs' means 'never occupy x positions' and 'stressed prosodically' means 'assigned to an arsis'.

[75] This finding provides further support for Momma's rejection of K2, which she supports with Old English evidence (ibid., pp. 65–75).

[76] *OEM*, §7.2.

stress. Such a stress would have created a mismatch with an x position and with an S position as well. Hence it seems reasonable, even necessary, to allow for varying assignment of finite main verbs to metrical positions near the beginning of the verse.

The behaviour of finite main verbs can be attributed to normal operation of rules R7–8.[77] When the verbal root is the first alliterating constituent in the verse, R8c will require this root to occupy an arsis, and the only arsis available will be the first S position. Any other arsis within the verse will then undergo subordination by R7b, as usual, and alliteration to the right of the verb will be constrained (the desired effect). When the verbal root stands before the first alliterating constituent of the verse, assignment of this root to an arsis will be blocked by R7a, which requires alliteration on the first arsis. Such a non-alliterating root will necessarily occupy an x position. The verbal root will therefore have no subordinating effect and will not constrain alliteration to its right (again the desired effect). In verse-final position, which coincides with clause-final or phrase-final position, finite verbs acquire additional prominence and must occupy an arsis. Metrical evidence points to secondary rather than primary stress in such verbs, as with the corresponding Modern German verbs.[78] Like the secondary root syllable of a compound, the root syllable of a finite verb may occupy a verse-final s position freely. Such a syllable contrasts with the fully stressed root syllable of a verse-final noun or adjective, which normally occupies an S position.[79]

In Old English poetry, finite main verbs seldom appear between the first alliterating word of the verse and its last word. The available evidence suggests that root syllables in such verse-medial verbs sometimes occupied an arsis and sometimes occupied an x position in Old English variants comparable to (22).[80] The much larger number of verse-medial verbs in Eddic poetry present some interesting problems of scansion:

---

[77] See *OEM*, §§9.4 and 9.6.
[78] For discussion within an early generative framework, see Kiparsky, 'Akzent'.
[79] See above, p. 89.
[80] In *God wāt on mec* (*Beo* 2650b), the medial verb *wāt* must occupy an arsis, since the Old English poet does not use the pattern Sxx/S. The medial verb *sæt* seems to occupy an x position in *æt fōtum sæt frēan Scyldinga* (*Beo* 1166a), a hypermetrical verse. See *OEM*, §9.6.

(26)   norðr horfa dyrr[81]   (*Vsp* 38/4)
(27)   Víg lýsir þú[82]   (*HH II* 10/1)
(28)   saman biuggo þau[83]   (*Rþ* 40/5)
       [alliteration on s-]

Example (28) has a resolvable word *saman* on the first S, and cannot be of Norse type E, which excludes resolvable sequences.[84] The type E analysis Ssx/S is problematic for examples (26)–(27) as well. In *Beowulf*, few type E verses have any sort of word group in the initial Ssx foot.[85] Considering the Norse bias against heavy verses, we would hardly expect complex Eddic variants of type E to proliferate. Clear cases of the S/Sxs pattern, type Db, are rare in Eddic poetry. If we analysed variants like (26)–(28) as S/Sxs, the percentage of Db verses would greatly increase, and the fact that so many had medial finite verbs would be very puzzling. The *Beowulf* poet, who makes considerably greater use of the Db pattern by any estimate, never places a trochaic finite verb on the Sx portion of the Sxs foot. Note, too, that in (26) the constituent occupying the last arsis is a lexical noun, the kind of word that usually forces alliteration on a preceding word within the same foot.[86] If such verses were properly analysed as S/Sxs, we would expect alliteration on the medial verb. I can think of no objection, on the other hand, to interpretation of verses like (26) as variants of the Norse pattern Sxx/S. Absence of comparable variants in *Beowulf* can be attributed to the fact that the Old English poet does not employ the Sxx/S pattern.

What we have yet to explain is the fact that variants like (27)–(28), with a verse-final pronoun, make up a disproportionate share of verses with a trochaic verb in medial position.[87] This would remain puzzling if (27)–(28) had the same analysis as (26). The solution to the puzzle presents itself when we recall that one member of the closed class of

---

[81] 'the doors open northward ...'   [82] 'You speak of war ...'
[83] 'they lived together...'   [84] See above, p. 104.
[85] *OEM*, §7.5.3.   [86] See above, p. 90.
[87] Others like (26) are *Hym* 6/4, 19/5, 31/1, 38/2; *Rþ* 2/7, 14/7, 15/1, 23/1, 25/1, 26/4, 31/5; *Hdl* 40/5 and 44/5. Some of these have function words rather than nouns verse-finally, and would scan as S/Sxx if the function words were enclitic. Others like (27)–(28) are *Vsp* 36/4, *Hym* 8/2, 9/2, 11/10, 12/3, 13/5, 15/1, 21/8; *HH* 7/1, 39/1, 43/1, 44/1; *Rþ* 3/1, 3/3, 5/1, 5/3, 11/2, 12/1, 13/1, 17/1, 19/5, 23/5, 24/1, 30/1, 30/3, 32/1, 33/1, 43/5, 47/5; *Hdl* 7/2, 31/1, 34/1, 35/5, 36/1, 39/1 and 46/2.

enclitics in Old Norse is the personal pronoun.[88] In (27)–(28), it seems best to suppose that the pronouns are enclitic.[89] On this hypothesis, the nuclear stress would fall on the preceding verbs and (27)–(28) would scan as S/Sxx, the light Da subtype posited in the word-foot theory. Incorporation of unstressed pronouns into the verse-final feet of (27)–(28) illustrates the special force of linguistic subordination in Old Norse and its link to metrical subordination, which also promoted incorporation of unstressed words into verse-initial feet, restricting employment of extra-metrical syllables.[90]

SUMMARY

Our Norse corpus provides little support for Kuhn's laws. The data supposedly explained by K1–2 can often be explained quite independently by universal syntactic constraints or by purely metrical constraints of the word-foot theory. Bliss's unstressed-verb hypothesis, which was designed to rationalize Old English counter-examples to K2, does not square with the Norse evidence. Finite main verbs that alliterate near the beginning of the clause in fornyrðislag cannot plausibly be regarded as unstressed because they so often suppress alliteration to the right, like nouns and adjectives. Such verbs cannot have a heavier stress in Old Norse because they occupy the thesis even more frequently than in *Beowulf*. What the Norse tradition supplies is clear evidence of varying metrical value in words with weak but significant stress.

---

[88] See Noreen, §465.

[89] Note that stress on the clause-final pronoun in *Þegi þú, Þórr* (*Þrk* 18/3) would yield a doubtful pattern Ss/S. If *þú* is enclitic, the verse has the most common short pattern, Sx/S.

[90] See above, p. 26.

10

Old Saxon alliterative verse

Anyone accustomed to the metrical norms of *Beowulf* or *Þrymsqviða* will be struck by the high frequency of unstressed words in the *Heliand*, which narrates the life of Jesus in alliterative metre. Sievers observes that liberal employment of extrametrical syllables in this Old Saxon work can make assignment of verses to metrical types quite difficult.[1] The *Heliand* is problematic in other respects as well. Its many exotic biblical names, for example, have uncertain metrical values.[2] In ch. 6 above, we used frequencies of optional alliteration to determine the metrical prominence of subordinate S and s positions. Frequencies for the *Heliand* are unfortunately not comparable, since the author tends to avoid the traditional heroic diction, with its stock of alliterating phrases. Old English evidence suggests that rejection of warlike epithets in favour of New Testament values made it significantly more difficult to supply a second alliterating syllable for the a-verse.[3]

Despite its problematic character, the *Heliand* provides valuable data for comparative study. Old Saxon alliterative frequencies may be skewed, but we can often determine the relative prominence of a metrical position by attending to the placement of resolvable sequences. Some Old Saxon verses may have uncertain scansions, but no special problems arise in two-word verses, which express their underlying patterns directly, providing crucial cases for all applicable rules. As we shall see, some rather complex verses also have unambiguous word-foot scansions; and verses with no determinate scansion prove surprisingly useful for some purposes. With

---

[1] *AGM*, p. 156. See Hofmann, *Versstrukturen* I, 110.
[2] Hofmann, *Versstrukturen* I, 98. [3] Russom, 'Verse Translations', pp. 570–1.

its nearly 6,000 lines, the *Heliand* often yields a good harvest of pertinent examples even after we winnow out the doubtful cases.

There are two nearly complete manuscripts of the *Heliand*, C and M, together with three small fragments.[4] Here we will be concerned primarily with C and M. Sievers noticed that the C scribe, though less diligent than the M scribe as a copyist, pays closer attention to metrical form. M gives us an idiomatic but clearly unmetrical word order in thirteen cases where C has poetic word order consistent with the alliterative rules. M has better word order than C in only three comparable cases.[5] With their distinct virtues, C and M offer independent testimony about many problems. Although we lack sufficient evidence for precise reconstruction of the original, Hofmann judges that the manuscripts are generally true to the author's style.[6] Additional support for this view will be provided below.

For a comparative metrist, the most valuable feature of *Heliand* is the structure of its language. Many peculiarities of Eddic versecraft result from syncopation of Old Norse unstressed vowels in positions where corresponding Old English vowels were retained. The forceful character of linguistic subordination in Old Norse yielded a correspondingly forceful metrical subordination, inhibiting use of extrametrical syllables. Old Saxon verse allows us to explore the metrical consequences of change in the opposite direction, since its weak linguistic stress did nothing to reduce or eliminate unstressed function words and permitted restoration of vowels like those that underwent syncopation in *Beowulf*.[7] Massive employment of extrametrical words in the *Heliand* can be attributed in part to a corresponding weakness of metrical subordination.[8]

---

[4] C = London, British Library, Cotton Caligula A. VII; M = München, cgm. 25. V, the Vatican fragment (Palat. Lat. 1447) extends from line 1279 to line 1358. The Prague fragment (P), now in Berlin (Museum für deutsche Geschichte, R56/2537), extends from 958 to 1006. The newly discovered Straubinger fragment (S), which is printed in Behaghel–Taeger (pp. 211–16), extends from 351 to 722, with several gaps. For further discussion of the manuscripts see Behaghel–Taeger, pp. xv–xix, and references cited there. For detailed description of C, Priebsch, *The Heliand Manuscript*, is still informative, though some of the author's conclusions are frankly speculative. A line number preceded by 'C' or 'M' identifies citations from the parallel-text *Heliand*, ed. Sievers.

[5] Sievers, 'Zum *Heliand*', pp. 56–7.   [6] Hofmann, *Versstrukturen* I, p. 50.

[7] See Holthausen, *Altsächsisches Elementarbuch*, §§137–40.

[8] See Lehmann, *DGV*, p. 90.

ADDED OR INESSENTIAL WORDS IN THE MANUSCRIPTS

In C and M, phrases like *quað he* 'said he' sometimes appear at the end of the verse, where they create striking metrical irregularities. Like Hofmann, I exclude such phrases from the scansion.[9] Transitions to direct discourse can occur quite abruptly in early Germanic poems, and may have been indicated during oral performance by gesture or intonation. Scribes must sometimes have felt a need to add discourse markers appropriate to their colder medium. The inessential character of these discourse markers is indicated by the fact that twelve of them appearing in one *Heliand* manuscript fail to appear in the corresponding verse of a parallel manuscript.[10]

Anyone familiar with Old English poetic formulas will often notice additional unstressed function words in the cognate Old Saxon formulas. These add little or nothing to the sense, though they usually make the verse more idiomatic. Consider the following:

(1) wordum ond weorcum[11] (*ChristC* 917a)
     [Sx/(x)Sx]

(2) mid uuordun endi mid uuercun[12] (*Hel* 5a)
     [(x)Sx/(xxx)Sx]

(3) uuordon endi uuercon (C3473a)
     [Sx/(xx)Sx]

(4) that he it gio an is hertan gehugda[13] (*Hel* 2505a)
     [(xxxxxx)Sx/(x)Sx]

Example (1) is an Old English formula that appears twice in *Christ*. This formula exploits an archaic construction in which the meaning 'with' is expressed solely by dative-instrumental endings. In the *ASPR* there are thirty verses containing the form *weorcum*, and of these five are identical to (1).[14] The cognate Old Saxon formula usually has a more idiomatic construction with an overt preposition, as in (2), where the first *mid* creates non-prefixal anacrusis. No comparable a-verses appear in *Beowulf*.

---

[9] See *Versstrukturen* I, p. 50.
[10] *Hel* 397, 825, 1597, 2419, 2432, 3052, 3057, 3203, 3948, 4516, 4638 and 4973.
[11] 'by words and deeds ...' Repeated as 1236a.
[12] 'by words and by deeds.' Repeated as 541a and 2107a.
[13] 'that he believed it previously in his heart ...'
[14] *Sat* 222a, *GuthA* 581a, 793a, *Whale* 84a, *Seasons* 74a; cf. also *Sat* 550b. See Bessinger and Smith, *Concordance*, p. 1409.

As with 'said he' phrases, semantically inessential words like OS *mid* are textually unstable and often fail to appear in one of the parallel manuscripts (see (3)).

Confronted with examples of this kind, we might be tempted to emend out the cognates of words that Old English poets omitted. Some researchers have even suggested that the *Heliand* was translated from Old English.[15] In many cases, however, very long strings of function words are necessary for the sense, as in (4), which looks like type A1 with a six-syllable anacrusis. The characteristic metrical features of Old Saxon verse are so pervasive as to render purely scribal explanations implausible.[16] As we shall see, these features are predictable results of composition in Old Saxon.

CONSTRAINTS ON OLD SAXON TYPE B VERSES

Although word-foot metres allow for extrametrical syllables before the foot, no such metre will permit additional syllables within the foot, which must correspond to the pattern of a native word. Like Old English, Old Saxon has compounds with two unstressed syllables between the stresses, but none with three or more (assuming resolution of any resolvable sequence in the primary constituent, which would be obligatory in verse). If Old Saxon poets employed a word-foot metre, they could have constructed long type B verses with a second foot of the form Sxxs, but not of the form Sxxxs, Sxxxxs, etc. Except for well-defined cases of elision, a two-stress Old Saxon verse should never have three or more syllables between the stresses when the second stress appears verse-finally and the first syllable of the verse is unstressed. Note that we are dealing with a straightforward empirical prediction here, not with a notational matter internal to the theory. The prediction should be falsified at once if it is incorrect because the Old Saxon poet employs unusually long strings of unstressed words in many locations. Words with the pattern Sxxs have special significance for our comparative project. Loss of such words from Old Norse initiated a cascade of metrical changes that gave fornyrðislag much of its distinct character. In the *Heliand* we should observe an

[15] See Kabell, *Metrische Studien* I, 179.
[16] As noted by Lehmann, *DGV*, pp. 103–12; and Hofmann, *Versstrukturen* I, p. 40.

opposite tendency, since Old Saxon has Sxxs words in some cases where the Old English cognate is reduced to Sxs.[17] Here as in other respects Old Saxon and Old Norse lie far apart, with Old English somewhere between them.

Our first task is to verify that Old Saxon long B verses still derive from an underlying two-word pattern with a verse-final Sxxs compound. Paradoxically, the most extreme deviations from the underlying pattern provide strong evidence for its existence. Consider first some relatively simple long B verses with two inter-stress syllables:

(5)	than sie / helligethuing[18]	(1500b)
	[xx/Sxxs]	
(6)	umbi thes / barnes giburd[19]	(697a)
	[xxx/Sxxs]	
(7)	Êr scal / bêðiu tefaran[20]	(1424b)
	[xx/Sxxs, s resolved]	
(8)	ef thu uuilt / hnîgan te mi[21]	(1102b)
	[xxx/Sxxs]	

In (5), the Sxxs foot is realized in the most direct way, as an Old Saxon Sxxs compound. All such compounds have the same type of morphological structure. The first constituent is a trochaic lexical item like *helli-*, with the pattern Sx. Next comes an unstressed internal prefix or 'infix' (e.g. *-ge-*). The final constituent is a stressed monosyllable like *-thuing* or an equivalent resolvable sequence. As in Old English poetry, word groups occupying an Sxxs foot often imitate the morphological structure of the corresponding compounds.[22] Verses (6) and (7), for example, have a trochaic word followed by a stressed monosyllable with a prefix. In Old Saxon poetry, we also find a number of variants like (8), where the preposition *te* occupies the place of its cognate prefix *te-* in (7).

Now consider some complex variants with three syllables between the stresses:

---

[17] Cf. OS *helligethuing* 'hell-confinement' (*Hel* 1500b), OE *hellgeþwing*; OS *uurdigiscapu* 'decree of fate' (*Hel* 197a and 3354b), OE *wyrdgesceap*; OS *metodogescapu* 'decree of fate' (*Hel* 2190a), OE *metodgesceaft, metodsceaft*.
[18] 'than that they (should seek out) hell ...'
[19] 'about this child's birth ...'   [20] 'Sooner shall both pass away...'
[21] 'if you will bow to me ...'   [22] See above, p. 53.

(9) hē þē æt / sunde oferflāt[23]   (*Beo* 517b)
     [xxx/Sxxs, adjacent vowels elided]
(10) endi it all mid / durðu oƀarsêu[24]   (*Hel* 2545b)
     [xxxxx/Sxxs, adjacent vowels elided]
(11) thea he / cûðde oƀar al[25]   (*Hel* 2345b)
     [xx/Sxxs, adjacent vowels elided]

Verse (9), an example of elision from *Beowulf*, has two adjacent unstressed vowels on the first x position of the Sxxs foot. Observe that (9) fills the Sxxs foot with the most common type of word group, a trochaic first constituent followed by a monosyllabic stressed word with an unstressed prefix. The complexity associated with elision here is mitigated by close adherence to the morphological structure from which the Sxxs foot derives. In example (10), the Old Saxon Sxxs foot is occupied by the same type of linguistic material that appears in the Old English Sxxs foot of (9). Example (11) and seven similar verses attest the more complex Old Saxon variant with a preposition substituting for its cognate prefix. Four verses have a non-prepositional function word in the site normally occupied by a prefix.[26]

In all, the *Heliand* manuscript contains twenty-nine long B verses with three or more syllables between the stresses. A large group of verses with two syllables between the stresses is available for comparison. I counted about 530 verses like (5)–(8), and of these fewer than one per cent had adjacent vowels eligible for elision. Unstressed vowels do not often fall together by chance between the stresses of a type B verse. The poet's obvious effort to arrange for adjacent vowels in the thirteen verses like (10) and (11) casts serious doubt on the sixteen remaining verses with three inter-stress syllables.

Eight of the sixteen anomalies appear in M only.[27] The C scribe, who is more alert to poetic form, has perfectly normal metre in corresponding verses. Consider the following pair of textual variants:

---

[23] 'he outdistanced you at swimming ...'
[24] 'and sowed it with weeds all over...'   [25] 'which he made known widely...'
[26] Like (11) are *Hel* 512b, 890b, 3230b, 3386b, 3646b, C4009b and C5376b. The form *endi* 'and' appears in 591a and 3581b; *allan* 'all' appears in 874b; and *is* 'his' appears in 3220b. See Kauffmann, 'Rhythmik des Heliand', p. 324.
[27] *Hel* 1699b, 1889b, 1890a, 2317b, 3097a, 3535a, 4369b and 4898a.

(12) ge- / tholon undar theru thiod[28]   (M1890a)
      [*x/Sxxxxs, S resolved]
(13) (gi-)tholon under / (thero) thioda   (C1890a)
      [(x)Sxx/(xx)Sx, first S resolved]

M's (12), an overstretched B verse, parallels C's (13), which scans as type A1 with anacrusis, a very common pattern in the *Heliand*. As Kauffmann observed, the regularity of (13) depends on employment of poetic *thioda*, which contrasts with M's more idiomatic *thiod*.[29] The form *thiod* causes exactly the same problem at M3097a and M3535a, also paralleled in C by unremarkable verses with *thioda*. Eight anomalies remain. In these it seems likely that inauthentic function words added at some point during manuscript transmission have evaded the scrutiny of the C scribe.[30] Such constituents are often missing in one or more of the parallel manuscripts.[31]

In thirteen cases, what looks like a third inter-stress syllable is purely scribal. Consider the following:

(14) thô imu is / thiodanes gisuêk[32]   (M5045b)
      [*xxxx/Sxxxs]
(15) thuo im is / thiednes gisuêk   (C5045b)
      [xxx/Sxxs]
(16) than mi / hunger endi thurst[33]   (4423b)
      [xx/Sxxs, not *xx/Sxxxs]
(17) mêðomhord / manag[34]   (3772a)
      [Ss/Sx, not *Sxs/Sx]

Sievers asserts that the poet employed syncopated bisyllabic forms along-

[28] 'suffer in this nation ...'   [29] 'Rhythmik des Heliand', p. 324.
[30] The possibly inauthentic constituents are *aftar thiu* (*Hel* 633b), *is* (twice in 2231a), *the* (twice in 2263a), *thîn* (second instance in 2429a), *that, thie* (2522a), prefixal *gi-* (3415a) and *âno* (second instance in 4483a). Verses 2134b and 2285b are excluded from consideration due to uncertainty about stress and vowel length in exotic personal names.
[31] Note for example the absence of unstable *sô* at C255b, C722b, CP975a, M1146b, C1336a, CV1341b, C1490a, C1889b, C2304b, C2587a, C3065b, C3515b, C3645b, M3894b, C4100b and C4122a. Representative examples with unstable possessive pronouns are C3234a and M615b; with unstable definite articles, C3812b and M2256b. Prefixal *gi-* seems to be optional in 3415a, since it is missing from the same word in M693a. The second *âno* of 4483a seems to be optional as well, since it is deleted from the same syntactic structure at 2871a.
[32] 'when his lord's (assistance) was withdrawn ...'
[33] 'when hunger and thirst (oppressed) me ...'   [34] 'many a treasure hoard ...'

side later trisyllabic forms with medial vowels restored by analogy.[35] Fulk describes a similar mixture of forms in some Old English poems.[36] It seems reasonable, then, to posit syncopated values for words such as *thiod(a)nes*, bringing the number of inter-stress syllables down to two in the twelve verses like (14). Observe that manuscript C has the old syncopated spelling in (15), a typical realization of the long type B pattern resembling example (6) above. Spellings attested in the manuscripts justify syncopated interpretation of later forms in several other cases like (14) as well.[37] With respect to another matter of prosody Sievers appears to be mistaken. He claims that epenthetic vowels spelled in the *Heliand* manuscript always count as syllabic, unlike the epenthetic vowels of the *Beowulf* manuscript, which must usually be disregarded.[38] In verse (16), however, a syllabic interpretation of the epenthetic *-e-* in *hunger* would raise the number of inter-stress syllables beyond the allowable limit.[39] Example (17) also tells against Sievers's view of Old Saxon epenthesis. If the epenthetic *-o-* of *međom-* counted as syllabic, (17) would have a poetic compound of the form Sxs in verse-initial position. Unambiguous Sxs compounds like OS *handgiuuerc* 'handiwork' are excluded from verse-initial position in the *Heliand* (see R5a), and the importance of this constraint has recently been emphasized by Hofmann.[40] If its epenthetic *-o-* is disregarded, example (17) scans as a typical instance of the Ss/Sx pattern.[41]

Compounds of the form Sxxs are not very common in Old English. Because these compounds do exist, however, the Sxxs foot is licensed, and

[35] *AGM*, §105. [36] *History of Old English Meter*, pp. 111 and 120.
[37] With *drohtines* (*Hel* 1571b), *hêlago* (3028b) and *hêlagon* (4064a), cf. *drihtnes* (C264b) and *hêlgost* (5739b). Five of the twelve verses like (14) have forms of *iungaro* (M1594b, M2171b, 3107b, 4270b and 4505b). The first two are paralleled by verses with syncopated spellings in the C manuscript (*iungron* C1594b and *iungrono* C2171b). The other long B verses requiring syncopation are 279b, 3838b and C5846b (see Kauffmann, 'Rhythmik des Heliand', p. 324). Verse 3352a is excluded, since it contains an exotic proper name. For discussion of the linguistic issues see Holthausen, *Altsächsisches Elementarbuch*, §138.
[38] *AGM*, §105.5.
[39] The epenthetic vowel must also be disregarded to enable normal scansion of verse 12b in the Old Saxon *Genesis* (*Nu thuingit mi giu hungar endi thrust*).
[40] *Versstrukturen* I, 133–8.
[41] Cf. *mãðþumfæt / mãre* (*Beo* 2405a). The Old Saxon example has the unresolved second S often encountered in variants like *guðrinc monig* (*Beo* 838b).

poets can exploit it as a convenient location for Sxxs word groups.[42] The higher frequency of Sxxs compounds in Old Saxon, which lowers the complexity of the corresponding foot, sanctions an elevated frequency of long type B in the *Heliand*, with its approximately 530 instances. The Old Saxon poem would have only about 300 instances if this pattern had the same relative frequency as the comparable pattern in *Beowulf*, a poem slightly more than half as large with about 170 long B verses. Prosodic ambiguities make exact counts of long type B problematic, but the discrepancy would be revealed by any consistent tally.[43] Reduced complexity of the Sxxs foot in the *Heliand* allows for more complex realizations. As we have seen, the *Beowulf* poet almost always employs a prefix on the second x position of this foot, but the Old Saxon poet frequently employs a cognate preposition instead, deviating farther from the structure of the corresponding compound.

METRICAL COMPLEXITY IN TYPE A1 VARIANTS

In *Beowulf*, two-word paradigms of type A1 usually have single alliteration, but complex variants usually have a second alliterating syllable that marks the leftward boundary of the second foot, facilitating intuitive scansion.[44] A similar tendency can be observed in the *Heliand*:

(18)   lengron / huîla[45]   (170a)
        [Sx/Sx]

(19)   uuârun / uuordun[46]   (406a)
        [Sx/Sx]

(20)   barn an / burgun[47]   (196a)
        [Sx/Sx, word group in first foot]

(21)   mildi / (uuas he im an is) môde[48]   (1259a)
        [Sx/(xxxxx)Sx, with extrametrical syllables]

(22)   faran fan / (themu is) folke[49]   (4617a)
        [Sx/(xxx)Sx, first S resolved, word group, extrametrical syllables]

---

[42] See *OEM*, p. 141.

[43] It is unclear, for example, whether elision is mandatory, forcing reduction from long B to normal B in all possible cases.

[44] See *OEM*, §8.1.   [45] 'for a longer time.'   [46] 'with true words ...'

[47] 'a child in the dwelling-places.'

[48] 'he was well disposed towards them in his mind ...'

[49] 'to depart from those people of his ...'

The Old Saxon poem contains about 980 Sx/Sx verses with two trochaic words. Of these 63 per cent are b-verses; 18 per cent are a-verses like (18), with single alliteration; and 19 per cent are a-verses like (19), with double alliteration. Percentages for complex Sx/Sx variants like (20)–(22) are strikingly different. There are about 1,250 such variants in the poem, and of these 30 per cent are b-verses; 7 per cent are a-verses with single alliteration; and 63 per cent are a-verses with double alliteration, like (20)–(22).[50] Note that the complex variants, which have a lower percentage of b-verses, also have a much higher percentage of a-verses with double alliteration. The poet's tendency to place complex variants in the first half of the line is explained in part by the principle of closure (U3), but there is an independent preference for double alliteration in such variants. The contrast would be even more dramatic if I had not excluded from consideration variants in which a finite verb with subordinate phrasal stress is the first alliterating word. In such variants the percentage of double alliteration may be further elevated by a preference for alliteration on the most strongly stressed syllable of the verse.[51]

Example (21) shows that the number of extrametrical words before the second foot in Old Saxon poetry can be rather large. We even encounter a few verses like (22) with a word group in the first foot and several extrametrical syllables as well. Verses like (21) are not too difficult to scan despite their length. When a stressed trochaic word appears at the beginning of a well-formed verse, the desired scansion can always be obtained by excluding all subsequent unstressed words as extrametrical. The second foot then begins with the first stressed syllable following the extrametrical words. This analytical procedure must have been quite automatic when the stressed syllable terminating the extrametrical

---

[50] Two-word variants like (18) and (19) are listed by Hofmann (*Versstrukturen* II) under subtype A2.2. Complex variants like (20)–(22) can be found under his subtypes A1.x2 and A⁵2.x2. I have of course excluded type A variants other than Sx/Sx, some of which will be found in Hofmann's more inclusive subtypes, e.g. *sinlíf sôkean* 2083a (Ss/Sx). Note, in particular, that the word-foot analysis for a variant like *gôdoro manno* 2135b or *craft endi cûsti* 2339a will be Sxx/Sx rather than Sx/Sx. For ease of comparison, I disregard verses with scansions considered uncertain by Hofmann, including a number with exotic proper names, and I count two syllables for *îu*, as Hofmann recommends, though I am not certain his analysis is correct. The gross statistical discrepancies of interest here would of course emerge from a variety of initial assumptions about proper scansion in doubtful cases.

[51] See *OEM*, §9.12.

sequence was marked by alliteration. Scansion is less straightforward in variants like (22) due to the uncertain status of an unstressed word after a stressed monosyllable.[52] Restrictions on the frequency of such variants kept analytical effort within reasonable bounds.[53]

THE SPECIAL STATUS OF EXTRAMETRICAL PREFIXES

The least disruptive extrametrical constituent is the unstressed prefix, a quasi-word so inconspicuous that it seldom appears as a foot in isolation. Alliterative evidence suggests that extrametrical prefixes caused relatively little complexity before the second foot of Old Saxon A1 verses:

(23)	uuîdost / (gi)uualdan[54]	(45a)
	[Sx/(x)Sx]	
(24)	rîki / (gi)uunnan[55]	(57b)
	[Sx/(x)Sx]	
(25)	helpa / (fan) himila[56]	(11a)
	[Sx/(x)Sx, second S resolved]	
(26)	managon / (te) helpun[57]	(51b)
	[Sx/(x)Sx, first S resolved]	

About 380 Sx/Sx verses like (23) and (24) have two trochaic words and an unstressed prefix or prefixal negative as the only extrametrical syllable. Of these, 54 per cent appear in the first half of the line, with double alliteration in 45 per cent of total occurrences. There are about 190 variants like (25) and (26). Of these, 91 per cent appear in the first half of the line, with double alliteration in 78 per cent of total occurrences. Variants like (23) and (24) are easy to scan because the extrametrical prefix practically begs to be ignored. In more complex variants like (25)

---

[52] In type A variants, such an unstressed word must be assigned to the x position of an Sx foot. In type D variants, the unstressed word might be excluded as extrametrical (*OEM*, §5.5).

[53] If we count as before, the only other Sx/Sx verses like (22), with a word group in the first foot and two or more extrametrical words (including prefixes), are *Hel* 153a, 3025a; 3138b, 3527b, 5529b, 5772b and 5812b (between hypermetrical a-verses). Sx/Sx variants with an alliterating finite verb in the first foot, which tend to constitute whole clauses, have long verse-medial strings of extrametrical words somewhat more often (e.g. *mîð is an thînumu môde* 3239a). See Hofmann's list for type A[v]II[v]2.

[54] 'to rule most widely ...'   [55] 'to win lordship ...'

[56] 'help from heaven ...'   [57] 'as a helper to many people ...'

and (26), the poet makes a more persistent effort to mark the leftward boundary of the second foot with an alliterating syllable.[58]

ANACRUSIS

Let us now consider some type A1 verses with a first foot preceded by one or more extrametrical syllables in anacrusis:

(27)	(ge)sîðos / mîne[59] [(x)Sx/Sx]	(3105a)
(28)	(gi)lêstead / (an thesumu) liohte[60] [(x)Sx/(xxxx)Sx]	(1626a)
(29)	(mid) uuordun / (endi mid) uuercun[61] [(x)Sx/(xxx)Sx]	(5a)
(30)	(an them is) uuârun / uuordun[62] [(xxx)Sx/Sx]	(3939a)

Examples like (27) pose no major problems of scansion. As in *Beowulf*, it is almost always safe to assume that an isolated unstressed prefix or negative particle at the beginning of an a-verse counts as extrametrical. Such constituents are seldom employed as light feet.[63] In the *Heliand*, there are about 220 Sx/Sx a-verses with a monosyllabic prefix in anacrusis.[64] In seven of these, represented above by (27), the main part – the part beginning with the first alliterating syllable – has the simplest possible type A1 structure, consisting of exactly two trochaic words. The

---

[58] Although prefixes are most characteristic of non-finite verbal forms, which have a strong stress, the group of verses with the metrical structure of (23)–(24) includes a number with prefixed finite verbs in final position, and one might suspect that the somewhat weaker stress on finite verbs affects the percentage of double alliteration. This is clearly not the case, however, since the percentage of double alliteration for examples with verse-final finite main verbs is actually somewhat higher than the percentage for the group as a whole (90 per cent, as compared with 83 per cent). Variants like (23)–(26) are included in Hofmann's list for A⁵2.x2. This list includes verse 863a, which is properly scanned but misprinted (with *mann* for *manno*).

[59] 'my companions . . .'

[60] 'performed in this light (i.e., this world) . . .'

[61] 'by words and by deeds.'   [62] 'in those true words of his . . .'

[63] A-verses like *for-* / *sehen selbo* (*Hel* 189a) are quite rare. Cf. 577a, 1394a, 1913a, 3199a, 3342a, 3350a, 3979a, 5796a and 5857a.

[64] Examples of type A1 variants other than Sx/Sx are excluded from consideration as before.

corresponding verses without anacrusis, represented by (18) and (19), have a rather low frequency of double alliteration, and this is also true of verses like (27), which have double alliteration in only two of the seven examples.[65] Anacrusis may increase the complexity of (27) somewhat, but the metrical simplicity of the main part seems to make double alliteration unnecessary. The remaining Sx/Sx variants with anacrusis have more complex main parts and a much higher frequency of double alliteration. We should probably set aside the eighty-nine examples with a complex main part in which the first alliterating word is a weakly stressed finite verb. All of these except *Hel* 4705a have double alliteration, but their testimony is problematic. More informative are the remaining 127 examples with complex main parts analogous to (20)–(22). In these the first alliterating word is a more strongly stressed constituent, such as a noun, adjective, or non-finite verb. All have double alliteration. As we have observed, single alliteration occurs in 7 per cent of the verses like (20)–(22). The complete absence of single alliteration in a group of 127 corresponding verses with anacrusis thus seems significant. Apparently, even the simplest form of anacrusis increases metrical complexity to some extent, making it still more desirable to mark the leftward boundary of the second foot with a second alliterating syllable when the main part of the verse has a complex structure.

The verse-initial syllable in (29) would be more difficult to identify as anacrusis, since an isolated monosyllabic preposition serves as the light foot of an a-verse occasionally in the *Heliand*. This happens less often than in *Beowulf*, however, and (29) may not have been very complex from the Old Saxon point of view.[66] Example (30) must have required considerably more analytical effort, since its string of verse-initial unstressed words

---

[65] Other examples like (27), with single alliteration: *Hel* 1257a, 2318a, 3077a and 5407a. With double alliteration: 1506a and 4844a. Hofmann classifies these as type *Ax2.2.

[66] The poem contains only fourteen a-verses like *an / êr-dagun* (*Hel* 362a), with a native word in the second foot. The other examples, listed under Hofmann's type dax3a, are 434a, 618a, 1053a, 1953a, 2605a, 2791a, 4515a, 4694a, 4708a, 4927a, 4999a, 5051a and 5704a. An additional eight putative examples with exotic proper names are set apart by Hofmann in his type *Dax4da: 61a, 461a, 532a, 833a, 910a, 4016a, 4126a and 5256a. These may have anacruses rather than light feet. My distinction between the light foot and anacrusis is equivalent, as far as practical scansion is concerned, to the distinction made by Hofmann between the *konstitutive Eingangssenkung* and the *Vorfeld* (*Versstrukturen* I, 111).

looks exactly like a light foot, hinting strongly that only one more foot will follow when in fact we will encounter two. The complexity of such variants seems to be mitigated by close adherence to metrical norms in the main part. There are seventy-eight Sx/Sx a-verses with three or more syllables in anacrusis. Of these, forty-four (56 per cent) have a two-word Sx/Sx structure as the main part.[67] In twenty-three cases (30 per cent), the main part is free of extrametrical syllables, like (20), or has an extrametrical prefix before the second foot, like (23) and (24).[68] There are perhaps eleven cases (14 per cent) in which an a-verse with three or more syllables in anacrusis also has an A1 variant of significant complexity as its main part.[69]

---

[67] Verses of this sort are classified by Hofmann as *Ax2.2. In the following list, examples with double alliteration are indicated by a parenthesized *d*: *Hel* 271a(d), 291a, 545a(d), 561a, 656a(d), 835a(d), 844a (assuming epenthesis), 1083a(d), 1759a, 1802a, 1812a, 1883a, 1974a(d), 1983a, 2380a, 2399a(d), 2452a, 2454a, 2595a(d), 2686a, 2901a, 2920a, 2954a, 3020a, 3026a, 3347a, 3605a(d), 3627a(d), 3715a(d), 3738a, 3939a(d), 4230a, 4251a, 4473a(d), 4860a(d), 4907a, 4983a, 5075a(d), 5142a, 5219a, 5227a(d), 5666a and 5826a. Note that the frequency of double alliteration remains low. There are no examples with a finite verb as the first alliterating word. As printed in Behaghel–Taeger, 879a would belong here as well, but Hofmann eliminates the anacrusis by assigning *ginâhid* to the previous verse, I think correctly.

[68] Verses in which the main part is occupied by a whole-verse compound with two Sx constituents: *Hel* 333a, 448a, 1811a, 1833a, 2056a and 2661a. With a word break in the first foot and no extrametrical syllables in the main part: 981a(d), 1218a, 1253a, 1917a, 2169a, 2347a, 2517a, 2518a(d), 3333a, 3336a and 3781a. Many of these are exact or partial repeats of 1218a, which may account for the unexpectedly low frequency of double alliteration. With extrametrical prefix or negative particle: 1469a(d), 1987a(d), 2505a(d), 3927a(d), 4265a and 5926a(d). There are no examples with a finite verb as the first alliterating word. The verses listed in this note are scanned quite variously or emended by Hofmann, and must be looked up individually in his *Versindex*. Doubtful cases with exotic proper nouns: 13a, 2075a and 5606a. I set aside 1554a because there is no alliteration in the line that contains it, and its scansion is therefore doubtful.

[69] All examples have double alliteration. I include *Hel* 5485a here, following editorial word division, but the constituent *thar* might be prefixal to *aftar* (cf. English *thereafter*). As *(obar ûsa) abaron / (thar-)after*, the verse would belong among those with a main part corresponding to simpler A1 variants like (23) and (24). The other cases with a complex main part and complex anacrusis are 2–3a, 410a, 496a, 592a, 1662a, 3481a, 4974a, 4993a, 5088a and 5091a. A finite verb is the first alliterating word in 1662a, 3481a and 5091a. The problems would disappear in some of these if inessential function words were excluded, e.g. *sulic* (592a), *Bethiu* (1662a) and *Thes* (5091a). Analogues like *uuordon endi uuercon* (C3473a) might justify reduction of 4974a to

Like Old English poets, the Old Saxon poet employs prefixal anacrusis less often in the second half of the line. Only forty-two b-verses with an Sx/Sx main part have such anacrusis. In these b-verses, the average number of extrametrical syllables before the second foot is only about 0.5, as compared with nearly 2.0 for the comparable a-verses. The difference must be due in part to the principle of closure (U3), which represses all kinds of complexity in the second half of the line. The poet might also avoid long strings of extrametrical words before the second foot in the b-verse because such strings could not be terminated by an alliterating syllable.

Old Saxon b-verses with prefixal anacrusis are often as simple as possible otherwise. Of the forty-two examples with a type A1 pattern as the main part, twenty-three consist of two trochaic words and a prefix. Consider the following:

(31)	(ge-)sîðos / mîne[70]	(*Hel* 4667b)
	[(x)Sx/Sx]	
(32)	*(ge-)gyrwed / golde	
	[(x)Sx/Sx]	
(33)	golde / (ge-)gyrwed[71]	(*Beo* 553a)
	[Sx/(x)Sx]	

Note that b-verse (31) is a repeat of a-verse (27). Such variants can be used in either half of the line, and within the Old Saxon system their simplicity relative to the many other variants with anacrusis seems to make them more suitable for the b-verse.[72] According to Bliss, Old English variants comparable to (31) had an undesirable breath-group

---

uuordun endi uuîson and of 5088a to *uuordun ni uuerkun.* The textual situation at line 2–3 is so confused that the editors assign it an ambivalent number. If the examples listed in this note are authentic, the double alliteration would have facilitated recovery of the underlying pattern.

[70] 'O my companions . . .'   [71] 'adorned with gold'.

[72] The other examples are *Hel* 17b, 146b, 520b, 1361b, 1389b, 2128b, 2388b, 2413b, 3003b, 3582b, 3641b, 3849b, 3912b, 3923b, 4162b, 4696b, 4807b, 5316b, 5543b, 5661b, 5675b and 5979b. More complex Sx/Sx variants with prefixal anacrusis are 148b, 857b, 888b, 1085b, 1221b, 1521b, 1887b, 2361b, 2363b, 2865b, 3482b, 3961b, 4197b, 4311b, 4643b, 4651b, 5120b (with prefixal negative in anacrusis), 5140b and 5468b. A finite verb is the first alliterating word in 3482b, 3961b, 4311b, 4643b, 4651b and 5120b.

structure, and were avoided for that reason.[73] Exclusion of such variants from *Beowulf* seems to follow trivially, however, from the poet's restricted employment of anacrusis in the b-verse.[74] In the Old English poem, a variant comparable to (31) would occur with significant frequency only in the a-verse, where, as Bliss observes, double alliteration is the rule. What we have to account for, then, is the absence of anything like (32). As soon as the missing variant is constructed, the reason for its absence seems obvious. The poet can easily reverse a variant like (32) to produce one like (33), in which the anacrusis has been removed and the possibility of confusion about the number of feet has been entirely eliminated. Note that variants like (31) cannot undergo reversal so easily. Here a change in word order would produce a change in the alliteration, and the first half of the line would have to be altered or replaced. In complex variants with a word group in the first foot or with extrametrical syllables before the second foot, a prefixed form cannot usually move due to syntactic constraints that come into play as the number of words increases. This simple fact explains why so many verses with prefixal anacrusis have a main part of significant metrical complexity.

TYPE A1 AND THE HYPERMETRICAL B-VERSE

The *Beowulf* poet never constructs a-verses comparable to (30), with more than two syllables in anacrusis. B-verses resembling (30) appear in *Beowulf*, but only in hypermetrical clusters. Hypermetrical b-verses consist of a normal verse, usually of the form Sx/Sx, preceded by a light *hypermetrical foot* of the form xx. Unlike an xx sequence in anacrusis, a hypermetrical foot usually contains one or more major function words and is often rendered more conspicuous by extrametrical syllables, like

---

[73] *Metre*, §49.

[74] Clear cases with non-prefixal anacrusis are *Beo* 93b, 666b, 1223b and 2247b. The anacrusis posited by Klaeber in 402b and 2592b might be eliminated by assigning the verse-initial function words to the preceding a-verse. Klaeber assigns *his* to the a-verse of line 2481b, eliminating the anacrusis posited by some previous editors, and he emends out the anacrusis in 9b. Clear cases with prefixal anacrusis are *(ðurh-)fōn ne / mihte* (*Beo* 1504b), *(ge-)sacan ne / tealde* (1773b) and *(for-)beran ne / mehte* (1877b). Hofmann notices violations of Bliss's constraint in Old Saxon poetry, but does not attempt an explanation (*Versstrukturen* I, 67).

Beowulf *and Old Germanic metre*

the light foot of type A3, B or C.[75] The *Heliand* poet does construct
seventy-eight a-verses like (30), as we have seen, but variants with this
structure appear most often as b-verses. Consider the following, in which
a double slash represents the leftward boundary of the main part
(adhering to our definition of 'main part' as the part beginning at the first
alliterating syllable, without regard for the metrical status of preceding
unstressed syllables):

(34) þǣr þā // gōdan / twēgen[76] (*Beo* 1163b)
      [xx//Sx/Sx]

(35) al sô it thar thô mid is // uuordun / sagde[77] (*Hel* 1333b)
      [xxxxxxx//Sx/Sx]

(36) endi sculun than // lôn ant- / fâhan[78] (*Hel* 2597b)
      [xxxxx//Sx/Sx]

(37) endi ni uuilliad êniga // fehta / (ge)uuirken[79] (*Hel* 1317b)
      [xxxxxxxx//Sx/(x)Sx]

(38) than mugi cuman thiu // siole / (te) himile[80] (*Hel* 3301b)
      [xxxxxx//Sx/(x)Sx, second S resolved]

A few b-verses with anacrusis appear in *Beowulf*, but the anacrusis never
extends beyond one syllable. In the second half of the line, the verse-
initial string *þǣr þā* constitutes an unambiguous light foot, so (34) scans
unambiguously as hypermetrical. The situation in the *Heliand* is more
complex. A-verses like (30) are not characteristic of hypermetrical
clusters, so they scan most plausibly as type A1 variants with long
anacruses.[81] The few a-verses resembling (30) that appear to lie within
hypermetrical clusters might be regarded as normal verses lying between

---

[75] See *OEM*, §6.4.   [76] 'where the two noble ones (sat) ...'
[77] 'just as he said with his words then and there ...'
[78] 'and they shall then receive a reward ...'
[79] 'and they will not cause any fights ...'
[80] 'then the soul may come to heaven ...'
[81] Placement of (30) in the a-verse seems to rule out its analysis as hypermetrical. In
general, the first foot of an a-verse appearing in a hypermetrical cluster will contain a
stressed alliterating word rather than an unstressed word (*OEM*, §6.2). This characteristic is readily observable in a large number of unambiguous examples from the
Heliand, listed by Hofmann as S-types (*Schwellverse*). Old Saxon examples like (*gi*)*fullit*
// (*thurh iro*) *ferhton* / *dâdi* (*Hel* 1310a) show that the first foot of a hypermetrical
a-verse may be preceded by anacrusis and that extrametrical words may appear before
the main part.

152

two clusters.[82] Corresponding b-verses like examples (35)–(38) scan unambiguously as hypermetrical when immediately adjacent to hypermetrical a-verses. About 184 examples like (35)–(38) seem to lie outside hypermetrical clusters, however, and it is uncertain whether these would be perceived as type A1 variants with long anacruses or as unclustered realizations of a hypermetrical pattern.

Among the Old Saxon b-verses comparable to (35)–(38), 109 variants may be regarded as unambiguously hypermetrical, since they are immediately preceded or followed by a hypermetrical a-verse.[83] Of these, sixty (55 per cent) are comparable to (35), with a main part consisting of two trochaic words (cf. the free-standing verse cited as example 18).[84] Twelve examples (11 per cent) are comparable to (36), with a word group in the first Sx foot of the main part and no extrametrical syllables before the second Sx foot (cf. the free-standing example 20).[85] Only one example (*Hel* 899b) has a word group in the first Sx foot and an extrametrical syllable before the second Sx foot. Another thirty-five examples (32 per cent) have the structure of (37), with two trochaic words and an extrametrical unstressed prefix in the main part (cf. the free-standing examples (23) and (24)).[86] The structure of (38) is represented by only

---

[82] See *OEM*, §6.5.

[83] As defined in *OEM*, ch. 6, a hypermetrical cluster may begin with a b-verse and end with an a-verse. Pope seems to assume that only whole lines can be hypermetrical, but his own lists show that many emendations would be required to sustain this hypothesis (*Rhythm*, pp. 99–104). The number of b-verses in question is not large, and the relative frequencies of interest here would emerge from any reasonable counting procedure.

[84] *Hel* 559b, 560b, 599b, 600b, 604b, 881b, 902b, 990b, 991b, 993b, 1301b, 1305b, 1312b, 1314b, 1315b, 1319b, 1542b, 1681b, 1682b, 1684b, 1686b, 1687b, 1688b, 1698b, 2208b, 2209b, 2211b, 2212b, 2213b, 2214b, 2215b, 2614b, 2825b, 3036b, 3038b, 3063b, 3064b, 3071b, 3493b, 3494b, 3499b, 3503b, 3504b, 3505b, 3563b, 4393b, 4394b, 4395b, 4396b, 4411b, 4414b, 5811b, 5891b, 5916b, 5918b, 5920(b)b, 5923b, 5929b, 5930b and 5931b. Most of the unambiguously hypermetrical verses will be found among Hofmann's S-types. I have included verse 5891b here as well, though Hofmann classifies it as *Ax2.2. Note that Hofmann scans the next a-verse, 5892a, as an S-type.

[85] *Hel* 900b, 989b, 1541b, 2597b, 2987b, 2989b, 3065b, 3498b, 3501b, 3677b, 4418b and 5228b.

[86] *Hel* 557b, 558b, 601b, 605b, 898b, 901b, 1307b, 1308b, 1310b, 1311b, 1317b, 1555b, 1683b, 2596b, 2822b, 2823b, 2903b, 2985b, 2988b, 2991b, 3037b, 3062b, 3495b, 3496b, 3497b, 3507b, 3562b, 4413b, 5654b, 5732b, 5917b, 5921b, 5922b, 5924b and 5933b.

one example (*Hel* 2824b), which has a main part with two trochaic words and a non-prefixal unstressed word before the second foot (cf. the free-standing examples 25 and 26). As we have observed, free-standing normal verses like (25) and (26) appear about half as frequently as normal verses like (23) and (24). Among hypermetrical b-verses, in which the poet takes special pains to restrict complexity, the relative frequency of main parts comparable to (25) and (26) is a mere 3 per cent (the unique example 38 as compared with the thirty-five verses like example 37). The status of the unstressed prefix as the least disruptive extrametrical constituent shows up with particular clarity in hypermetrical verses.

B-verses with the structure of examples (35)–(38) are complex on any analysis, but the strategy of clustering would have provided a useful clue to proper scansion of the 109 unambiguously hypermetrical examples. The 184 comparable b-verses lying outside hypermetrical clusters must have been significantly more difficult to scan, and in these we would expect even more severe restrictions on the complexity of the main part. As expected, the proportion of verses like (35), with a main part of two trochaic words, rises significantly in the group of unclustered examples, from 55 per cent to 71 per cent (130/184).[87] There are eight somewhat more complex variants in which the main part is free of extrametrical words (4 per cent), including seven variants like example (36).[88] The second-largest group of variants again has the structure of (37), with two

[87] *Hel* 7b, 157b, 290b, 482b, 518b, 561b, 656b, 706b, 849b, 854b, 1129b, 1147b, 1176b, 1235b, 1255b, 1268b, 1284b, 1286b, 1295b, 1333b, 1386b, 1470b, 1471b, 1472b, 1511b, 1553b, 1609b, 1628b, 1641b, 1718b, 1808b, 1974b, 1994b, 2068b, 2074b, 2125b, 2261b, 2297b, 2313b, 2448b, 2456b, 2479b, 2544b, 2586b, 2609b, 2690b, 2761b, 2820b, 2891b, 2924b, 2982b, 2997b, 3016b, 3035b, 3039b, 3104b, 3131b, 3192b, 3246b, 3258b, 3359b, 3508b, 3518b, 3635b, 3708b, 3847b, 3926b, 4002b, 4066b, 4125b, 4132b, 4179b, 4236b, 4239b, 4243b, 4497b, 4566b, 4577b, 4657b, 4714b, 4725b, 4830b, 4836b, 4837b, 4843b, 4846b, 4847b, 4900b, 4936b, 4950b, 4972b, 4988b, 5004b, 5029b, 5051b, 5096b, 5114b, 5127b, 5129b, 5176b, 5187b, 5233b, 5234b, 5341b, 5366b, 5375b, 5450b, 5470b, 5487b, 5495b, 5541b, 5555b, 5588b, 5649b, 5651b, 5736b, 5799b, 5807b, 5818b, 5820b, 5830b, 5832b, 5859b, 5871b, 5876b, 5894b, 5911b, 5935b, 5939b and 5941b. Most of the unclustered verses comparable to examples (34)–(38) will be found in Hofmann's lists for types a^{v}II^{v}2, *Ax1.x2, *Ax2.2, *A^{5}x2.x2 and *A^{5}x3a.2. Hofmann's criteria for hypermetrical verses differ slightly from my criteria for unambiguous examples, and a few items listed above will accordingly be found among his S-types.

[88] Like (36) are *Hel* 1804b, 1858b, 2826b, 3936b, 4092b, 4584b and 5165b. The main part in 5946b is wholly occupied by a compound with two Sx constituents.

trochaic words in the main part and an extrametrical prefix between them. There are forty such examples (22 per cent).[89] Four examples (2 per cent) have two trochaic words and one or more non-prefixal unstressed words in the main part, like (38).[90] The most complex type of variant, with a word group in the first foot of the main part and extrametrical constituents following, occurs twice (1 per cent).[91] We should probably not attribute much significance to the small increase in relative frequency for the two most complex categories, taken together (about 1 per cent). This is more than offset by the 16 per cent increase for verses with a main part of two trochaic words.

Although many verses like (35)–(38) seem to have indeterminate scansion, such verses provide valuable insight into gradations of metrical complexity. If we restricted our attention to free-standing Sx/Sx variants without anacrusis, it might seem possible to explain their relative frequencies on non-metrical grounds. When we inspect the corresponding main parts of verses with long strings of verse-initial function words, however, the link between relative frequency and deviation from the two-word norm becomes unmistakably clear.

Although the *Beowulf* poet confines bisyllabic anacrusis to the a-verse, the *Heliand* poet seems to allow it in the b-verse as well:

(39)	(themu) flôde / nâhor[92]		(2382b)
	{(xx)Sx/Sx}		
(40)	quâðun that // uualdand / selbo[93]		(2213b)
	{xxx//Sx/Sx}		
(41)	(thesoro) thiodo / drohtin[94]		(1994b)
	{(xxx)Sx/Sx}		

Old Saxon b-verses like example (39) do not appear in hypermetrical clusters and scan most plausibly as type A1 with anacrusis. Only when the number of verse-initial unstressed syllables rises to three do we begin to observe clustering, as with example (40), which appears beside an

---

[89] *Hel* 285b, 471b, 1232b, 1535b, 1569b, 2067b, 2196b, 2331b, 2371b, 2453b, 2562b, 2795b, 2828b, 3077b, 3626b, 3627b, 3648b, 3864b, 3900b, 3948b, 3973b, 3979b, 4170b, 4300b, 4334b, 4603b, 4650b, 4977b, 5028b, 5108b, 5115b, 5215b, 5321b, 5480b, 5486b, 5496b, 5503b, 5581b, 5682b and 5754b.
[90] *Hel* 47b, 3301b, 4724b and 5566b.
[91] *Hel* 4963b and 5537b.   [92] 'nearer to the sea ...'
[93] 'they said that the lord himself (would come) ...'   [94] 'lord of this people ...'

unambiguously hypermetrical a-verse.[95] Some sequences of three un-stressed syllables were probably insufficient to constitute the initial thesis of a hypermetrical b-verse in the *Heliand*. Old Saxon variants like example (41), which begins with an isolated minor function word of three syllables, do not appear in hypermetrical clusters. The trisyllabic initial sequences of clustered variants always contain two or more words, one of which is always a major function word (see 40).[96] Clustered variants with a main part of type A1 often exceed the minimum of three unstressed verse-initial syllables, having more than five on average. This dramatic expansion of the light hypermetrical foot represents a significant effort to distinguish hypermetrical b-verses from b-verses with anacrusis, though the boundary is less sharply drawn than in *Beowulf*.

DETERMINERS AND TRISYLLABIC ANACRUSIS

A-verses like the following, with an isolated definite article or demonstrative in anacrusis, occur with remarkably high frequency in the *Heliand*:

> (42) (That) uuîf uuarð / (thuo an) uuunnon[97]   (5939a)
> [(x)Sx/(xx)Sx]
> (43) (thero) thegno / (ge-)thâhti[98]   (1741a)
> [(xx)Sx/(x)Sx]

The Old Saxon poem contains about 450 Sx/Sx a-verses with an isolated constituent in anacrusis.[99] Familiar variants with an isolated prefix, which have analogues in *Beowulf*, account for 48 per cent of this sample (see examples (27) and (28)). Variants like (42) and (43), with an isolated definite article or demonstrative, have a frequency more than half that of the prefixal variants, accounting for 29 per cent of total verses in the sample. The *Beowulf* poet deletes articles and demonstratives verse-

---

[95] See Hofmann, *Versstrukturen* I, 170.

[96] Hofmann's S-verses include *Hel* 658b and 5755b, which have isolated determiners before the main part, but these are clearly not adjacent to hypermetrical a-verses and I do not regard them as hypermetrical.

[97] 'The woman was happy then ...'   [98] 'the beliefs of the thanes'.

[99] I restrict attention to examples with a main part of the form Sx/Sx listed under Hofmann's types *Ax1.x2, *Ax2.2 and *A⁵x2.x2. Examples with bisyllabic and trisyllabic anacruses are included. Statistics for articles and demonstratives are lumped together by necessity, since the distinction between these categories is not clear in early Germanic languages. See Mitchell, *Old English Syntax* I, §§220 and 238.

initially to eliminate anacrusis; variants like (42) and (43) do not appear in the Old English poem. This type of deletion had evidently become less acceptable in Old Saxon, however, as in later English.[100]

Within the word-foot theory, definite articles and demonstratives can be regarded as natural additions to the set of proclitics employed in anacrusis. Like prefixes, these closely-bound determiners make inconspicuous light feet and do not often appear in isolation at the beginning of an Old Saxon type B or C verse.[101] The light foot rule (R6) predicts that isolated determiners will constitute anacruses when they can no longer simply be deleted. The possibility of trisyllabic anacrusis then arises because some Old Saxon determiners have three syllables, like *thesoro* in example (41). Forms like *thesoro* have no analogues in *Beowulf*, since Old English function words were reduced to one or two syllables by a more forceful linguistic stress. With definite articles and demonstratives established as legitimate anacruses, the way lay open for freer employment of other non-prefixal words. Not all such words were equally acceptable as anacruses, however. Among the remaining verses in the sample, the largest category consists of Sx/Sx verses with an isolated possessive pronoun or noun quantifier in anacrusis (10 per cent). Such words are often classified as determiners, and their deletion may have been inhibited in Old Saxon, as with definite articles. The remaining 13 per cent of the sample consists of variants with miscellaneous isolated constituents in anacrusis, including several verses with isolated prepositions or intensifiers (notably *sô*). There is only one example with an isolated finite verb, however.[102] Recall that the prominence of the finite verb, as compared with other weakly stressed constituents, makes it most suitable as a light

---

[100] Article deletion seems to have become less acceptable by the time of *The Battle of Maldon*, composed no earlier than 991. Here we find Sx/Sx verses with articles in anacrusis like *(Se) eorl wæs / (þē) blīþra* 146a (cf. *Mald* 72b and 202b). The unusual anacruses of *Maldon* do not appear in *The Battle of Brunanburh*, composed no earlier than 937. A trisyllabic anacrusis represented at *Brun* 62b in manuscript A would certainly be unusual, but it seems best to scan according to manuscripts B, C, and D, which attest an unremarkable variant of type C here.

[101] See Hofmann, *Versstrukturen* I, 112 and 139.

[102] Verse 5515a, *gengun uuîf mid uuôpu* (xx//Sx/Sx), where the verb in anacrusis has high frequency and little semantic force. Though rare, this type of anacrusis does seem legitimate; cf. 5400a, *uuas mâri meginthiof* (x//Sx/Ss, second S resolved) with a form of the verb *to be* in anacrusis.

foot in two-word Norse verses of type A3.[103] This prominence makes the finite verb least suitable as an anacrusis.

Employment of non-prefixal constituents for anacrusis adds considerable ambiguity to the Old Saxon metrical system. The poet makes a significant effort, however, to restrict the frequency of the more complex variants, allowing us to distinguish fine shades of relative prominence among constituents with weak stress. Provided with a rich assortment of Old Saxon anacruses, we observe a distinct gradation from prefixes, which are least disruptive in this role, to non-prefixal minor function words (determiners), then to more disruptive major function words such as prepositions and auxiliaries, finally to finite main verbs, the most prominent and therefore most disruptive of the weakly stressed constituents. This gradation is predicted by provision R6b of the Light Foot Rule, but not by Kuhn's laws.

THEORIZING OLD SAXON ANACRUSIS

In clause-initial verses like example (42), the determiner violates K2, which would forbid placement of an isolated Satzteilpartikel in the first thesis. Kuhn attributes such counterexamples to innovations in the natural language, but his remarks leave much unexplained and seem inconsistent with his further suggestion that the *Heliand* dates from a transitional period when K1–2 still had some force.[104] During such a period, function words of the kind omitted by the *Beowulf* poet would be expected to occur first and most frequently in positions where the laws allowed them. Liberalization of constraints on anacrusis in type A1, for example, might be expected to encourage placement of Satzpartikeln in the old positions of the prefixes as allowed by K2. Consider the following examples in which the first alliterating word is a finite verb and the anacrusis is non-prefixal:

(44) (thar he) hêlde / (mid is) handun[105]   (1213a)
      [(xx)Sx/(xx)Sx]

(45) (sie) uuêgeat / (mi te) uundron[106]   (3530a)
      [(x)Sx/(xx)Sx]

---

[103] See above, p. 51.   [104] 'Wortstellung', p. 16.
[105] 'where he healed with his hands ...'
[106] 'they will torture me shockingly ...'

In example (44), the anacrusis consists of an adverb and a pronoun, both defined as Satzpartikeln by Kuhn. The two words occupy the same thesis, as required by K1. Since Kuhn defines *mid* and *is* as Satzteilpartikeln, K1 allows for their placement in the second thesis. We would have good evidence for Kuhn's transitional period if verses like (44) were unusually abundant. As it turns out, verses like (45) have the higher frequency.[107] Although the clause-initial thesis in (45) is licensed by a pronominal Satzpartikel, satisfying K2, another pronoun appears after the alliterating verb *uuêgeat*. Kuhn classifies all alliterating main verbs as stressed words and accordingly lists verses like (45) as exceptions to K1, which would require grouping of *sie* with *mi* in the first or second thesis.[108] If Kuhn's analysis is correct, it is hard to understand why verses like (45) should occur more frequently than those like (44), which obeys both K1 and K2. In the *Heliand*, after all, an a-verse like **sie mi uuêgeat te wundron* would have an unremarkable stress pattern. Within the word-foot framework, the poet's choice of word order in (45) is explained by reference to the complexity of anacruses with two major function words, which bear a confusing resemblance to light feet (see R6b). The violation of K1 in (45) would of course disappear if *uuêgeat* were redefined as an unstressed Satzpartikel occupying the first thesis. On that hypothesis, however, we could no longer explain why comparable verses are so rare in Old English poetry.[109] In the *Heliand*, then, anacrusis has been generalized in a way that is puzzling from the standpoint of Kuhn's laws but quite as expected from the standpoint of the word-foot theory.

RESOLUTION

A crucial linguistic precondition for Norse fornyrðislag is the forceful primary stress that effects deep subordination of less prominent syllables

---

[107] The relevant examples are unambiguous Sx/Sx verses with anacrusis, necessarily in the a-verse, that contain at least two Satzpartikeln. Like (44) are *Hel* 2118a, 3481a, 4282a and 4340a. Like (45) are 551a, 699a, 1576a, 1632a, 1644a, 1948a, 2381a, 2427a, 2582a, 2716a, 2773a, 4226a, 4549a, 4583a, 4724a, 4728a, 4833a, 4886a, 4976a, 5098a, 5201a, 5292a, 5357a, 5388a and 5430a. The only cases listed are those in which the first alliterating word is a finite verb, as in typical examples of anacrusis from *Beowulf*. The examples from *Beowulf*, of course, almost always have prefixal anacrusis in the a-verse, but it is interesting to note that a rare instance of non-prefixal anacrusis, *Hū lomp ēow on lāde* (*Beo* 1987a), violates K1, like example (45).

[108] 'Wortstellung', p. 16.   [109] Ibid., pp. 11–12.

in Old Norse words. The word-foot theory predicts that this linguistic stress will yield a correspondingly forceful metrical stress on an alliterating S position to the left, with deep subordination of S and s positions to the right. As we have seen, the subordinate arsis of a fornyrðislag verse pattern is in fact considered unsuitable for resolved sequences, which are associated with high metrical prominence.[110] In Old Saxon, primary stress is insufficiently forceful to eliminate weak syllables of a kind that were lost in Old English as well as Old Norse. Metrical subordination is predicted to be weakest in the *Heliand*, and we should expect an increase in the frequency of resolved sequences on subordinate S and s positions.

In Old Saxon type B verses, placement of resolved sequences is indeed much freer than in comparable Old English or Old Norse verses:

(46)   sô môsta siu mid ira / brûdigumon[111]   (*Hel* 509a)
       {xxxxxxx/Sxs, s resolved}

(47)   bêd / metodogiscapu[112]   (*Hel* 4827b)
       {x/Sxxs, S and s resolved, alliteration on m-}

(48)   þurh / rūmne sefan[113]   (*Beo* 278a)
       {x/Sxs, s resolved}

Resolution is somewhat unnatural in the subordinate constituent of a compound (see R9a) and also on the secondary arsis of a compound foot (see R9b). The effects of R9a and R9b are summed when both apply to the same metrical position (see U4). From an Old English perspective, examples (46) and (47) are quite unnatural, since they resolve a subordinate constituent on a secondary arsis. In *Beowulf*, we do find variants like example (48), with an unsubordinated constituent resolved on a secondary arsis, but these are unnatural by R9b only. Norse poets never resolve any kind of constituent on a secondary arsis.

Examples (46) and (47) may have no genuine analogues in *Beowulf*. Terasawa shows that apparent examples of resolved s in Old English type B can be otherwise explained.[114] The situation is very different in the

---

[110] See above, p. 100.   [111] 'so, with her bridegroom, she was able ...'
[112] 'he awaited the decree of fate ...' Cf. 2593b and 3347b.
[113] 'with a generous heart ...'
[114] 'Metrical Constraints', pp. 5–8. Because the *Beowulf* poet employs pre-epenthetic forms, for example, scansion as type C rather than type B is justified in cases like *æfter / māþðųm-gife* (*Beo* 1301a), which has the form xx/Ssx if we disregard the epenthetic -*u*- of *māþðum*-. In cases like *wið / Hrefna-wudu* (*Beo* 2925b), the second foot may

Heliand. I found eighteen clear cases of Old Saxon type B with a native Germanic compound containing a resolvable sequence.[115] All of these violate Terasawa's constraint. The only two examples with a resolved sequence on the S position also have a resolved sequence on the s position, like (47).[116] The number of crucial cases is relatively small in the *Heliand* because the author employs poetic compounds so seldom. In other Germanic traditions, poetic compounds are typically derived from ordinary words by addition of semantically inessential elements meaning 'war' or 'warlike', but these elements attribute positive value to martial ferocity, and would be quite inappropriate in a poem emphasizing New Testament values.[117]

Secondary constituents also resolve on the s position in some Old Saxon type Db verses with two alliterating syllables:

> (49) haldan / hôhgisetu[118]   (*Hel* 365a)
>   [Sx/Sxs, s resolved]
>
> (50) mâri / metodogescapu[119]   (*Hel* 2190a)
>   [Sx/Sxxs, S and s resolved]

---

contain a word group rather than a genitive compound. For fuller discussion consult the word index in Terasawa, *Nominal Compounds.*

[115] Cf. *Hel* 284a, 586a, 634a, 1118a, 1329a, 1660a, 2050a, 2527a, 4522a; 127b, 3354b, 4127b, 4211b and 4652b. Long loan words are excluded from consideration here because their morphological structures are problematic and their stress patterns are correspondingly uncertain; but verse 5179a, with a native secondary constituent, seems a fairly clear violation of Terasawa's constraint. For discussion of such forms see Hofmann, *Versstrukturen* I, ch. 4. If Hofmann's analysis of OS *íu* is accepted, 1340b, 1437b and 5353b would belong on the list above as well. Putative examples with epenthetic vowels are 4105a, 5066a; 2249b, 2779b, 4889b and 5687b (as scanned by Hofmann).

[116] Old English poems have no Sxs or Sxxs compounds with a resolvable sequence in the primary constituent for purely linguistic reasons (*OEG*, §§341–59). As we have frequently observed, Germanic languages had no short stressed syllables word-finally, so Germanic poets could not leave a syllable unresolved on the last arsis of an Sxs or Sxxs foot. In types B and Db, Sievers's rule of resolution would 'forbid' assignment of an unresolved short syllable to the final arsis, but ordinary linguistic rules will produce the results we observe and no additional rules of metre are required. Sievers's rule 'permits' an unresolved syllable on the s position of the Ss foot, but this is blocked by linguistic rules. Scansion of (51) as S/Sxs rather than S/Sxxs excludes an epenthetic *-o-* in *wundor-*.

[117] See Russom, 'Verse Translations'.   [118] 'to occupy the high seat'.

[119] 'the well-known decree of fate . . .'

(51)   wōm / wundọrbebodum[120]   (*Beo* 1747a)
        [S/Sxs, s resolved]

Twelve Db variants in the *Heliand* contain a native Germanic Sxs or Sxxs compound with a resolvable sequence. All twelve violate Terasawa's constraint.[121] Example (50), the only Db variant with resolution on the second S position, also has resolved s. *Beowulf*, with its much larger proportion of compounds, yields only one comparable verse, example (51). The Old Saxon poet is clearly more tolerant of resolution on weak metrical positions, as predicted.[122]

According to rule R9e, the most deeply subordinated s positions in type Da, those preceded by two alliterating syllables, are most appropriately filled by unresolved short syllables. Such deeply subordinated s positions are never filled by resolvable sequences in *Beowulf*, but this sometimes occurs in the *Heliand*. Consider the following Old Saxon variants:

(52)   uuârsaguno / uuord[123]   (3399a)
        [Ssx/S, s resolved]
(53)   erlos aðalborana[124]   (4003a)
        [Sx/Ssx, second S and s resolved]

Thirteen type E variants like example (52) have a resolved sequence on the relatively strong s position of the first foot. Nine of these are a-verses, five with double alliteration.[125] The *Beowulf* poet creates four similar verses, two of them a-verses with double alliteration.[126] Five Old Saxon Da verses like example (53) have a resolved sequence on the

---

[120] 'with perverse, strange suggestions ...'

[121] The others are *Hel* 92a, 110a, 197a, 512a, 725a, 1186a, 1324a, 4729a, 5064a and 3628b. All the a-verses have double alliteration. Putative examples with *îu* or epenthetic vowels, as scanned by Hofmann: 1200a, 1904a, 3882a, 4810a, 4568a, 5379a, 5590a and 5609a.

[122] With regard to the Old Saxon poet's employment of adjacent resolvable sequences, see Terasawa, 'Old English *here-toga*'.

[123] 'the word of the prophets ...'   [124] 'noble men ...'

[125] Other examples with double alliteration: *Hel* 537a, 2735a, 4935a and 5491a. With single alliteration: 317a, 619a, 1202a, 2893a; 1461b, 2087b, 2700b and 5427b.

[126] *Beo* 911a, 1187a, 2583b and 2661b.

weaker s of the second foot.[127] These have no analogues in *Beowulf*.[128] An Old English verse comparable to (53) would be quite unnatural, since it would contravene both R9a and R9b on a deeply subordinated arsis. When metrical subordination is in general less deep, as in Old Saxon poetry, simultaneous contravention of R9a and R9b causes less complexity.

In ch. 8, we saw how Old English and Old Norse poets assigned syllables to s positions in type Da, restricting attention to two-word variants that contained Ssx compounds and were free of resolved sequences on S positions. Only a few Old Saxon verses satisfy these criteria:

> (54) glau / anduuordi[129]   (930b)
> [S/Ssx, single alliteration, long s]
>
> (55) suart / sinnahti[130]   (2146a)
> [S/Ssx, double alliteration, long s]
>
> (56) hard / harmscare[131]   (240a)
> [S/Ssx, double alliteration, short s]

Four examples like (54) have single alliteration and long s. No corresponding examples with short s occur. Among the examples with double alliteration, six are like (55), with long s, and five are like (56), with short s.[132] If these meagre statistics can be taken at face value, they suggest that long s is unrestricted in Old Saxon Da variants with double alliteration. As we have observed, the other Germanic poets restrict the frequency of long s in Da variants with double alliteration and allow short s in variants with single alliteration.[133] These comparative relation-

---

[127] Cf. *Hel* 521a, 5742a and 5748a. The similar verse 902a occurs inside a hypermetrical cluster, and might attest a hypermetrical pattern Sx//S/Ssx, with the last S unresolved. A foot of the form Ssxx appears occasionally in the *Heliand*, but is apparently restricted to first position in heavy verses, ruling out analysis of (53) as Sx/Ssxx. The fairly large number of examples like (52) seems to rule out analysis as Ssxx/S, which has a much lower frequency than Ssx/S. See below, p. 190.

[128] A resolved sequence on the s position of type Da violates the 'law of the coda' proposed by Fulk in *History of Old English Meter*, chs. 7–8; cf. Cable, *English Alliterative Tradition*, pp. 19, 25 and 26.

[129] 'a wise answer...'   [130] 'dark, everlasting night...'

[131] 'hard, painful injury...'

[132] Like (54) are *Hel* 153b, 1759b and 5781b. Like (55) are 2446a, 2574a, 3512a, 4350a and 5781b. Like (56) are 1396a, 3044a, 4128a and 4866a.

[133] See above, p. 108. The Old English poet has short s in seven of thirty-two examples with single alliteration and long s in only three of twenty-six examples with double alliteration. The Old Norse poet has short s in twenty-five of fifty-three examples

ships are again as expected, since the less deeply subordinated s position
in the Old Saxon variants would provide a more appropriate location for a
long syllable.

The Old Saxon poet allows long and short s to alternate rather freely in
the expanded Da pattern Sx/Ssx:

(57)	manno / mêndâdi[134] [Sx/Ssx]	(1007a)
(58)	mirki / mênscaðo[135] [Sx/Ssx or Sx/Ss]	(1062a)
(59)	stênfatu / sehsi[136] [Ss/Sx]	(2037a)

Our comparison here must stay within the West Germanic area. Long
heavy verses seldom occur in the Old Norse corpus, and there are no
relevant two-word examples of expanded Da. The *Heliand* contains
twenty-eight verses like example (57), with long s, and another twenty-
eight like example (58), with short s.[137] Single alliteration occurs in one
a-verse (*Hel* 381a). In *Beowulf*, there are twenty-five verses comparable to
(57) and thirty-six comparable to (58).[138] Again we find a larger
percentage of long s in the *Heliand* due to the weaker effect of metrical
subordination. The expanded variant with short s can undergo reversal to
produce a variant with the normal number of metrical positions. In
example (59), resolution applies on the relatively strong s position of the

---

with single alliteration and long s in only seven of thirty-one examples with double
alliteration.

[134] 'men's sinful deeds'.

[135] 'the dark, sinful attacker ...'   [136] 'six stone vessels'.

[137] Like (57): *Hel* 233a, 381a, 494a, 581a, 967a, 974a, 1119a, 1361a, 1515a, 1574a,
1722a, 1842a, 1919a, 2238a, 2396a, 2542a, 3029a, 3043a, 3253a, 3602a, 3879a,
4221a, 4698a, 5173a, 5864a; 483b and 2585b. Like (58): 424a, 627a, 1228a, 1544a,
1722a, 1783a, 1886a, 1961a, 1981a, 2229a, 2300a, 2361a, 2400a, 2730a, 2796a,
3053a, 3686a, 3879a, 4028a, 4033a, 4127a, 4762a, 4766a, 4897a, 4971a, 5242a and
5734a. These are Hofmann's type Da⁵2.3a.

[138] Comparable to (57): *Beo* 223a, 325a, 326a, 411a, 770a, 987a, 1002a, 1097a, 1440a,
1512a, 1532a, 1565a, 1749a, 1865a, 1874a, 1886a, 2051a, 2065a, 2396a, 2646a,
2648a, 2725a, 2810a, 3031a and 3099a. Comparable to (58): 103a, 275a, 392a,
450a, 606a, 614a, 616a, 689a, 818a, 839a, 966a, 986a, 1212a, 1231a, 1298a, 1339a,
1348a, 1410a, 1468a, 1568a, 1678a, 1793a, 1969a, 2123a, 2205a (reading *hild-*),
2496a, 2545a, 2603a, 2649a, 2674a, 2689a, 2719a, 2760a, 2800a, 2811a and 2847a.
All of these are two-word variants with no resolution on S positions.

first foot, yielding a common variant of the A2 pattern Ss/Sx. This sort of reversal does not often occur in the *Heliand*. There are only seven other examples like (59).[139] In the shorter *Beowulf*, by contrast, there are forty-eight comparable examples.[140] The Old English poet seems much less tolerant of expanded verses, as we would expect if deeper metrical subordination tended to restrict the number of unstressed syllables.

Of the forty-eight Old English reversals, only one stands in the second half of the line, where the s position is more deeply subordinated and therefore less appropriate for occupation by resolved sequences. On the other hand, four of the eight Old Saxon examples appear as b-verses, evidently because the b-verse was less strongly subordinated to the a-verse in this tradition. It is worth emphasizing that reversal tends to decrease the frequency of verses like example (58) relative to those like example (57). If the *Beowulf* poet employed reversal less often, expanded Da variants with short s would preponderate even more obviously.

The s position of an Old Saxon type C verse can contain a long syllable or an unresolved short syllable, as in the cognate traditions:

$$(60) \quad \text{an / suefrestu}^{141} \qquad\qquad (4356\text{b})$$
$$[\text{x/Ssx, long s}]$$
$$(61) \quad \text{an / nîðhugi}^{142} \qquad\qquad (5704\text{a})$$
$$[\text{x/Ssx, short s}]$$

I found twelve two-word examples like (60), with long s, and fifteen like (61), with short s.[143] Short s has a higher frequency, as expected, in the traditions with deeper metrical subordination. In *Beowulf*, there are sixteen examples with long s and forty-seven with short s.[144] The

---

[139] Cf. *Hel* 4544a, 4712a, 4756a; 2056b, 3452b, 3745b and 3873b (Hofmann's A⁵3a.2).

[140] In the b-verse: *Beo* 1369b. In the a-verse: 76a, 136a, 156a, 208a, 222a, 226a, 430a, 622a, 640a, 753a, 1079a, 1116a, 1121a, 1122a, 1147a, 1177a, 1243a, 1284a, 1343a, 1463a, 1470a, 1516a, 1619a, 1676a, 1722a, 1738a, 1778a, 1940a, 2046a, 2069a, 2077a, 2120a, 2133a, 2250a, 2265a, 2320a, 2357a, 2419a, 2429a, 2456a, 2535a, 2537a, 2584a, 2622a, 2742a, 3007a and 3149a.

[141] 'on a sleeping couch ...'   [142] 'with hostile intent ...'

[143] Like (60) are *Hel* 1053a, 1953a, 3424a, 3592a, 5051a; 248b, 1036b, 1615b, 4356b, 4979b and 5063b. Like (61) are 362a, 2783a, 5704a; 1046b, 2575b, 2783b, 3327b, 3348b, 4014b, 4362b, 4553b, 4754b, 5002b and 5199b. Example (60) is misprinted in Behaghel–Taeger, and has been corrected (see Hofmann, *Versstrukturen* II, 171). As in previous chapters, only examples of the form x/Ssx are considered.

[144] Lists of comparable Old English and Old Norse type C variants are provided above, pp. 112–13.

165

Beowulf *and Old Germanic metre*

frequency of Old English type C with long s is low in part because a word pair of the sort that constitutes (60) can sometimes undergo reversal, yielding a type E variant with a non-clitic preposition on the verse-final S position. Fornyrðislag poets also employ reversal in such cases, though less often, since they tend to avoid heavy patterns generally.[145] In the *Heliand*, type E is never derived by reversal of type C variants like (60).

In all three Germanic traditions, the s position of type E normally contains a long syllable. There are a few instances of resolved s in some West Germanic E verses (e.g. example (53)), and short s, though rare, does seem to be allowed in this type as well:

(62) Sūð-Dena / folc[146]   (*Beo* 463b)
      [Ssx/S, short s]

(63) orlegas / uuord[147]   (*Hel* 3697b)
      [Ssx/S, short s]

Beowulf has five examples of type E like (62), with an unresolved syllable on the s position. These unusual variants seem to be tolerable only in the second half of the line, where the s position is more deeply subordinated and therefore more appropriate for occupation by a short syllable.[148] In the *Heliand*, which is nearly twice as long, we find only one analogue to (62), example (63). The less deeply subordinated s position of Old Saxon type E seems quite inhospitable to short syllables.[149]

In general, then, assignment of syllables to metrical positions follows the expected trend in Old Saxon poetry. The higher frequency of resolution on subordinate metrical positions may be attributable in part to the larger number of resolvable sequences in Old Saxon, though the trend seems much too prominent to explain entirely on such grounds. A purely metrical explanation is required, of course, for the higher frequency of long syllables on subordinate metrical positions and the lower frequency of resolvable sequences left unresolved.

[145] On reversal of type C in Old English and Old Norse poetry, see above, p. 110.
[146] 'the people of the South-Danes ...'
[147] 'declaration of war ...'   [148] See above, p. 111.
[149] A medial *d* has been simplified in *Hel* 4628b, inuuid{d}eas gern, repeated as 5060b. These two verses are probably not examples of type E with short s (cf. the spelling *inuuiddies* at 4594a). *Hel* 1742a, uuînberi uuesan, might be analysed as Ss/Sx, with the secondary constituent resolved, or as Ssx/S, with *uuesan* resolved and short s.

OLD SAXON SXX WORDS

In the *Heliand*, as in the cognate traditions, we find trisyllabic words with no perceptible stress on the medial syllable. Consider the following:

(64)	stênfatu / sehsi[150]	(2037a)
	[Ss/Sx]	
(65)	folgode / fruokno[151]	(2995a)
	[Sxx/Sx]	
(66)	uuardode / (uuið the) uurêðon[152]	(3837a)
	[Sxx/(xx)Sx]	
(67)	mâridun / (is) megincraft[153]	(2268a)
	[Sxx/(x)Ss]	
(68)	liof endi / luttil[154]	(740a)
	[Sxx/Sx]	
(69)	uuord endi / uuîsdôm[155]	(848a)
	[Sxx/Sx]	

In example (64), discussed above as (59), the resolvable constituent *-fatu* fills the s position of an Ss foot. As we observed, the *Heliand* poet employs only eight such verses. These eight verses all consist of exactly two words, no doubt because further deviation from the norm would have caused intolerable complexity in a heavy, reversed pattern with an unusual type of resolution. On the other hand, there are thirty-five examples like (65) and (66), with a trisyllabic weak preterite or infinitive of class II in the first foot. Only nine of the Old Saxon examples are like (65), with exactly two words; the other twenty-six are like (66), with one or more extrametrical words.[156] It seems clear, then, that the pattern of (65) and (66) differed significantly from the pattern of (64). The *Heliand* contains only three somewhat doubtful cases of the ultra-heavy pattern Ss/Ss.[157] These have exactly two words, with no extrametrical syllables. It would be quite implausible to represent the four verses like (67) as complex

---

[150] 'six stone vessels'.   [151] 'they followed the bold (man) ...'
[152] 'guarded against the adversaries ...'   [153] 'they praised his power'.
[154] 'loveable and little ...'   [155] 'word and wisdom ...'
[156] Like (65) are *Hel* 2042a, 5205a; 384b, 2910b, 4633b, 5372b, 5511b and 5782b. Like (66) are 83a, 203a, 1077a, 1156a, 1204a, 3311a, 3586a, 3664a, 3786a, 3904a, 3970a, 4109a, 4286a, 4791a, 4835a, 4985a, 4989a, 5099a, 5138a, 5211a, 5613a, 5618a, 5974a; 2069b and 5465b.
[157] *Hel* 2343a (possibly Sx/Ss) and 3747a, repeated as 3842a (possibly Ss/Sx).

variants of Ss/Ss with the first s resolved and extrametrical syllables before the second foot.[158] Within the framework employed here, such verses scan as variants of Sxx/Ss, which are heavy but not ultra-heavy.

The patterns Sxx/Sx and Sxx/Ss are independently required to account for variants like examples (68) and (69). In such cases, the bisyllabic function word could not be excluded as extrametrical without making the verse too small. Because bracketing rule R2a forbids treatment of a function word as half-extrametrical, *endi* must be assigned to an Sxx foot in (68) and (69), along with the verse-initial stressed word.

Perhaps the most noteworthy feature of Old Saxon is its restoration of medial syllables formerly subject to syncopation. Since these syllables actually disappeared at one point, they could hardly retain stress from an earlier period of Germanic. From the perspective of the word-foot theory, it is not surprising to discover that the innovative forms appear in type C and Da variants:

(70)	is / engilun[159]		(1087a)
	[x/Sxx]		
(71)	Sô / gornode[160]		(5021a)
	[x/Sxx]		
(72)	drôm / drohtines[161]		(2084a)
	[S/Sxx]		
(73)	folc / folgoda[162]		(2370a)
	[S/Sxx]		

If trisyllabic weak class II verbs have the metrical value Sxx, forms with restored medial syllables should have the same value and the same distribution. That is what we observe. Examples (70) and (72) clearly contain unsyncopated forms, since corresponding earlier forms would make these verses too short.[163] Here the new Sxx nouns have moved into

---

[158] Like (67) are *Hel* 5116a, 5299a and 5497a; cf. 5276a, which would be an ultra-heavy type Da if the verb were analysed as Ss. In *Beowulf*, the only clear cases of Ss/Ss with resolved first s are *nȳdwracu / nīþgrim* (193a) and *drihtsele / drēorfāh* (485a). *Beo* 1246a and 2618a would be comparable, however, if word-final *-līc* bore significant stress. There are no clear cases of an ultra-heavy type D pattern in *Beowulf* (*OEM*, §1.7, n. 20).

[159] 'to his angels ...'   [160] 'Thus he mourned ...' Cf. 3671a.

[161] 'pleasure given by God ...'   [162] 'a multitude followed ...'

[163] Verses of the form x/Sx or S/Sx are unacceptable in the *Heliand*. Such verses are extremely rare even in native Eddic fornyrðislag, where short verses of other kinds are

positions characteristic of Sxx verbs (see examples (71) and (73)). Examples like (70) and (72) are unexpected if types C and Da necessarily have a stressed syllable before the last unstressed syllable of the verse, as Sievers supposes. On Sievers's hypothesis, new Sxx words would be expected to appear only in type A verses of the form Sxx/Sx or Sxx/Ss.[164]

SUMMARY

Lehmann detects a 'relaxation of rhythm' in the *Heliand*, taking *Beowulf* as his paradigm for West Germanic verse.[165] He argues that linguistic developments in Old Saxon made it impossible for poets to observe traditional standards. Hofmann disagrees, arguing that Old Saxon poets simply had different standards.[166] The word-foot theory posits a decisive influence of language on metre, but this influence changes metrical standards in addition to promoting deviation from them. When isolated articles could no longer be deleted at the beginning of the verse, for example, they were best employed as anacruses, since they were insufficiently conspicuous for routine employment as light feet. The presence of trisyllabic articles in Old Saxon then led to employment of trisyllabic anacrusis, which could create confusion about the number of feet in the second half of the line. Such confusion was not simply tolerated. By adding unstressed constituents verse-initially, the poet could and quite often did distinguish hypermetrical b-verses from normal b-verses with anacrusis. This procedure was sanctioned by the weakness of metrical

---

permitted. For a few doubtful exceptions, see Hofmann's list of *Unternormale Verse* (*Versstrukturen* II, 213).

[164] The number of two-word verses like (70) is relatively small (cf. *Hel* 877a and 4250a). As we have observed, the Old Saxon poet most often supports light feet with extrametrical words. Variants like *that sie ûses / drohtines* (1229a) have uncertain evidential value because they can be scanned as type A3 if syncopated forms are posited. In type Da, on the other hand, there are many verses like (72) that scan only with the innovative value: cf. 446a, 2366a, 2808a, 2815a, 2999a, 4026a, 5110a, 5207a, 5431a, 5568a, 5788a, 5837a, 5850a; 534b, 834b, 1045b, 1596b, 2073b, 2199b, 2621b, 2969b, 2974b, 3115b, 3350b, 3542b, 3682b, 3787b, 3980b, 3984b, 4012b, 4053b, 4259b, 4272b, 4631b, 4744b, 4800b, 4992b and 5288b. These are classified by Hofmann as Da1.3a, except for verse 2815a, which he classifies, I think incorrectly, as Da⁵2.3a. The larger number of such verses suggests that the innovative value has become the unmarked or default value for the poet.

[165] *DGV*, p. 105.   [166] *Versstrukturen* I, 35.

169

subordination, which reflects the weak stress of the natural language but is not reducible to a purely linguistic phenomenon. It is important to remember that the number of unstressed syllables was still carefully restricted under certain metrical conditions discussed above, notably between the stresses of type B, in the main part of a-verses with complex anacruses, and in the main part of unclustered b-verses otherwise identical to hypermetrical variants.

Despite the efforts of its author, the *Heliand* probably represents a tradition in decline, as Lehmann argues.[167] Fundamental principles of word-foot metre must have been especially difficult to implement in a Germanic language with weakened stress and an increasing number of obligatory proclitics. The degree of metrical ambiguity in the *Heliand* may be somewhat lower than Sievers suspected. Further research may provide principled scansions for some difficult verses. To judge from our study of type A1, however, average verse complexity was quite high, imposing many difficult problems of scansion on the audience.

[167] *DGV*, p. 50. To the extent that this holds true, of course, no theory of Old Saxon metre can rationalize the poet's practice. The reader should bear in mind that the concept of anacrusis and the normal / hypermetrical distinction are derived from the systematic practice of the *Beowulf* poet. The attempt here has been to determine whether my theoretical explanations for these features of Old English versecraft predict the characteristic Old Saxon forms of anacrusis and hypermetrical patterning (not at all the same thing as building up a theory of anacrusis and hypermetricality from Old Saxon evidence in isolation). As noted just above, the word-foot theory predicts that the normal / hypermetrical distinction will be more difficult for an Old Saxon poet to make. Borderline Old Saxon cases of a kind unattested in *Beowulf* validate this prediction.

11

Hildebrandslied

The apparent mixture of High and Low German forms in *Hildebrandslied* is often explained as Saxonization of an Old High German original. The provenance of the poem remains uncertain, however.[1] Here I simply assume that the author composed in an Old German dialect of some kind. Narrower description of the author's language seems unnecessary for most of our comparative purposes. The High German consonant shift, for example, has no significant bearing on issues emphasized in previous chapters. The special advantage of *Hildebrandslied* for the comparative metrist is its native legendary content, which would not have interfered with traditional methods of composition. Although the text that survives to us has less than seventy lines, it provides valuable support for claims about continental Germanic metre derived from the *Heliand*.

In the *Heliand* we observed a number of metrically intractable phrases marking direct discourse boundaries. Three similar phrases appear in *Hildebrandslied*. All three take the same form, *quad Hiltibrant* 'quoth Hildebrand'. All three stand between verses that constitute a well-formed

---

[1] Robinson includes *Hildebrandslied* in his list of Old Saxon works and also in his list of Old High German works (*Old English and its Closest Relatives*, pp. 109 and 227). According to Sonderegger, the manuscript of *Hildebrandslied* is a copy or paraphrase made at Fulda, based on a Bavarian exemplar but converted partially into Old Saxon, with some false or hypercorrect Low German forms (*Althochdeutsche Sprache und Literatur*, p. 55). Bostock–King–McLintock (p. 79) claim that the poem was composed in a High German dialect, if we include Langobardic under that description, citing as evidence the alliteration of *rīche* with High German *reccheo* (line 48) and the metrical desirability of disyllabic High German *suāsat* (line 53). The other poems regarded as Old High German have limited value for metrical analysis (see Hofmann, *Versstrukturen* I, 11).

line when *quad Hiltibrant* is removed.[2] A fourth phrase, *Heribrantes sunu* 'son of Heribrand', causes severe metrical problems in the middle of the otherwise unremarkable line 7. These four phrases are bracketed in Braune–Ebbinghaus, and it seems best to exclude them from the metrical analysis. Sievers identifies a few passages as prose interpolations that may contain remnants of poetic language.[3] Of these I exclude three from consideration: *dat Hiltibrant hætti mīn fater: ih heittu Hadubrant* (line 17); *chūd was her chōnnem mannum* (line 28); *dat dū neo dana halt mit sus sippan man dinc ni gileitos* (lines 31–2).[4] Finally, incomplete understanding of the linguistic material dictates exclusion of verse 65b, *staim bort chludun*. Excluded material will be discussed separately when it has some bearing on the argument.

COINCIDENCE OF THE CLAUSE WITH THE VERSE AND LINE

Hildebrandslied shows a high frequency of one-verse clauses, with forty-three clear cases in about sixty-eight lines.[5] The Light Foot Rule (R6) explains Kuhn's-law effects in these one-verse clauses. *Hildebrandslied* also contains nineteen one-verse adjuncts that have no Satzpartikeln of their own and could not provide landing sites for Satzpartikeln.[6] Kuhn's first law (K1) does not of course apply in such cases, since it regulates Satzpartikeln. Being heavy phrases, the nineteen adjuncts have undergone

---

[2] Lines 30, 49 and 58. [3] *AGM*, §125.

[4] Most metrists would I think agree that these three lines are unmetrical, though Sievers's system of classification makes no principled distinction between rare metrical subtypes and unmetrical verses (*OEM*, §10.1; Stanley, *Foreground*, p. 212). The word-foot theory, which employs natural rules applying across the board to all relevant verses, makes it possible to isolate spurious material with somewhat more confidence. It is difficult to rule out the possibility that some unmetrical lines in *Hildebrandslied* were due to imperfect control of the metre by the poet or to a decline in poetic tradition, but as we shall see, several types of evidence point toward textual corruption instead.

[5] *Hld* 5a, 7a, 12a, 14a, 18a, 27a, 30a, 36a, 40a, 41a, 44a, 45a, 46a, 49a, 54a, 59a, 65a, 68a; 5b, 6b, 7b, 8b, 9b, 11b, 12b, 13b, 16b, 18b, 22b, 24b, 27b, 34b, 35b, 40b, 41b, 43b, 49b, 54b, 55b, 57b, 59b, 60b and 64b. The remaining parts of lines 1 and 29 also appear to be one-verse clauses.

[6] The adjuncts appear after clauses that would be syntactically complete without them, and are semantically inessential in all but one case. Note that although the epithet *Hūneo truhtin* 'lord of the Huns' (35a) seems essential to identify the king mentioned in 34b, 34b is syntactically complete. The semantically inessential adjuncts are *Hld* 6a, 8a, 9a, 10a, 13a, 16a, 34a, 38a, 43a, 57a, 60a, 64a, 68a; 14b, 30b, 36b, 44b and 45b.

the expected shift towards the end of the clause.[7] None of them begin with Satzteilpartikeln, so their placement within the clause cannot be attributed to Kuhn's second law (K2). In *Hildebrandslied*, as in *Þrymsqviða*, placement of words and phrases is often determined by factors quite independent of Kuhn's laws.

Six clauses in *Hildebrandslied* seem to extend beyond two verses, comprising a total of twenty-three verses in all.[8] The poet creates these clauses primarily by adjunction. Consider the largest clause of the poem (20–22a):

> (1) her furlaet in lante   luttila sitten,[9]
> (2) prūt in būre,   barn unwahsan[10]
> (3) arbeo laosa[11]

The first line of the clause, example (1), is almost complete syntactically, or perhaps entirely so, if the adjective *luttila* functions as a noun.[12] If (1) is syntactically complete, the following phrase *prūt in būre* is an adjunct comparable to *Hūneo truhtin* (*Hld* 35a). The case ending on *luttila* has the normal form for the feminine. In (2), the b-verse, with neuter *barn*, lies outside the scope of the adjective, and cannot be closely construed with the preceding line. Example (3) looks like an adjunct to *barn unwahsan*.[13]

---

[7] See above, pp. 118–19.

[8] Lines 2–3, 18–19, 20–22a, 23–24a, 55–56 and 60b–61. Line 61 is a one-line clause embedded in the higher clause initiated at 60b.

[9] 'he left (his) young (one) to stay in this land ... '

[10] '(his) bride in (her) bower, and a young child ... '   [11] 'bereft of inheritance ... '

[12] This type of construction is not characteristic of native Eddic fornyrðislag, but there are many examples in Old English poetry, e.g. *forlēt forheardne faran eft ongēan* 'he caused the very keen (thing) to go back again' (*Mald* 156). For substantized adjectives in an Old High German alliterative poem, see *Muspilli* 86b, *tōten enti quekkhen* '(the) dead and (the) quick'. The constituent *ēnan* '(the) former' is used substantively in *Hld* 12a, so *ōdre* '(the) latter' in 12b would appear to be substantival as well. This implies that *Hld* 13a is an appositional adjunct (i.e., a variation) rather than a noun phrase modified directly by adjectival *ōdre*.

[13] Cf. the translation in Bostock–King–McLintock, p. 45: 'He left at home sitting in the dwelling a young wife and an ungrown child bereft of inheritance.' The authors seem to construe *in būre* rather closely with *sitten*, but do not discuss the matter explicitly, and may be more concerned about accurate representation of meaning than about exact reproduction of the original syntax. Translations in this chapter often follow Bostock–King–McLintock, with some alterations to represent the syntax of individual verses and lines more directly.

Hildebrandslied contains nineteen clauses that fill an entire line.[14] The principle of closure (U3), which restricts the complexity of the b-verse, has a strong influence on word order in these clauses:

(4) (nū scal) mih / suāsat chind // suertu / hauwan[15]   (53)
[(xx)x/Sxs // Sx/Sx]

(5) (der sī doh) nū / argosto // ōstar- / liuto[16]   (58)
[(xxx)x/Ssx // Sx/Sx]

(6) mit / gēru scal man // geba in- / fāhan[17]   (37)
[x/Sxxs // Sx/Sx, first S resolved]

(7) (dat dū noh bi) desemo / rīche // reccheo / (ni) wurti[18]   (48)
[(xxxx)xxx/Sx // Sx/(x)Sx]

Of the nineteen one-line clauses, eleven are like example (4), with a b-verse of exactly two words. Satzpartikeln are present in sixteen of the one-line clauses, and nine of these have two-word b-verses.[19] As in *Þrymsqviða*, the poet frees the b-verse of movable function words whenever possible to produce variants that express their underlying patterns directly. Two one-line clauses like example (5) have b-verses consisting of a single compound. These b-verses are not particularly complex, having no extrametrical words and no word groups within the foot. In example (6), the b-verse has a word group in the first foot, but is free of extrametrical words. In the two examples like (7), the b-verse has the least disruptive

---

[14] Lines 2, 4, 15, 25, 33, 37, 39, 42, 47, 48, 50, 51, 52, 53, 58, 62, 63, 66 and 67. Line 61 clearly belongs here as well if we accept the analysis of Hofmann, who reads *hru{o}men* rather than *rūmen* for MS *hrumen* and divides the line immediately before this word (*Versstrukturen* II, 294). Essentially the same analysis is proposed by McLintock ('Metre and Rhythm', 571). One might also add line 28, *chūd was her ... chōnnem mannum* ('he was known ... to bold men'). The alliterative link between *chūd* and *chōnnem* suggests that this is a one-line clause with some words missing, and it is so represented in Braune–Ebbinghaus. I exclude from consideration here line 20, the possible one-line clause cited as example (1).

[15] 'now my own child must hew me with a sword ... '

[16] 'yet let him now be the most wretched of easterners ... ' Cf. line 42.

[17] 'gifts are to be received with the spear ... '

[18] 'that you have not yet become an outlaw in this kingdom'. Cf. line 52.

[19] Other two-word b-verses in one-line clauses containing Satzpartikeln: *Hld* 2b, 15b, 25b, 33b, 39b, 47b, 63b and 67b. *Hld* 28b and 61b probably belong here as well. More complex b-verses in one-line clauses containing Satzpartikeln: *Hld* 37b, 42b, 48b, 50b, 51b, 52b and 58b. Among the one-line clauses without Satzpartikeln, *Hld* 62 and 66 have two-word b-verses.

type of extrametrical constituent before the second foot, a negative particle or prefix. It is worth emphasizing that Kuhn's laws do not apply to prefixes, negative particles, or other Satzteilpartikeln when they appear after the first thesis of the clause. By repressing employment of the more disruptive extrametrical words in the b-verse of a one-line clause, the principle of closure also represses employment of the only constituents that could violate Kuhn's laws there. *Hld* 50 and 51 are the only one-line clauses with b-verses of significant complexity. *Hld* 50 was excluded from consideration by Sievers due to other problems in the line that led him to classify it as a prose interpolation.[20] The b-verse of *Hld* 51 has an extremely peculiar alliterative pattern (discussed below), and may not originally have contained an extrametrical preposition. However we may decide such matters, it is clear that the universal principle of closure imposed strict constraints on the b-verse in the one-line clauses of *Hildebrandslied*. U3 independently explains why the poet did not produce violations of K1 such as **suertu mih hauwan* or **reccheo noh ni wurti* (see examples (4) and (7)).

A conspicuous violation of K2 occurs in the a-verse of example (6), where the isolated Satzteilpartikel *mit* stands before *geru*, the first stressed word of the clause.[21] An equally conspicuous violation of K1 occurs in *Hld* 11b, where the Satzpartikeln *eddo* and *dū* fail to cluster, appearing on opposite sides of a stressed noun:

(8)   (eddo) hwelīhhes / cnuosles dū sīs[22]
      [(xx)xxx/Sxxs]

Kuhn concludes from such evidence that K1–2 had little force in *Hildebrandslied* and related works.[23] U3, on the other hand, applies just as

---

[20] *AGM*, §125.

[21] Movement of prepositional phrases to absolute clause-initial position is rare in *Beowulf*, but not unattested (see *Æt þǣm / āde wæs* 1110a, *Æfter þǣm / wordum* 1492a). Kuhn deals with such exceptions by *ad-hoc* redefinition of the article as a relative pronoun ('Wortstellung', p. 44).

[22] 'or to what family you belong . . . '

[23] 'In diesen ahd. Stabreimgedichten scheint das alte Satzpartikelgesetz kaum noch wirksam gewesen zu sein' ('Wortstellung', p. 24). Kuhn finds similar violations in *Muspilli*, lines 39, 40, 57 and 66. Such violations of K2 are discussed further by Kuhn on pp. 45–6. Bostock–King–McLintock (p. 71) argue on grammatical grounds that there is a lacuna before example (8) in which a verb of saying once stood, but there is no reason to be suspicious of example (8) itself.

Beowulf *and Old Germanic metre*

strictly in *Hildebrandslied* as in *Þrymsqviða*. Among the one-line clauses of *Þrymsqviða* that contain Satzpartikeln, the proportion of two-word b-verses is 25/48.[24] In *Hildebrandslied*, as we have seen, the proportion is 9/16, about the same.[25] Since U3 is independently necessary, and since it rules out so many of the constructions forbidden by Kuhn's laws, the range of cases in which Kuhn's laws perform meaningful work must be quite restricted.

PLACEMENT OF ADJUNCTS

A familiar type of b-verse adjunct in fornyrðislag is the two-word prepositional phrase. *Þrymsqviða* contains nine of these, all type C, like *ór Nóatúnom*.[26] Treatment of prepositional phrases is quite different in *Hildebrandslied*:

(9) miti / Deotrīchhe[27] (26b)
[xx/Ssx]

(10) in sus / hēremo man[28] (56a)
[xx/Sxxs]

(11) helidos, ubar hringa[29] (6a)
[Sx/(xx)Sx, first S resolved]

Example (9), which resembles the Norse type of prepositional adjunct, is the only such verse in *Hildebrandslied* as it survives to us.[30] Three prepositional phrases with more than two words occupy a whole verse, as in example (10), but the poet uses prepositional phrases most often as

---

[24] See above, p. 122.

[25] The proportion would rise to 12/19 if lines 20, 28 and 61 were included in the count; it would fall to 8/15 if line 15 were excluded due to lack of alliteration. Note that the unproblematic *Hld* 42, which strongly resembles *Hld* 15, allows for principled division of *Hld* 15 into verses without reference to alliterative patterning.

[26] See above, p. 123.   [27] 'with Dietrich'.

[28] 'from such a distinguished man ... '

[29] '[those] heroes, over [their] ring-mail ... '

[30] Hld 51b (discussed below) would constitute a two-word adjunct of the Norse type if the word *folc* were removed as inauthentic. Example (9) requires emendation of *unti* to *miti*, but the emendation seems straightforward paleographically (see Bostock–King–McLintock, p. 46). Since I take an agnostic position with regard to the provenance of the poem, I do not mark length in inflectional vowels of forms like *hringa*, which would be *hringā* if it were Old High German.

176

subconstituents of the verse, usually in the first half of the line.[31] Example (11) is one of seven semantically inessential adjuncts that consist of an alliterating word followed by a prepositional phrase. Six of these are a-verses like (11), with the prepositional object alliterating on the second S position.[32] Alliteration is especially appropriate on this position, which would be expected to retain considerable prominence in a continental West Germanic poem.[33]

When we consider the whole range of adjuncts employed in *Hildebrandslied*, the contrast with North Germanic practice stands out even more clearly:

(12)	Hadubrant gimahalta,	Hiltibrantes sunu[34]	(14)
(13)	wēttu irmingot	obana ab hevane[35]	(30)
(14)	ferahes frōtoro;	her frāgen gistuont[36]	(8)

Only five adjuncts appear as b-verses in *Hildebrandslied*. Four of these are patronymics in lines like example (12).[37] Example (13) contains the only b-verse adjunct with an embedded prepositional phrase. The remaining fourteen adjuncts are clause-final a-verses. Nine of these have double alliteration, like the a-verse of example (14). Only four of the fourteen are two-word paradigms.[38] In six cases, a one-verse clause following the

---

[31] Like (10) are *Hld* 2b (type A1) and 51b (see previous note). B-verses with embedded prepositional phrases are *Hld* 6b (type B), 30b (A1), 35b (B), 54b (C) and 64b (B). A-verses with embedded prepositional phrases are *Hld* 6a (example 11), 10a (type A1), 13a (Da), 19a (C), 20a (A1 with anacrusis), 21a (A1), 27a (?A1 with long anacrusis), 33a (A1), 37a (B), 38a (A1), 40a (A1), 43a (Db), 46a (probably A3), 48a (A3), 52a (unclassifiable), 54a (A1), 65a and 68a (both A1 with anacrusis).

[32] Cf. *Hld* 10a, 13a, 38a, 43a and 68a. *Hld* 30b has single alliteration in the second half of the line.

[33] The percentage of total verses with double alliteration is low in *Hildebrandslied* (Bostock–King–McLintock, p. 319); but this results primarily from a high percentage of verses with a single primary arsis (types A3, B and C), in which double alliteration would be less likely to occur. Verses 33a and 40a have sole alliteration on the finite verb, and may have been derived from variants in which the verb did not alliterate.

[34] 'Hadubrand, son of Hildebrand, spoke out ... '

[35] 'you know, great God, from heaven above ... '

[36] 'more experienced in life; he began to ask ... '

[37] See *Hld* 36b, 44b and 45b. Employment of patronymics in the b-verse, an ancient device for filling out the line, is richly attested in Eddic and Old English verse.

[38] The two-word paradigms with double alliteration are the a-verse of example (14) and *scarpen scūrim* (*Hld* 64a). Single alliteration is present in *fōhem uuortum* (Hld 9a) and

adjunct brings the sentence to an end.[39] In five other cases, however, the sentence continues beyond the b-verse, as in (14).[40] In *Hildebrandslied*, then, the clause-final adjunct is typically used to provide double alliteration in the a-verse. Such an adjunct will displace the opening of an immediately following clause to the b-verse, and this clause will often continue into the next line. Although it is more than twice the size of *Hildebrandslied*, *Þrymsqviða* has only two a-verse adjuncts. These are two-word paradigms with single alliteration, and they are both followed in the b-verse by an additional adjunct rather than by a new clause.[41] In *Þrymsqviða*, as we have seen, the typical adjuncts are two-word b-verses like *ór Nóatúnom* and *þursa dróttinn*, which provide metrical closure for the line as they round out a clause or sentence.

In both North and West Germanic poetry, syntactic principles of ordinary speech promote shifting of adjuncts to clause-final position. Within the poetic line, differing placement of adjuncts will result in differing placement of clause boundaries. The less stichic, 'S-hook' style of West Germanic poetry is attributable in part to relatively weak subordination of the rightward arsis, which makes double alliteration more desirable in the a-verse, promoting use of formulaic adjuncts that displace the following clause rightward.[42] Differing syntactic properties of b-verses in the two traditions highlight the universal character of U3, which applies with about equal strength in *Þrymsqviða* and *Hildebrandslied*. Despite major differences in technique, both poems achieve a high degree of metrical closure. Kendall attributes the Kuhn's-law effects to archaic syntax preserved in traditional formulas 'without reinforcement from the patterns of everyday speech and writing'.[43] As we have seen, however, many of these effects are attributable to U3, which supervenes

---

Hūneo truhtin (*Hld* 35a). The other examples with double alliteration are 6a, 10a (missing b-verse), 13a, 38a (missing b-verse), 43a, 57a and 68a (missing b-verse). The other examples with single alliteration are 16a, 34a and 60a. It is possible, though I think quite unlikely, that the examples with missing b-verses were not clause-final.

[39] *Hld* 6b, 13b, 35b, 43b, 57b and 64b. Verse 13b might be regarded as a complete sentence, in which case 13a would be sentence-final. I would put a period rather than a comma at the end of verse 6b and a comma rather than a period at the end of verse 4b.

[40] See *Hld* 9b, 16b, 34b and 60b.

[41] *Þrk* 22/7, *Niarðar dóttur*, and 29/9, *ástir mínar* (a repetition of the preceding b-verse).

[42] See Stanley, *Foreground*, pp. 110–14.   [43] *Metrical Grammar*, p. 28.

independently of formulaic structure and applies even in poems that violate Kuhn's laws.

The type C verses of *Hildebrandslied* have a remarkably consistent distribution. Consider the following examples:

> (15) (erdo) desero / brunnono[44]   (62a)
>   {(xx)xxx/Sxx}
> (16) đat sih / urhēttun[45]   (2a)
>   [xx/Ssx]
> (17) iro / saro rihtun[46]   (4b)
>   [xx/Ssx, S resolved]

I set aside example (15), an ultra-light variant of type C with an Sxx simplex in the second foot. This is the only such variant in the poem, and it appears in the first half of the line, the most appropriate site for verses of significant complexity. What deserves special notice is the distribution of more familiar type C variants with an Ssx foot. A-verses of this kind conform to the style of (16). All are syntactically incomplete, and in all cases this element of complexity is mitigated by the fact that the Ssx foot is filled by a single word.[47] Comparable b-verses, represented by example (17), exhibit a different kind of metrical kinship. With the exception of *Hld* 26b, each one has a word group in the Ssx foot, a significant element of complexity. On the other hand, all of these b-verses are syntactically complete, so their complexity is mitigated by strict adherence to the principle of syntactic integrity (U1). It is worth adding that the last word in every Ssx group is a trochaic verb that provides a good match for the subordinated sx sequence.[48] Such careful distribution of variants tells against the claim of Lehmann that the poet's versecraft was relaxed in some general sense.[49]

---

[44] 'or of these mail-coats ... '   [45] 'that warriors (encountered) each other ... '
[46] 'arranged their equipment'.   [47] Cf. *Hld* 19a, 23a, 25a, 55a and 58a.
[48] See *Hld* 9b, 40b, 54b, 57b and 59b. The verbs in 40b and 54b are infinitives, which were more strongly stressed than finite verbs, but probably provided a better match than nouns or adjectives (*OEM*, §9.9). The weak line-final arsis is also a favoured location for verb roots in Old Norse poetry (see above, p. 126).
[49] *DGV*, pp. 113–14.

In the *Heliand,* Sxx simplexes with unsyncopated vowels occupy the same metrical locations as Sxx preterites of weak class II.[50] *Hildebrandslied* contains no relevant class II forms, but Sxx simplexes are placed very much as in the *Heliand*:

(18) luttilo / wurtun[51]   (67b)
      [Sxx/Sx]

(19) ferahes / frōtoro[52]   (8a)
      [Sx/Sxx, first S resolved]

If these trisyllabic simplexes had the metrical value Ssx, we would expect the poet to locate them most often in the second foot of type C, creating a verse with the normal number of stresses. Example (15) is the only variant of its kind in the poem, however, and there are five variants like example (18).[53] Example (19) is a long, heavy verse on the Ssx analysis but has standard weight on the Sxx analysis.[54]

Morphological constraints on the Ssx foot in heavy verses seem quite strict in *Hildebrandslied,* as the following examples illustrate:

(20) barn / unwahsan[55]   (21b)
      [S/Ssx]

(21) sēo- / līdante[56]   (42b)
      [S/Ssx]

(22) chind, / (in) chunincrīche[57]   (13a)
      [S/(x)Ssx, second S resolved]

(23) gurtun / (sih iro) suert ana[58]   (5b)
      [Sx/(xxx)Ssx]

(24) Heribrantes / suno[59]   (44b)
      [Ssx/S, first and second S resolved]

The poem contains eight Da variants of the form S/Ssx and Sx/Ssx. Three of these examples are two-word paradigms with an Ssx word in the second foot, like (20). Two others like (21) are wholly filled by large compounds. In two cases like (22), the only elements of complexity are extrametrical

---

50 See above, p. 168.   51 'became small ...'   52 'more experienced in life ...'
53 See *Hld* 15b, 20b, 33b and 62b. The relevant medial vowels in the Sxx words would be short even in Old High German.
54 If we are dealing with an OHG *frōtōro,* the long medial vowel might have been stressed, in which case the Ssx analysis might be forced.
55 'a young child ...'   56 'seafarers ...'   57 'boy, in the kingdom ...'
58 'girded on their swords ...'   59 'Heribrand's son'. Repeated as 45b.

words before the second foot.[60] Example (23), which also has extra-metrical words before the second foot, is the only type Da variant in the poem with an Ssx word group. The *Beowulf* poet permits extrametrical words before the second foot in only about eighteen of more than 350 comparable S/Ssx verses and in only three or four of more than 120 Sx/Ssx verses.[61] Like the *Heliand, Hildebrandslied* is much less strict in this regard. On the other hand, the author of *Hildebrandslied* makes a respectable effort to fill the Ssx foot of type Da with a compound, doing so in seven of eight cases. In the simpler type C, as we saw, six of thirteen examples have a word group in the Ssx foot. Example (24) and its repetition at *Hld* 45b provide the only examples of type E in the poem. The inherent complexity of this reversed pattern is mitigated by its simple two-word realization.

In the most common B subtype, the second foot corresponds to the low-frequency compound pattern Sxs. The *Beowulf* poet must often coin a poetic compound to fill the Sxs foot of this subtype in the most desirable way, and manages to do so in about 9 per cent of total instances. Two of eighteen comparable verses in *Hildebrandslied* have a compound in the second foot, a respectable 11 per cent of total instances.[62] The proportion of variants with an Sxs compound rises, as expected, in the heavy type

---

[60] With example (20) cf. the two-word Sx/Ssx variants *Hld* 26a and 66a. With (21) cf. *Hld* 4a. With (22) cf. *Hld* 5a, an Sx/Ssx variant with two extrametrical words before the second foot.

[61] Old English S/Ssx with extrametrical words before the second foot (excluding variants with anacrusis): *Beo* 356a, 473a, 612a, 896a, 1162a, 1454a, 1727a, 1790a, 1863a, 2471a, 2751a, 2936a, 3077a (assuming stressed *oft*); 1323b, 1724b, 1840b, 1997b and 2863b. In *Beo* 612a, the second foot might have the form Sxx rather than Ssx. Old English Sx/Ssx variants with extrametrical words before the second foot: *Beo* 712a, 1941a and 2562a. Example 1724b is probably S/Ssx, but would be Sx/Ssx if the epenthetic vowel was recognized in the scansion. Example 2047a is probably type C, since auxiliaries like *meaht* do not normally occupy an arsis even when their onsets match those of alliterating constituents.

[62] The type B verses with compounds are *Hld* 30a and 44a. Observe that both appear in the first half of the line, perhaps in accord with a weaker form of the principle operative in type C, which always has a compound in the a-verse. The other a-verses of type B are *Hld* 12a, 15a, 39a, 41a, 42a and 53a. Of these only *Hld* 12a ends with a finite verb, but there are six such b-verses (*Hld* 6b, 12b, 35b, 43b, 55b and 64b). The b-verses that do not end with a finite verb are *Hld* 3b, 19b, 22b and 24b. Here again a principle operative in type C seems to act in a weaker form, assigning verb-final variants preferentially to the second half of the line.

Db, an inherently complex pattern that is intolerant of additional complexity (see U4):

> (25) chūd / (ist mir al) irmindeot[63]   (13b)
>   [S/(xxx)Sxs]
> (26) westar / (ubar) wentilsẹ̄o[64]   (43a)
>   [Sx/(xx)Sxs]
> (27) welaga / (nū,) waltant got[65]   (49a)
>   [Sx/(x)Sxs, first S resolved]

The *Beowulf* poet has an Sxs compound in 28 per cent of Db verses that reduce to S/Sxs when unstressed words are excluded as extrametrical. Example (25), the only comparable verse in *Hildebrandslied*, contains an Sxs compound. Examples (26) and (27) must be analysed as Sx/Sxs variants because their verse-initial trochaic words cannot be split by the foot boundary (see R2a). Of the verses with this pattern in *Beowulf*, about half have a compound in the second foot. *Hildebrandslied* seems at first to show the same proportion in its two examples, but (27) probably contains a compound *waltantgot* rather than a word group.[66]

In *Beowulf*, S/Sxs verses never have three extrametrical words before the second foot, and Sx/Sxs verses never have any extrametrical words before the second foot. The parenthesized constituents in examples (25)–(27) would probably have been unacceptable by strict Old English standards. Standards were different for continental West Germanic poets, however. In *Hildebrandslied*, as in the *Heliand*, the weak linguistic stress of the natural language yielded a weak metrical stress that sanctioned relatively free employment of extrametrical words.[67]

Hildebrandslied bears a close resemblance to the *Heliand* in its high frequency of long type B variants:

---

[63] 'I know about all the important people.'
[64] 'west over the [Mediterranean?] sea ... '   [65] 'Woe now, ruling God ... '
[66] In *Heliand*, ed. Sievers, the cognate OS constituent is printed as a word group at line 20b (no doubt because the case form has uncertain status), but Sievers remarks in his note, 'besser wäre vielleicht mit Heyne und Rückert stets *uualdandgod*' (p. 508). A cognate Old English compound is attested in the *Paris Psalter*, where uninflected *wealdend-* appears twice in the dative singular form *wealdendgode* (at metrical psalms 56.2, 2 and 67.16, 3). Lack of alliteration on *irmin-deot* of example (25) suggests that this is not a poetic compound (*OEM*, §8.5). Note that the term is not a redundant phrase meaning simply 'people'.
[67] See above, p. 137.

(28)   forn her / ōstar giweit[68]   (*Hld* 18a)
      [xx/Sxxs]

(29)   hue queðad / gi, that ik sî[69]   (*Hel* 3052a)
      [xxx/Sxxs]

In *Beowulf*, long variants with a second foot of the form Sxxs account for about 20 per cent of total type B verses. The proportion of long type B in *Hildebrandslied* is 31 per cent (8/26).[70] Principle P2 predicts this significantly higher percentage for a language with restricted syncopation in which Sxxs compounds are more familiar and the corresponding foot is therefore less complex. As in the *Heliand*, the less marginal status of the Sxxs foot seems to license Sxxs word groups that seldom or never appear in *Beowulf*. In the Old English poem, the vast majority of Sxxs word groups contain a trochaic word and a prefixed monosyllabic stressed word, imitating the structure of compounds like *sibbe-ge-driht*.[71] Of eight long B verses in *Hildebrandslied*, on the other hand, only example (28) and one other verse have this type of structure (see *Hld* 8b). One might think of eliminating the exception to K1 by removing *dū* from the offending *eddo hwelīhhes / cnuosles dū sīs* (example (8) above). If this were grammatically acceptable, the line would reduce to a less complex type B variant with a second foot of the form Sxs. Placement of a personal pronoun on the second x of an Sxxs foot is clearly permissible, however, in Old Saxon variants like example (29), which may occur as a-verses or b-verses.[72] There is no easy emendation for *mit / gēru scal man* (example (6)), another long B verse with a kind of Sxxs word group unattested in *Beowulf*. It seems best to suppose that traditions in which syncopation had limited scope could exploit the Sxxs foot rather freely as a useful location for word groups.[73] Note, however, that this freedom is exercised primarily in verses with the normal number of stresses. In the inherently complex

---

[68] 'long ago he went east ... '   [69] 'who do you say that I am ... '

[70] Long B variants: *Hld* 18a (example 28), 37a, 56a; 7b, 8b, 11b, 18b and 27b. Normal B variants: *Hld* 12a, 15a, 30a, 39a, 41a, 42a, 44a, 53a; 3b, 6b, 12b, 19b, 22b, 24b, 35b, 43b, 55b and 64b.

[71] See above, p. 53.   [72] Cf. *Hel* 1522a, 2510a, 3404a, 2028b and 5542b.

[73] In Ælfric's rhythmical prose, where word-foot constraints are disregarded, the proportion of verses analysable as long type B rises sharply, and we encounter many Sxxs word groups that the *Beowulf* poet would not employ (*OEM*, §10.5, pp. 141–2). The long type B pattern must have been quite useful.

heavy verses, as we have seen, the poet avoids the additional complexity caused by word groups within the foot.

Certain Old High German inflectional vowels retained etymological length even though they had no stress.[74] If unstressed vowels could be long, we would expect a relatively weak bias against long syllables and resolved sequences on deeply subordinated s positions of an Old High German poem, even weaker than the bias in the *Heliand*. The distribution of long syllables in *Hildebrandslied* seems consistent with Old High German provenance, but this evidence can hardly be regarded as conclusive, since the number of relevant verses is quite small. Our analysis of syllable placement in the *Heliand* focused on two-word verses with an Ssx compound.[75] All six comparable examples from *Hildebrandslied* have a long syllable on the s position. Three of these correspond to Old Saxon types in which the s position is always or nearly always occupied by a long syllable. The three others, however, correspond to Old Saxon types that often have a short syllable on the s position.[76] The total number of type C verses in *Hildebrandslied*, including all putative variants, is thirteen. The only one of these with a short syllable on the s position is *Hld* 57b. More than a third of the corresponding Old Saxon variants have a short syllable on this position.[77] In *Beowulf*, no more than 8 per cent of the type B verses have a resolved syllable on the s position of an Sxs foot, and about a third of these should probably be analysed as type C.[78] In

---

[76] With *Hld* 26a and 66a (Sx/Ssx) compare *Hel* 1007a. With *Hld* 26b (type C) compare *Hel* 4356b. *Hld* 21b (S/Ssx), with single alliteration, corresponds to four OS variants like *Hel* 2146a, which all have a long syllable on the s position. *Hld* 44b and 45b (Ssx/S) correspond to Old Saxon type E variants that almost always have a long syllable on the s position, with the single exception of *Hel* 3697b.

[77] See Hofmann, *Versstrukturen* II, 143–62. *Hld* 5a and 5b probably exemplify use of a short syllable on the s position of the type Da pattern, the most favourable site for non-resolution, but these are not clear two-word cases. It would in fact be quite difficult to prove that short syllables could stand unresolved if we restricted our attention to *Hildebrandslied*. The one clear case in Old High German poetry is *Wessobrunner Gebet* 2b, *noh / ūf-himil*, which would be too short if *-himil* underwent resolution.

[78] Terasawa, 'Metrical Constraints', p. 7.

Hildebrandslied, there are eighteen type B verses with a second foot of the form Sxs, and five of these (28 per cent) provide clear cases of resolved s.[79] Such verses are also common in the *Heliand*, however, so they provide no special evidence for High German authorship.

Few clear cases of the Ss foot appear in *Hildebrandslied*. There are some putative examples of the A2 subtype Ss/Sx, but these cannot bear much theoretical weight:

(30)	ummet / spāher[80]	(39b)
	[Ss/Sx or Sx/Sx]	
(31)	wēwurt / skihit[81]	(49b)
	[Ss/Sx, second S unresolved]	
(32)	staim bort chludun[82]	(65b)
	[?Ss/Sx, second S unresolved]	

The scribal spelling *ummet* in example (30) attests lexicalization of earlier *un-met*, with assimilation of *n* to following *m*. If this form was lexicalized in the poet's language as well, losing the stress on its secondary constituent, (30) would be a two-word expression of the standard pattern Sx/Sx. The same analysis would then apply to the similar *Hld* 25b. Another putative Ss/Sx variant is example (31). This has uncertain value, however, since the self-alliterating compound *wēwurt* violates the constraint against double alliteration in the b-verse. Example (32) would scan as Ss/Sx if the obscure string *staim bort* represents an Ss compound.[83]

The light type A3 pattern xx/Sx behaves as expected in *Hildebrandslied*, but there are some odd variants of the heavier A3 pattern xx/Ss:

(33)	(dat dū) habes / hēme[84]	(*Hld* 47a)
	[(xx)xx/Sx]	
(34)	(sō imo) se der / chuning gap[85]	(*Hld* 34b)
	[(xxx)xx/Ss, S resolved]	
(35)	thar the / heri dranc[86]	(*Hel* 2001b)
	[xx/Ss, S resolved]	

---

[79] *Hld* 6b, 12a, 19b, 22b and 35b. [80] 'very clever...' Cf. 25b.
[81] 'an evil fate is coming to pass'. [82] Meaning uncertain.
[83] See Hofmann, *Versstrukturen* II, 294. [84] 'that you have at home...'
[85] 'which the king had given him...' [86] 'where the people drank...'

All the xx/Sx variants of *Hildebrandslied* appear in the a-verse, and all have at least one extrametrical word to support the xx foot, like example (33).[87] The continental Germanic poet handles this pattern with the same care evident in *Beowulf*.[88] Examples (34) and (35), on the other hand, look like unusual variants of the xx/Ss pattern with resolved S and a word group in the second foot. In *Beowulf*, heavy A3 verses always have a compound in the second foot, and always occur in the first half of the line. Variants like (34) and (35) are not peculiar to *Hildebrandslied*. The *Heliand* contains a number of b-verses like (108c), and *Muspilli* provides an analogous Old High German example.[89] Observe that the second element of the Ss word group in (34) and (35) is a finite verb, which provides a good match for the s position.

The *Beowulf* poet probably restricts the xx/Ss pattern to the a-verse along with the xx/Sx pattern because the boundary between Ss words and Sx words is somewhat blurred.[90] Since all instances of xx/Ss in the Old English poem contain Ss compounds, they all look rather like xx/Sx verses, which are excluded from the second half of the line to avoid overlap with the opening segment of the most common hypermetrical b-verse pattern, xx//Sx/Sx.[91] Continental Germanic variants like (34) and (35) bear no significant resemblance to this opening segment, however, and may have caused no significant problems of metrical ambiguity. The analogues in *Muspilli* and the *Heliand* make it implausible to characterize verses like (19) as unmetrical.[92]

The name *Hiltibrant* appears in several peculiar verses. One of these may be a type A1 variant:

$$\text{(36)} \quad \text{Hiltibrant / (gi-)mahalta}^{93} \qquad \text{(7a)}$$
$$[?\text{Sxx}/(\text{x})\text{Sx, second S resolved}]$$

Even the relatively tolerant *Heliand* poet excludes unambiguous Sxs compounds from initial position. Verse (36) has normal scansion,

---

[87] See above, p. 48. Other clear cases of xx/Sx are *Hld* 48a, 51a, 63a and 67a. The isolated verses at lines 1 and 46 may belong here as well.

[88] See above, p. 50.

[89] Cf. *Hel* 2014b, 2572b, 2780b, 2930b, 5730b and 5738b. Comparable examples in the first half of the line are *Hel* 3805a and 4226a. Sievers (*AGM*, §128.5) notes that *Muspilli* 11a has a similar structure.

[90] *OEG*, §88.   [91] *OEM*, §5.3, n. 10.   [92] *Pace* Sievers, *AGM*, §128.5.

[93] 'Hildebrand spoke ... ' Repeated as 45a.

however, if the secondary constituent of the proper name occupies an x position rather than an s position, something that happens occasionally in Old English verse. The only examples in *Beowulf* involve the Ssx forms *Bēowulfes* (501b), *Æschere* (1329b) and *Higelāce* (1830b). Since secondary root syllables usually occupy s positions even in proper names, we would not expect to find comparable examples among the rarer Sxs proper name forms, of which there are only eleven in the Old English poem.[94]

Some heavy verses in *Hildebrandslied* deviate more conspicuously from Old English practice:

(37)	Hiltibrantes / sunu[95] [?Sxsx/S]	(*Hld* 14b)
(38)	cheisuringu / (gi-)tān[96] [?Sxsx/(x)S]	(*Hld* 34a)
(39)	sundilôsan / (gi-)sald[97] [?Sxsx/(x)S]	(*C5*148a)
(40)	giâmarlîcara / (for-)gang[98] [?Sxsxx/(x)S]	(*Hel* 735a)
(41)	ôðar- / lîcora[99] [Sx/Sxx]	(*Hel* 3123b)

The twice-repeated (37) appears on both occasions in the familiar 'X spoke, Y's son' formula. Unlike the grammatically identical *Heribrantes suno* (example (24)), example (37) cannot undergo resolution of the first two syllables in the compound proper name, and cannot therefore be analysed as type E (Ssx/S). Example (38) would scan as type E with an extrametrical syllable before the second foot if *cheisur-* could be resolved, but *ei* generally represents a long diphthong, and analogous borrowings in other Germanic languages have long diphthongs or long vowels in the first syllable.[100] Turning to the *Heliand*, we find the same type of reversed pattern with a long first foot (example (39)). The Old Saxon poem contains some variants like example (40) with even longer feet in verse-initial position, and these feet sometimes overlap short verses like

---

[94] These appear in *Beo* 1071a, 1114a, 2486a, 2924a, 2951a, 2961a, 2986a; 2477b, 2925b, 2935b and 3031b. The names of major characters may have been the most likely to appear in reduced form, which probably correlated with familiarity and repetition.

[95] 'Hildebrand's son ... ' Repeated as 36b.   [96] 'made of imperial gold ... '

[97] 'betrayed the sinless one'.   [98] 'a sadder death ... '

[99] 'otherwise ... ' Cf. *Hel* 155b.   [100] Gothic *kaisar*, OE *cāsere*, OS *kêsur*.

example (41). It must have been somewhat difficult to determine that the long verse-initial word in (40) counted as one foot, while the same type of word counted as two feet in (41). The form *Hiltibrantes* would have posed the same type of problem in (37). Sxsx compounds like *ōstarliuto* can constitute whole Sx/Sx verses, as in example (5) above. If the audience interpreted *Hiltibrantes* as Sx/Sx, the following *sunu* would present the appearance of an unmetrical third foot. Example (38) poses a somewhat different problem. In this verse, the form *cheisuringu* is long, but cannot be analysed as two word feet because *-ingu* does not correspond to an independent lexical item. We cannot determine what constraints would be imposed on such words in *Beowulf* because the poem contains none.[101] The available evidence, then, suggests that *Hildebrandslied* derived from a tradition with relatively weak constraints on overlap and reversal. The higher frequency of long words in continental West Germanic languages seems to have diminished the complexity of the corresponding feet, allowing for freer experimentation with reversed patterns. Note, however, that the overlapping feet of (37) and (38) are occupied by words rather than word groups. In these examples, as in other complex heavy variants, the poet takes special pains to fill the compound foot in the simplest way (see U4).[102]

Most examples of anacrusis in *Hildebrandslied* have no parallels in *Beowulf*, and many are peculiar even by the standards of the *Heliand*:

(42) (gi-)wigan miti / wābnum[103]   (*Hld* 68a)
     [(x)Sxx/Sx, first S resolved]

(43) (her fur-)laet in / lante[104]   (*Hld* 20a)
     [(xx)Sx/Sx]

(44) (ih wallota) sumaro / (enti) wintro[105]   (*Hld* 50a)
     [(xxxx)Sx/(xx)Sx, first S resolved]

(45) (folgodun ênun) berhtun / bôkne[106]   (*Hel* 545a)
     [(xxxxx)Sx/Sx]

---

[101] On the metrical value of non-Germanic words in other Old English poems, see *OEG*, §§548, 549 and 551.

[102] The *Heliand* poet employs a few verses like *uuîsas mannas / uuord* (503a). If we divide this at the major syntactic break (indicated by the slash), the result is a variant comparable to examples (37)–(38), but with a word group in the first foot. Sxsx/S verses are listed as heavy variants of type E in Hofmann, *Versstrukturen* II, 210–12.

[103] 'damaged in battle by weapons ...'   [104] 'he left behind in this land ...'

[105] 'I wandered (sixty) summers and winters ...'   [106] 'followed a bright beacon ...'

The most common type of a-verse anacrusis in the *Heliand* consists of an isolated prefix. *Hildebrandslied* does contain one such verse, example (42), but there are five verses like (43) and (44), which seem to have major function words in anacrusis, and in four cases the anacrusis seems to extend beyond two syllables, something that never happens in *Beowulf*.[107] In the *Heliand*, where unusually long anacruses do occur, they have about one-fourth the frequency of variants comparable to (42).[108] Example (44), with a trisyllabic verb in anacrusis, has no close parallel in the cognate traditions. One verse from the *Heliand* seems to have such a verb in anacrusis (45), but this example has a main part of the form Sx/Sx occupied by two trochaic words. Here as elsewhere in the *Heliand* the simplicity of the main part mitigates the complexity of the anacrusis. No such mitigation is evident in (44), which has a major function word as an extrametrical constituent before the second foot of the main part. If all putative examples in *Hildebrandslied* were authentic, the poem would attest a tradition with no evident constraints on anacrusis in the a-verse, differing utterly in this respect from the cognate traditions. Sievers had good reasons to regard (44) as interpolated prose.[109] It is worth adding, simply as further evidence of corruption, that most of the problematic anacruses could be repaired by deletion of inessential words.[110]

---

[107] Other putative examples from the first half of the line with major function words in anacrusis: *Hld* 27a, 59a and 65a. *Hld* 61a belongs here as well if we divide the line in the way recommended by Hofmann (*Versstrukturen* II, 294). Other putative examples like (44), with three or more syllables in anacrusis: *Hld* 27a, 59a and 61a. *Hld* 52a might have four syllables in anacrusis, but its metrical pattern is difficult to specify, since words like *ēnigeru* are unparalleled in the Old English and Old Norse traditions. If we are dealing with a long vocalic affix in an OHG *ēnīgeru*, the word might be interpretable as Ssxx, but words with this pattern were not usually employed at the end of the line, to judge from the *Heliand.*

[108] See above, p. 147.   [109] *AGM*, §125.

[110] Removal of *her* from example (43) would yield a variant like (42) with the normal sort of prefixal anacrusis. Removal of *hiutu* from *Hld* 61a would yield an ordinary a-verse of type A3 if we divide the line after *hregilo*. Removal of *dō* from *Hld* 65a would eliminate the anacrusis, yielding a type A1 variant *stōptun tō samane*. Alternatively, *dō* could be relocated after the verb, as in Old English variants with cognate *þā*, e.g. *Grāp þā tōgēanes* (*Beo* 1501a). Finally, deletion of *her was eo* from *Hld* 27a would yield the A1 variant *folches at ente*, which might do as an adjunct to the sentence above, though verses with this structure tend to have double alliteration. I can think of no plausible way to eliminate the anacrusis in *Hld* 59a, *(der dir nū) wīges / warne*. This is not problematic in a continental Germanic poem, however, since the main part of the

Some b-verses in *Hildebrandslied* have anacruses of a kind not found in *Beowulf*:

(46) (sō dū ēwin) inwit / fōrtos[111]   (*Hld* 41b)
      [(xxxx)Sx/Sx]
(47) (Than sat im the) landes / hirdi[112]   (*Hel* 1286b)
      [(xxxx)Sx/Sx]
(48) (in) folc / sceotantero[113]   (*Hld* 51b)
      [(x)S/Ssxx?]
(49) þæs ic on / scēotendum[114]   (*GenA* 2144b)
      [xxx/Ssx]

The complexity of example (46) is mitigated by the simplicity of its main part, which has two trochaic words, as with many comparable b-verses in the *Heliand* (e.g. (47)). Example (48) looks like a heavy verse with anacrusis, but is suspect for two quite different reasons. Note, first, that the genitive plural simplex *sceotantero* has the pattern Ssxx, with a long second syllable and two unstressed syllables word-finally. Words of this form appear in the *Heliand*, but never as the second foot of a b-verse like (48).[115] Note too the absence of alliteration on the fully stressed noun *folc*, which is not preceded by any other stressed word in (48). A verse with this sort of alliterative pattern would be unmetrical in any of the cognate traditions.[116] If (48) is authentic, it testifies to an unparalleled

verse consists of two trochaic words, as in numerous examples from the *Heliand*. The trisyllabic anacrusis in *Hld* 59a is expected due to the presence of trisyllabic articles in the language, e.g. *desero* in *Hld* 62a (see above, p. 157). Line 50 remains a desperate case.
[111] 'because you always used cunning'.
[112] 'the guardian of the land then sat down ...'
[113] 'among the troop of warriors ...'   [114] 'which I among warriors ...'
[115] Ssxx simplexes seem to be confined for most part to first position in the verse pattern Ssxx/S, as in *hêleandero* / *bezt* (*Hel* 3156b). Similar Old Saxon b-verses are *Hel* 2635b, 2678b, 2811b, 3606b, 3630b and 4036b. A-verses: 2031a, 2180a, 3061a, 3558a, 4915a (as emended by Hofmann), 5218a and 5858a. Ssxx compounds also prefer the first foot of the Ssxx/S pattern: cf. *Hel* 670a, 698a, 736a, 745a, 1192a, 2055a, 2085a, 2120a, 2472a, 2819a, 2878a, 4326a, 4331a, 4948a (assuming syncopation), 5977a; 660b and 4225b. An Ssxx simplex appears as the second foot of the relatively light a-verse *that he im thero* / *costondero* (*Hel* 4741a), but I found no other examples of this kind in the poem.
[116] Monosyllabic nouns and adjectives may appear without alliteration at the beginning of the verse when used predicatively (Kuhn, 'Wortstellung', pp. 82–4). Example (48)

Hildebrandslied

alliterative practice. We may have to deal here with a type of scribal trivialization that substituted 'troop of shooting ones' for a more compressed and less idiomatic 'shooting ones'.[117] The phrase *on sceotantem* would constitute a simple two-word variant of type C and would be good Germanic idiom, if we may judge from example (49) and two other Old English analogues.[118] Accepting all alliterative patterns in the poem as evidence for continental Germanic practice would be quite implausible, of course. The otherwise unremarkable line 15 has no alliteration at all, and both alliterating words in line 60 are badly misplaced according to standards observed in all cognate traditions, as Sievers pointed out.[119] We should not claim to know for certain what the poet intended at *Hld* 51b, but it would be equally inappropriate to declare such a verse well-formed.[120]

I would distinguish violations like those in lines 15, 51 and 60 from another kind of deviance pointed out by Sievers.[121] It seems clear that the author of *Hildebrandslied* sanctioned alliteration on a finite verb when the following noun did not alliterate, something that happens three times in this brief work.[122] The testimony of *Hildebrandslied* casts further doubt

is anomalous, but there are no problems in *Mæl is mē tō fēran* (*Beo* 316a, alliteration on *fēran*); *Mál er mér at ríða* (*HH II* 49/1, alliteration on *ríða*); or *tōt ist Hiltibrant* (*Hld* 44a, alliteration on *Hiltibrant*). Kuhn's point is worth reiterating, since verses of this kind are apparently regarded as unmetrical even by such careful observers as McLintock ('Metre and Rhythm', p. 571) and Kendall (*Metrical Grammar*, p. 51 n. 23).

[117] See *OEM*, §10.3. An anonymous reviewer suggested dividing line 51 after *folc* (*dar man mih eo / scerita in folc // sceo- / tantero*). The a-verse then analyses as (xxx)x/Sxxs and the b-verse as S/Sxx. This seems to me the best way to divide the line as it stands, though there may be a problem with the principle of syntactic integrity (U1), since the posited midline syntactic break after *folc* seems significantly weaker than the break after *scerita*.

[118] *Ex* 112a, *Beo* 1026a.   [119] *AGM*, §126.

[120] Most textual critics acknowledge some degree of corruption in *Hildebrandslied* (see McLintock, 'Metre and Rhythm', p. 573). Another remarkable b-verse with anacrusis is 16b, evidently an Sxx/Sx variant. Such variants never have anacrusis in *Beowulf*, but the enhanced frequency of Sxx words in continental Germanic may have made the Sxx/Sx pattern less complex and Sxx/Sx variants with anacrusis more acceptable.

[121] *AGM*, §126.

[122] *Hld* 5b, 33a and 40a. *Hld* 33a and 40a are the only well-formed a-verses in which a prepositional object on the second primary arsis fails to alliterate (setting aside *Hld* 27a, with its peculiar anacrusis). The non-alliterating word group *suert ana* in the

191

on the theory that alliterating finite verbs counted as unstressed when placed near the beginning of the verse.[123]

SUMMARY

Some unusual variants in *Hildebrandslied* exhibit authentic features of continental Germanic versecraft. Parallel variants in the *Heliand* show that this tradition imposed relatively few constraints on reversal, allowing for employment of heavy patterns unattested in the Old English and Old Norse traditions. Assignment of a single word to the first foot of reversed patterns often mitigated their complexity, however.

According to the word-foot theory, the less forceful primary stress of continental Germanic languages, which eliminated relatively few weak syllables, should yield a less forceful metrical stress, allowing for more weak syllables in the verse. As expected, we observe a distinctly higher frequency of extrametrical words in *Hildebrandslied* and the *Heliand*. To the extent that unstressed words took over the functions of case endings, their incorporation into the verse would have been a practical necessity, of course. What I wish to emphasize is that bowing to any such necessity would have been sanctioned by natural evolution of the rule system.

Some verses in *Hildebrandslied* have no analogues in the *Heliand* and seem to result from problems of manuscript transmission. Easy emendations are available for most of these, but it is often difficult to reconstruct the author's intention, especially when more than one familiar type of scribal error could produce the result we observe. The number of verses isolated as unmetrical by the word-foot theory is consistent with the generally problematic character of the text, which exhibits obvious

second foot of 5b also seems unusual (see ch. 7 and *OEM*, §8.4). Verses with this type of alliteration may have been derived from formulas of type A3, B or C in which the finite verb did not normally alliterate. The useful option of alliterating on the verb would have produced verses that were metrically unusual, though not unmetrical.

[123] *Hld* 17 would violate widespread constraints on alliteration if the alliterating finite verbs *hǣtti* and *heittu* occupied an arsis. These forms might be taken as auxiliaries, in which case they could occupy x positions and their alliterative matching could be disregarded (see Stanley, 'Alliterative Ornament', p. 212). Within the framework employed here, the line is problematic quite independently of its alliterative peculiarities. The a-verse, *dat Hiltibrant hǣtti mīn fater*, seems to scan as Sxs/S, a complex pattern not reliably attested in the *Heliand*; and the complexity of this pattern is further aggravated by an unusual anacrusis consisting of a conjunction.

irregularities such as lack of alliteration, lack of a second verse within the line and interpolation of discourse markers.

Systematic distribution of familiar variants, notably in types C and A3, tells against the hypothesis that *Hildebrandslied* is metrically casual rather than distorted by transmission. Violations of Kuhn's laws clearly do not indicate a general relaxation of metrical standards, since the poet continues to respect the principle of closure (U3), which imposes many similar requirements. Metrical features shared with the *Heliand* have important implications for analysis of the Old Saxon work. Scribes might sometimes have altered the original text of the *Heliand* for theological reasons, but there is no comparable motive for altering a poem on a native heroic subject. *Hildebrandslied* supports the impression of Hofmann that the *Heliand* manuscripts give us authentic information about continental Germanic versecraft.[124]

[124] *Versstrukturen* I, 50.

12

Conclusions

In this study I have sought comparative evidence for the word-foot theory of *OEM*, which was derived primarily from *Beowulf*, and I have also attempted to validate Lehmann's claim that the development of Germanic verse form was influenced by changes in stress and associated linguistic processes. Analysis of relevant problems at the level of fine detail has necessarily been somewhat piecemeal. Here I offer a synthesis. The survey of evidence for the word-foot theory takes the form of a comparison to the five-types system of Sievers, with attention to descriptive as well as explanatory issues.

LIMITATIONS OF THE FIVE-TYPES SYSTEM

Though often designated *Sievers's Theory*, the five-types system is primarily a method of classification, taxonomic rather than explanatory. As a taxonomist, Sievers has proved remarkably successful. Verses excluded from his system have been found wanting again and again by editors for reasons quite independent of the metre.[1] The refinement of Sievers's system by Bliss is the current standard for philological application in the Old English field.[2] Sievers's theoretical proposals are less widely accepted. As Bliss points out, the five-types system fails to explain just why certain verse patterns occur freely while others are avoided or subject to special constraints.[3]

Sievers claims that the metrical constant of the verse is its number of stresses, supposedly two, but he applies this principle quite inconsistently, counting secondary stress as significant for classes B and C but not

---

[1] *OEM*, ch. 10.   [2] See Fulk, *History of Old English Meter*, §30.   [3] *Metre*, §122.

for classes A, D or E. As he assigns subtypes to types and types to his two-stress paradigm, Sievers too often proceeds *ad hoc*, diminishing the empirical content of his claim that the types form a manageably small, coherent system.[4] The secondary stress of type A2, for example, interacts crucially with Sievers's rule of resolution, but must be disregarded when A2 verses are subsumed under type A.[5] Bliss realizes that his own sharpening of Sievers's system has resulted in a further proliferation of types, making it extremely difficult to understand how Germanic metre could have been learned or appreciated – perhaps, he thinks, impossible.[6]

PROBLEMS OF DESCRIPTION

Word-foot scansions are very concrete. They often correspond exactly to the detailed scansions used by Sievers to represent his subtypes. Thus the word-foot scansion Ss/Sx corresponds exactly to the detailed scansion for subtype A2a, apart from trivial matters of notation.[7] In types D and E, the detailed scansion for a given Sievers subtype can be derived from the corresponding word-foot notation by substituting his acute accent for my S, his grave accent for my *s* and his vertical bar for my slash (*x* remaining unchanged). The same procedure works for other subdivisions of subtype A2, represented in the word-foot theory as distinct verse patterns of the form Sx/Ss and Ss/Ss. Within the five-types system, detailed scansions for subtypes and their further subdivisions constitute an unmotivated, purely descriptive device, a necessary evil, in fact, since the system is justified by a supposed constraint on the number of verse patterns. The theory proposed here suffers no loss of explanatory power in granting independent status to Sievers's subtypes because it is justified by the naturalness and simplicity of the equation *foot* = *word*.

If we set aside the *ad-hoc* devices employed by Sievers to reduce the number of types, it becomes clear that his system does not employ significantly fewer verse patterns than the word-foot theory. The real work of the five-types system is done by unmotivated subtypes. The ill-defined character of Sievers's types makes it awkward to relate important metrical constraints to basic patterns and leads to proliferation of distinct types as new constraints are discovered. In the word-foot theory, the

---

[4] See Russom, 'Constraints on Resolution', p. 154.
[5] *AGM*, §§9.2 and 15.   [6] *Metre*, §129.   [7] *AGM*, §16.

number of types is limited by the number of word patterns in the natural language and cannot proliferate arbitrarily. Constraints attributed by Bliss to the placement of his caesura can be attributed to deviations from two-word norms. Thus the word-foot theory provides a more precise descriptive method in addition to its more plausible explanatory account.

HEAVY VERSES

Many verses of types A2, D and E consist of a compound and a stressed simplex. Representative heavy a-verses with double alliteration are *Hym* 10/3, *harðráðr* / *Hymir* (Ss/Sx); *Vsp* 33/7, *vá* / *Valhallar* (S/Ssx); *Beo* 1747a, *wōm* / *wundǫrbebodum* (S/Sxs); and *Hel* 3399a, *uuársaguno* / *uuord* (Ssx/S). There are also a number of verses like *Þrk* 21/7, *óc* / *Óðins sonr* (S/Sxs), with a heavy foot occupied by a word group. Division of these verses at the point indicated by the slash is forced by bracketing rule R2, which requires that the verse-medial foot boundary coincide with the major syntactic break. Sievers uses the same syntactic criterion for division of heavy verses and his scansions usually correspond to mine.[8]

The five-types system restricts alliteration to the primary arsis of the foot. This restriction fails to account for the small but significant number of verses like *Vsp* 32/5, *Baldrs bróðir* / *var* (Ssx/S), which has two alliterating constituents in the first foot when divided at the major syntactic break. Sievers defends his alliterative rule against selected counter-examples with *ad-hoc* syntactic divisions.[9] The counter-examples with a compound word in the first foot, which he simply ignores, seem decisive, however (cf. *Beo* 1538a, *Gūð-Gēata* / *lēod* (Ssx/S); *Hel* 1433a, *uuorduuîse* / *man* (Ssx/S)). The word-foot theory predicts, correctly, that heavy verses will sometimes alliterate on a secondary arsis in the first foot, which is the weak constituent of a strong constituent, but never on a secondary arsis in the second foot, which is the weak constituent of a weak constituent (see R8b). The number of heavy variants like *Beo* 1538a and *Hel* 1433a is predicted, correctly, to be small, since the primary arsis of the second foot has the second-greatest metrical prominence within the a-verse and is therefore the more natural site for optional alliteration, though not the only one. If we restricted attention to *Beowulf*, variants like 1538a might be dismissed as oversights of the poet, but comparative

---

[8] Ibid., §23.3.   [9] Ibid., §23.3a.

evidence makes such a manoeuvre less credible. The cognate traditions show the predicted small number of cases with double alliteration in the first foot and no cases of double alliteration in the second foot of type D or A2. This systematic gap seems especially significant because a high percentage of heavy verses have a second foot occupied by a compound or word group.[10]

THE SXX FOOT

Sievers's scansion of A1 verses usually corresponds to mine, trivial details of notation aside. For some variants, however, the word-foot scansion has a first foot with the pattern Sxx. This pattern cannot be expressed within the five-types system, which employs an undifferentiated thesis. The word-foot scansion for verses like *folgode / fruokno* (*Hel* 2995a) must be Sxx/Sx because labelling rule R1b mandates assignment of the unstressed syllables in *folgode* to separate x positions. Bracketing rule R2a, which requires that the foot boundary coincide with a word boundary, mandates a scansion of Sxx/Sx for verses like *liof endi / luttil* (*Hel* 740a), where the first foot is occupied by an Sxx word group. For the same reason, A2 variants like *uuord endi / uuîsdôm* (*Hel* 848a) must be scanned as Sxx/Ss.

Paradigmatic type C verses with the ultra-light pattern x/Sxx are *um / sacnaði* (*Þrk* 1/4) and *Sô / gornode* (*Hel* 5021a). Paradigmatic S/Sxx verses, representing the type D pattern of standard weight, are *mǫn / iafnaði* (*Þrk* 6/6) and *drôm / drohtines* (*Hel* 2084a). Sievers posits a light stress on the medial syllable in weak class II forms like *sacnaði* and *gornode*. He would assign this type of syllable to a secondary arsis when scanning C variants like *um / sacnaði* and *Sô / gornode*, bringing the number of significant stresses up to two, as required by the five-types system. There is no independent linguistic evidence, however, for preservation of medial stress in weak class II after shortening of medial vowels, which occurred before the period of interest here.[11] Stress seems very unlikely on the medial syllable of OS *drohtines*, which was restored after syncopation. Relative frequencies for verses with word-foot scansions of x/Sxx and S/Sxx indicate, as expected, that the former were lighter than normal and that the latter had standard weight.[12] Thus the Sxx pattern required by

---

[10] See above, p. 41.
[11] Fulk, *History of Old English Meter*, §261.   [12] See above, p. 115.

197

the word-foot theory for internal systematic reasons is required on empirical grounds as well.

TYPE A3

The word-foot scansion for type A3 has a light xx foot in first position. A paradigmatic two-word example is *spurði* / *Helgi* (*HH* 23/5), which alliterates on *H*- and is therefore scanned as xx/Sx. The type A designation is used here as a familiar label only; xx/Sx is posited as a distinct pattern with no special relation to type A1 (Sx/Sx). The five-types system, with its undifferentiated thesis, has no means for representation of an xx foot. To obtain the required number of four metrical positions for A3 verses, Sievers must scan them as type A1 variants with peculiar alliteration. The initial syllable of *spurði* in *spurði* / *Helgi* would be assigned to a primary arsis in a five-types scansion despite the fact that it fails to alliterate.[13] Sievers's analysis seems entirely *ad hoc*, since it often requires assignment to a primary arsis of a function word otherwise confined to the thesis. In an A3 variant like *í inom* / *mæra* (*Vsp* 28/9), Sievers would have to assign the non-alliterating preposition *í* to the primary arsis of the first foot. If this type of analysis is allowed, it is not at all clear what empirical content remains in the crucial term *arsis*.

According to Sievers, type A3 is confined to the a-verse by the head-stave rule, which requires alliteration on the first arsis of the b-verse. A b-verse with the structure of *í inom* / *mæra* would violate this rule if the non-alliterating preposition *í* occupied an arsis, as Sievers supposes. In the word-foot theory, type A3 is excluded from the b-verse only when it would overlap the opening segment of a hypermetrical pattern, creating confusion about the number of word feet. Comparative evidence shows that the five-types analysis is not only *ad hoc* but descriptively inadequate. In fornyrðislag, which abandoned hypermetrical patterns, type A3 does appear in the b-verse, as predicted by the word-foot analysis.[14]

TYPES B AND C

Ultra-light C verses with an Sxx word in the second foot have been discussed above. For the remaining B and C verses, the word-foot theory

[13] *AGM*, §19.2. Sievers gives the head-stave rule in this section.
[14] See above, p. 50.

posits a light first foot followed by a heavy foot with the pattern of a compound word. Paradigmatic two-word examples are *Vsp* 50/3, *snýz / iormungandr* (x/Sxs); and *Vsp* 9/2, *á / rǫcstóla* (x/Ssx). When a B or C verse has double alliteration, the second alliterating syllable usually lies within an independent word, and the second foot is then occupied by a word group. Typical examples with double alliteration are *HH* 54/3, *óx / geira gnýr* (x/Sxs); and *HH II* 16/3, *enn / iofur annan* (x/Ssx, S resolved). Assignment of heavy word groups to the second foot is independently necessary in type D. Word groups comparable to *geira gnýr* and *iofur annan* are routinely assigned by Sievers to the heavy second foot of D variants like *Þrk* 21/7, *óc / Óðins sonr* (S/Sxs); and *HH* 51/1, *Renni / raucn bitluð* (Sx/Ssx).

Sievers claims that all feet employed in Germanic metres had to contain a stress, like the feet of more familiar metres.[15] I see no reason why the equation *foot = word* should not sometimes apply in full generality, however, yielding light feet as well as heavy feet. The word-foot theory provides a straightforward account of an important artistic technique, the balancing of light feet against heavy feet in the B and C types, which have significantly higher frequency than the heavy D and E types.[16] This technique cannot easily be explained or even described by the five-types system proper, which posits the same number of significant stresses for every type. The relevant distinctions can only be notated *ad hoc*, in detailed scansions, a necessary evil for Sievers here as elsewhere. It would be absurd, of course, to claim that unstressed function words are imperceptible, though they are certainly less prominent than words of major category and do pose potential problems for intuitive scansion. As we saw in ch. 4, however, Germanic poets could avoid such problems by imposing constraints on isolated verse-initial constituents.

The five-types system forbids alliteration on the secondary arsis and must therefore supply a primary arsis in each foot to allow for double alliteration. As scanned by Sievers, the first foot in types B and C has rising rhythm, with a primary arsis for the first alliterating syllable. A second primary arsis, which can accommodate a second alliterating syllable, is supplied in the second foot. Sievers's rhythmical analyses for the B and C types seem quite implausible from a music-theoretical point

---

[15] *AGM*, §12.   [16] See above, p. 8.

of view.[17] His scansions also involve him in a major inconsistency here.[18] Although Sievers imposes syntactic criteria on division of heavy verses, he must often divide a B or C verse at the least plausible location, inside a simplex constituent. Thus *Vsp* 50/3 would have to be divided as *snýz ior- / mungandr*. *Hel* 5021a, an ultra-light C verse, would have to be divided as *Sô gor- / node*. In the latter case, Sievers is obliged to fill the second primary arsis with a short, non-root syllable of doubtful stress.

The higher frequency of verse-final word groups in types B and C, as compared with types Da and Db, lends some initial plausibility to Sievers's scansion. All other things being equal, these frequencies might be interpreted as evidence for a second primary arsis in B and C verses. Within the framework employed here, however, distribution of heavy word groups can be otherwise explained. Since heavy verse patterns are inherently complex, deviation from their paradigmatic two-word expressions would naturally be restricted (see U4). In the balanced types B and C, which have the normal number of stresses, more deviation would be tolerable. The word-foot analysis has an obvious appeal in type C, where the frequency of verse-final compounds is quite high, as Sievers himself observes.[19] The word-foot analysis of long type B, with a second foot of the form Sxxs, may seem less plausible initially. Sxxs compounds like OE *sibbegedriht* and OS *helligithuuing* are not very common, and the second foot of long type B is usually occupied by a word group. As we have observed, however, word groups assigned to an Sxxs foot normally conform to the morphological structure of an Sxxs compound, with a trochaic first constituent followed by a prefixed monosyllable. Even in the *Heliand*, where long strings of unstressed syllables are very common, the syllables between the stresses of a type B verse stay within limits imposed by the Sxxs pattern.[20] Sievers is well aware that the *Beowulf* poet never places more than two syllables in the second thesis of type B, apart from cases of elision, but this fact calls for differentiation of the thesis into distinct x positions, and cannot be explained within the five-types framework.[21] Word-foot analyses for types B and C are strikingly confirmed by the practice of the regularizing skalds, who normally use a

---

[17] See above, p. 12.
[18] This inconsistency was pointed out in von See, *Germanische Verskunst*, pp. 4 and 5.
[19] *AGM*, §9.3.   [20] See above, p. 139.
[21] See Sievers, 'Rhythmik', pp. 241–2.

function word and a compound to fill corresponding segments of the dróttkvætt a-verse.[22]

On Sievers's analysis, the verse-initial thesis of type B has the same metrical status as the verse-medial thesis. Since Sievers cannot explain preferential assignment of movable function words to the verse-initial thesis, Kuhn's laws are a necessary adjunct to the five-types system. In the word-foot theory, the first thesis of type B is a light foot, an enumerated structural component of the metrical pattern that should be as conspicuous as possible, whereas the second thesis is internal to the second foot and should be as inconspicuous as possible, since it corresponds to an inflectional or derivational syllable (ch. 4). On this analysis, movement of function words to the verse-initial thesis would be metrically advantageous in type B, and no other explanation seems to be required (see R6). Here and in many other cases the word-foot theory derives Kuhn's-law effects from general principles of verse construction. Any remaining Kuhn's-law effects can be attributed to universal syntactic constraints that apply in prose as well as poetry (ch. 9).

LIGHT FEET AND ANACRUSIS

In the five-types scansion of a-verses like *gi-lêstead an thesumu liohte* (*Hel* 1626a), unstressed linguistic material before the first alliteration, typically an isolated prefix, is interpreted as an anacrusis and excluded from the metrical pattern. The isolated prefix *gi-* in *Hel* 1626a would also be represented as an anacrusis in word-foot scansion. Treatment of such constituents as extrametrical is explained by their 'light' character.[23] Even in the *Heliand*, where constraints on unstressed syllables are relatively weak, we observe a distinct gradation of anacruses favouring the lighter function words.[24]

Because prefixes are so inconspicuous, they are relatively ineffective as enumerated structural components of the verse. Type B verses seldom have an isolated unstressed prefix as the verse-initial thesis, represented in word-foot scansion as a light foot. Variants like *Beo* 1696a, *ge-* / *seted ond gesǣd* (x/Sxxs), are quite rare.[25] Type C variants like *Beo* 511b, *be-* / *lēan mihte* (x/Ssx), occur somewhat more often, but primarily in the second

---

[22] See above, p. 24.   [23] Kuhn, *Füllwort*, p. 55.   [24] See above, p. 158.
[25] See *OEM*, §3.5.

half of the line, where the prefix is unlikely to be taken for an anacrusis. The word-foot scansions for such B and C variants are quite unnatural, providing straightforward representations for the unnatural verses.[26] There is nothing unnatural, on the other hand, about the corresponding five-types scansions (*geseted* / *ond gesǣd, belēan* / *mihte*). As analysed by Sievers, these marginal variants look like paradigmatic expressions of their types, and it is hard to see why special constraints should be imposed on them. Sievers's concept of anacrusis seems inconsistent with his scansion of types B and C.

RESOLUTION

According to Sievers, a short syllable may occupy an arsis only when immediately preceded by a stressed syllable or the resolved equivalent.[27] In all other cases, an arsis must be occupied by a long syllable or a resolved sequence. Sievers's rule of resolution must apply to *ad-hoc* detailed scansions rather than to the five types proper. In a significant number of A2 verses like *Hel* 2037a, *stênfatu* / *sehsi* (Ss/Sx), resolution is obligatory on the secondary arsis of the first foot, an arsis disregarded by Sievers as insignificant for purposes of assignment to class A. There are more than forty verses comparable to *Hel* 2037a in *Beowulf* alone.[28]

Within the word-foot framework, resolution applies directly to an S or s position in a basic verse pattern. There is no need to stipulate rules of resolution as such; the detail rules of R9 are corollaries derivable from linguistic rules for syllable structure and from independently necessary principles of verse construction, notably P3, the principle of metrical subordination. Rule R9a, which states that the syllables most suitable for resolution are those with the most prominent stress, is a purely linguistic rule.[29] Rule R9b, the equivalent poetic rule, is a straightforward application of R9a to metrical positions of the verse, with the most prominent type of position (S) being most suitable for resolution. The detail rule R7, which implements the principle of metrical subordination, creates hierarchies of relative prominence for metrical positions at the level of the line, increasing the prominence of some positions while

---

[26] See above, p. 7.   [27] *AGM*, §9.2.
[28] Russom, 'Constraints on Resolution', p. 153.
[29] Appropriated from Dresher and Lahiri, 'Germanic Foot'.

Conclusions

diminishing the prominence of others (ch. 6). Detail rules R9c and R9e simply state that resolution bears the expected relation to these independently motivated hierarchies, with the most prominent of the S positions being most suitable for resolution and the least prominent of the s positions least suitable (ch. 8). Detail rule R9d, Kaluza's law, is a linguistic footnote to R9a.[30]

Distribution of type A1 variants in West Germanic verse lends some initial plausibility to Sievers's resolution rule. As Sievers predicts, unresolved short syllables occupy the second S position less frequently in the type A1 pattern Sx/Sx, where the unresolved syllable is immediately preceded by a syllable with zero stress, than in the type Da pattern S/Ssx, where the unresolved syllable is immediately preceded by a stressed syllable. Most of the relevant Da verses, however, are wholly occupied by a compound, e.g. *Beo* 2a, *þēod- / cyninga* (S/Ssx). In these, assignment of a short syllable to the second S position can be explained by detail rule R9a, which states that resolution is less natural in a syllable of secondary stress. Within the restricted set of verses having a short syllable on the second S position, Da variants like *Beo* 1210b, *feorh / cyninges* (S/Ssx), have about the same very low frequency as A1 variants like *Beo* 2430b, *Hrēðel / cyning* (Sx/Sx). These low frequencies can be attributed to the combined influence of R9a and R9b, which inhibit assignment of a short syllable under primary stress to a primary arsis.

All other things being equal, we would expect unresolved short syllables to appear somewhat more frequently on the rightward primary arsis of the type A1 pattern, which is metrically simpler than the Da pattern and should be more tolerant of mismatches. Yet we observe about the same low frequency of non-resolution in type A1 as in type Da. The especially low frequency of non-resolution in type A1 can be attributed to the overlap constraint (U2), which discourages employment of verses resembling feet. A1 variants like *Hrēðel / cyning* are rare in Old English poetry because they look too much like the second foot of B variants with resolution on the secondary arsis, e.g. *Beo* 2356a, *syððan / Gēata cyning* (xx/Sxs). Since Old Norse poets have abandoned resolution on the secondary arsis, they do not have this problem of overlap, and fornyrðislag exhibits a distinct rise, as predicted, in the frequency of non-resolved A1 variants like *HH II* 21/3, *sáttir / saman*.

[30] Russom, 'Constraints on Resolution', p. 151.

203

Sievers has no way to explain why the preferred sites for unresolved short syllables are the secondary arsis of his type Da and the second primary arsis of his type C. Within the word-foot theory, the rightward arsis of type C is an s position, not an S position, and the high frequency of verses with a short syllable on this arsis is attributable to R9b, which makes resolution less natural on the s position of any pattern, across the board. R9b explains why non-resolution occurs most often on the s position of the Da pattern S/Ssx, rather than on the second S position of this type, which is also immediately preceded by a stressed constituent and should be strictly parallel, on Sievers's analysis, to the second arsis of type C. Since the poet often employs verse-final Ssx compounds in type C as well as type Da, assignment of a short syllable to the s position in these types will be further promoted by R9a, which inhibits resolution of subordinate constituents in compounds.

THE DEVELOPMENT OF GERMANIC VERSE FORM

The five-types system is presented as a hypostatic, transhistorical phenomenon. After stating the head-stave rule, for example, Sievers characterizes Norse A3 verses occupying the second half of the line as exceptions to this rule rather than as metrical innovations.[31] Since he adopts Sievers's system for *DGV*, Lehmann inevitably represents metrical differences as differing realizations of unchanging archetypes. Lehmann rightly underscores the importance of developments in stress and associated linguistic processes, which deserve the closest attention in any account of alliterative versecraft. The five-types system, which dismisses variants of obvious interest as casual errors, seems unsuitable as a framework for comparative analysis, however. When changes in stress and syllable count are in question, it seems particularly inappropriate to assume that fixed patterns of stresses and syllables served as metrical targets throughout the history of the form.

According to the word-foot theory, ideals of verse form derive from the lexicon of the poet's historical moment and are themselves subject to change. Loss of a word pattern is predicted to eliminate the corresponding foot pattern. If a word pattern is employed with greater or diminished frequency over historical time, employment of the corresponding foot is

---

[31] *AGM*, §19.2.

Conclusions

predicted to be freer or more restricted. A change in the forcefulness of primary stress is predicted to bring about changes in alliterative patterning, resolution and employment of extrametrical syllables. Such explicit predictions have made it possible to investigate the development of Germanic verse form at the level of fine detail. Below I provide a fairly complete historical summary consistent with the word-foot theory. For ease of cross-reference, related developments in the cognate traditions are presented in parallel entries.

PREHISTORIC DEVELOPMENTS

In some of the earliest Celtic and Italic poetry, the verse normally consists of two stressed words, with occasional addition of extrametrical function words.[32] The word foot may have been employed very early in Western Europe, perhaps before Germanic was fully differentiated from other Indo-European dialects. In the Germanic sphere, derivation of word feet attained full generality, yielding light feet corresponding to unstressed words and heavy feet corresponding to compounds in addition to the more familiar type of foot that corresponds to a stressed simplex (see P1–2).

Italic, Celtic and Germanic experienced a shift of stress to the root syllable at an early period, and alliterative poetry developed in all three dialects as a technique for binding metrical constituents together.[33] The term for alliteration used by Old Irish poets is úaim, literally 'stitching' – hence, according to Murphy, 'joining' in a poetic sense.[34] In the Germanic sphere, the rule for placement of alliteration was associated with the compound stress rule, which created a hierarchy of prominence for root syllables as it bound them into larger linguistic constituents (see P3–4).

From the earliest times, Germanic poets would have needed to respect certain universal constraints on poetic form that facilitate intuitive scansion. The variety of verse patterns made it important to realize them as coherent syntactic constituents in most cases (see U1) and to restrict overlap with foot patterns (see U2). A principle of closure (U3) no doubt provided relief from metrical complexity in the b-verse, and unambiguous closure of the b-verse would have foregrounded the leftward boundary of

---

[32] See Travis, *Celtic Versecraft*, pp. 1–14; Whitman, *Comparative Study*, pp. 41–2.
[33] Murphy, *Early Irish Metrics*, pp. 6–7.   [34] Ibid., p. 36.

the following a-verse, preparing the audience for the next analytical challenge. Simultaneous deviation from underlying two-word norms must have been restricted or forbidden in many ways (see U4).

OLD ENGLISH VERSE

OE1. The language of *Beowulf* differed significantly from the language of the Gallehus inscription, *(ek) HlewagastiR HoltijaR / horna tawido.* By the historical Old English period, average word length had decreased due to the subordinating effect of a moderately forceful stress.

a At some time before the composition of *Beowulf,* short unstressed syllables underwent syncopation in medial position after long stressed syllables.

b Medial syllables in certain weak class II forms retained stress and length throughout the period of syncopation. After these syllables were destressed and shortened, weak class II forms provided models for Sxx feet.[35]

c Epenthetic vowels had developed, but were usually disregarded by the *Beowulf* poet (ch. 5).

d Most polysyllabic inflectional endings had been reduced to monosyllables.[36]

e Loss of vowel length was far advanced in unstressed syllables and may have been completed in ordinary speech just before *Beowulf* was composed, though the poet was still sensitive to etymological length in the old circumflex vowels.[37]

f Prefixes and unstressed function words underwent reduction to one or two syllables. Prefixes retained some wordlike characteristics.[38]

OE2. The poet needed to employ a variety of unstressed prefixes and negative particles, which called for special constraints (ch. 4).

a Due to their 'light' character, prefixes and negative particles were often treated as anacruses verse-initially. Other constituents were occasionally

---

[35] Russom, 'Constraints on Resolution', pp. 154–6.
[36] See Fulk, *History of Old English Meter*, Appendix C, for recent reconstructions of earlier endings.
[37] Ibid., ch. 6.   [38] *OEM*, §§1.1 and 1.4.

employed as anacruses, but the number of syllables in an anacrusis never exceeded two, the number of syllables in an Old English unstressed prefix.

b To keep metrical ambiguity within tolerable limits, employment of isolated prefixes as light feet was severely restricted.

c In certain cases, as with isolated verse-initial articles, anacrusis was avoided by deletion.

d Because the number of unstressed syllables in anacrusis never exceeded two, extrametrical function words could provide unambiguous markers for light feet. Because most anacruses had only one syllable, an isolated bisyllabic function word was significantly more effective as a light foot than a monosyllable of the same syntactic category. In types B and C, there was a perceptible bias against isolated monosyllables.

e Two-word type A3 was ruled out by the overlap constraint because it looked too much like the first foot of a type A1 verse with anacrusis. In all but a handful of A3 verses, an extrametrical unstressed word provided an unambiguous marker for the light foot.

OE3. The moderately forceful Old English stress was reflected in metrical compounding (P3), which had a moderately forceful subordinating effect.

a Operating analogously to linguistic subordination, metrical subordination permitted moderate employment of extrametrical constituents.[39]

b The rightward arsis of the verse was moderately subordinated, retaining sufficient strength in the a-verse to promote optional alliteration, which in complex variants often served to mark the leftward boundary of the second foot (ch. 7).

c The secondary arsis retained sufficient strength to allow for resolution in certain cases, but resolution was rare or non-existent on the most deeply subordinated s positions (ch. 8).

OE4. A number of large compounds existed, and employment of the corresponding feet had to be carefully regulated.

a Large compounds like *middangeardes* were often treated as two words because they overlapped the most highly favoured verse pattern, Sx/Sx. Some other large compounds were treated in the same way.[40]

---

[39] See above, p. 26.   [40] See above, p. 34.

b Hypermetrical clustering signalled a displacement of the metrical norm, allowing for employment of compounds like *middangeardes* as Sxsx feet.[41] Large compounds with other phonological patterns also served as 'giant feet' in hypermetrical verses, though less frequently.

c Type A3 was excluded from the second half of the line to avoid overlap with the opening portion of the hypermetrical b-verse.[42]

d An Sxs foot was derived from compounds like *middangeard*, with a trochaic first constituent, and *handgeweorc*, with a medial infix.

e Compounds like *sibbegedriht*, with a trochaic first constituent and a medial infix, provided models for a four-position foot with the pattern Sxxs. Word groups assigned to this complex foot pattern generally conformed to the morphological structure of an Sxxs compound, with a trochaic first constituent followed by a prefixed monosyllable. Employment of an Sxx/S verse pattern was blocked by the overlap constraint (U2).

f The poet often coined poetic compounds to fill compound feet in the most desirable way. Because subordination of the secondary constituent in such compounds was somewhat unclear, it was reinforced by obligatory alliteration on the primary constituent, as with certain heavy word groups, which could occupy a compound foot at a cost in complexity (ch. 7).

g In heavy verses with more than two stressed words, the verse-medial foot boundary had to fall at the major syntactic break. There was little enjambment.

OE5. Near the end of the tenth century, changes in Old English put pressure on the metrical system. In *The Battle of Maldon*, deletion of determiners was apparently inhibited, leading to new forms of anacrusis and a higher degree of metrical ambiguity.[43] After the Norman Conquest, lexical iambs and other exotic word patterns were introduced. A poet who wished to use French borrowings with social or academic prestige must have found the old system totally unworkable. By the time of *Sir Gawain and the Green Knight*, a fourteenth-century alliterative poem, two-word verses were quite obviously not favoured and placement of alliterating syllables in the a-verse was no longer governed by the major syntactic break. Declining productivity of linguistic compounding in the Early

---

[41] *OEM*, §6.6.   [42] See above, p. 49.   [43] See above, p. 157.

Middle English period may have hastened the demise of metrical compounding as a principle of verse construction.[44]

OLD NORSE VERSE

ON1. Native Eddic fornyrðislag attests a stage of linguistic development at which average word size had been drastically reduced due to the subordinating effect of an extremely forceful stress (ch. 2).

a Syncopation occurred after short as well as long syllables, and many resolvable sequences were eliminated.

b Employment of enclitic forms with the status of secondary affixes yielded new Sxx words, which were treated by the poets as equivalent to Sxx forms of weak class II verbs.

c Epenthetic vowels had not developed at this stage (ch. 5).

d Some inflectional endings had become non-syllabic (e.g. gen. sg. -s).

e Vowel length in unstressed syllables had been lost entirely.

f Most unstressed prefixes were eliminated, with the minor exception of *fyr-*. A single infix, -*u*-, survived in a handful of compounds. The Norse cognate of *ge-*, a prefix of high frequency in Old English, was reduced to non-syllabic *g-* and absorbed into the root onset, retaining no word-like properties of its own. Preverbal negative particles and some other function words were replaced by new enclitic forms with the status of non-words (affixes). Simplex function words underwent reduction to one or two syllables, but new xxx words were created from function-word groups by enclisis, and a new verse pattern xxx/S was sanctioned.

ON2. The Norse poet did not need to employ prefixes or preverbal negative particles at the beginning of the verse, and special constraints of the West Germanic type were unnecessary (ch. 4).

a Anacrusis was eliminated from the metrical system.

b The filler word *of* / *um* had the 'light' character of a prefix, and made an ineffective light foot, though like the prefixes of cognate traditions it was used as a foot occasionally.

c Filler words could be deleted freely, and were employed only to improve the metre, as with articles.

---

[44] See Sauer, *Nominalkomposita*, p. 719.

d Because anacrusis had been abandoned, isolated monosyllabic function
words were easier to identify as light feet, and there was no bias against
use of such words for the first foot of type B and C verses.

e The light foot of type A3 could no longer be confused with an
anacrusis. Two-word A3 verses appeared, and A3 variants with the
minimum number of syllables were employed with much higher
frequency.

ON3. The extremely forceful Old Norse stress was reflected in metrical
compounding (P3), which had an extremely forceful subordinating effect.

a Operating analogously to linguistic subordination, which promoted
incorporation of clitics into words, metrical subordination restricted
employment of extrametrical constituents, promoting incorporation of
x positions into feet.[45]

b The rightward arsis of the verse was more deeply subordinated than in
West Germanic traditions and accordingly less suitable for optional
alliteration (ch. 6). In complex variants, alliteration served less often to
mark the leftward boundary of the second foot. Restricted employment
of extrametrical syllables lowered the frequency of complex variants,
making an alliterative boundary marker less necessary.

c Resolution was sharply restricted on the second primary arsis, which
was more frequently occupied by an unresolved short syllable (ch. 8).
The secondary arsis was deeply subordinated and totally unsuitable for
resolution. A secondary constituent could be reduced to the status of an
unstressed syllable when subordinated by two alliterating constituents
in the same foot.[46] As a more marginal phenomenon, resolution made
a greater contribution to overall verse complexity, and was restricted to
the more prominent locations in relatively simple verse patterns (see
U4). There was no resolution within the complex Sxs foot, and
resolvable sequences were excluded altogether from type E.

ON4. The frequency of large compounds was significantly diminished by
syncopation, loss of inflectional syllables and loss of infixes (cf. OE
middangeardes, ON *miðgarðs*).

a Large compounds like *Gullinkambi* were always treated as two words

[45] See above, p. 26.   [46] See above, p. 95.

210

Conclusions

and occupied an Sx/Sx verse pattern. Some other large compounds were treated in the same way.

b Constraints on mismatch allowed for employment of short patterns in fornyrðislag, primarily of the form Sx/S. Loss of syllables from traditional formulas provided influential precedents for short patterns, leading to the abandonment of hypermetrical patterns.[47] In ljóðaháttr, a variety of short patterns were employed as the first verse of the half-stanza, with their fixed positions signalling a displacement of the metrical norm.[48] When the balance shifted toward lighter patterns, the frequency of heavy verses was restricted. Although the trochaic word pattern was still paradigmatic in the natural language, long heavy verses with an Sx word in first position became extremely rare.

c Since there was no danger of overlap with hypermetrical b-verses, type A3 could be employed in the second half of the line.

d Most forms with medial infixes had been eliminated, apart from a handful of forms like bekkj-u-nautr. The Sxs foot was now derived almost exclusively from forms like iormungandr. Marginalization of Sxs compounds restricted employment of the Sxs foot, producing a sharp drop in the relative frequency of type B and a dramatic shift of this type toward the a-verse.[49] A verse pattern Sx/S could be employed with less risk of overlap.

e Since words comparable to OE sibbegedriht no longer occurred in Old Norse, the Sxxs foot was eliminated, allowing for employment of Sxx/S verses with no risk of overlap.

f In native Eddic fornyrðislag, poetic compounds were sometimes employed, but not as systematically as in Beowulf. The subordinate status of the secondary constituent was more readily perceptible due to the more forceful character of subordination in Old Norse. Alliteration on the first constituent often provided a further mark of subordination, but was not obligatory.

g In heavy verses with more than two stressed words, the verse-medial foot boundary had to fall at the major syntactic break. Enjambment sometimes created a particularly sharp syntactic break before the second stress in complex D variants, and this marked the leftward

[47] See above, p. 34. [48] See above, p. 37.
[49] See above, p. 39.

211

boundary of the second foot quite distinctly, making alliteration less necessary for that purpose.[50]

ON5. Changes in phrasal stress seem to have obscured the old relationship between word class and alliteration by the time of Snorri.[51] Placement of alliterating syllables was fixed artificially in skaldic metres and metrical compounding was abandoned as a principle of verse construction. Since information about phrasal stress is required for scansion of the more complex Eddic variants, especially those with more than two stressed words, the word-foot structure of traditional models may not have been accessible to intuition at this time. Word-foot structure was maintained in the skaldic a-verse, but in the b-verse demands of syllable count and internal rhyme seem to have predominated.[52] The integrity of the line as a metrical domain was enhanced by exaggerating the asymmetry of its subcomponents, with two alliterating syllables required in the dróttkvætt a-verse and strongly preferred in the a-verse of the málaháttr form, which had abandoned word-foot structure. Norse metres with exotic content may have been subject to continental West Germanic influence.

CONTINENTAL WEST GERMANIC VERSE

CG1. Hildebrandslied and the *Heliand* attest a stage of linguistic development at which average word size had increased due to recent weakening of stress.

a Syllables formerly subject to syncopation were restored and the number of resolvable sequences increased. Old syncopated forms could still be used as metrical variants, however.

b Restoration of syncopated syllables created new Sxx words, which were treated by the poets as equivalent to Sxx forms of weak class II verbs.[53]

c Epenthetic vowels normally counted as significant, though not always.[54]

d A number of bisyllabic inflectional endings survived in forms like *sceotantero.*

e In Old High German, some unstressed syllables were long.

---

[50] See above, p. 94.   [51] See Faulkes, *Háttatal*, p. xxii.

[52] Kuhn, *Dróttkvætt*, §66.   [53] See above, p. 180.   [54] See above, p. 143.

f Unstressed prefixes were retained and there were some trisyllabic function words, notably demonstratives and articles (e.g. *thesoro*).

CG2. The poet needed to employ a variety of unstressed prefixes, prefixal negatives and determiners, which called for special constraints.

a Due to their light character, prefixal elements and determiners were often treated as anacruses verse-initially. Other parts of speech could occur as anacruses, but the heavier unstressed words, notably finite verbs, were seldom employed in this way. Since some determiners had three syllables, trisyllabic anacrusis was sanctioned.
b To reduce the level of metrical ambiguity in the system, employment of isolated prefixes and determiners as light feet was severely restricted.
c Deletion of articles to avoid anacrusis was inhibited at this stage of the language. Deletion of other determiners, such as possessive pronouns, may have been inhibited as well.[55]
d Because the average number of unstressed syllables in anacruses had grown, longer strings of extrametrical function words were required to mark light feet unambiguously. The complexity of the main part of the verse was restricted in the variants with the most complex anacruses.[56]
e As in *Beowulf*, the overlap constraint ruled out two-word type A3, which looked too much like the first foot of a type A1 verse with anacrusis. In most A3 verses, a long string of extrametrical words provided a marker for the light foot.

CG3. The weak continental West Germanic stress was reflected in metrical compounding (P3), which had a weakly subordinating effect.

a Operating analogously to linguistic subordination, which did little to reduce or incorporate function words, metrical subordination permitted extensive employment of extrametrical constituents.
b A subordinate arsis retained sufficient strength in the a-verse to promote optional alliteration, which in complex variants often served to mark the leftward boundary of the second foot. The increased frequency of extrametrical syllables made such a marker more necessary, but rejection of formulas with a pronounced martial character made double alliteration more difficult to achieve in the *Heliand*.

[55] See above, p. 157. [56] See above, p. 149.

c The secondary arsis retained sufficient strength to allow for resolution, even when subordinated by two alliterating S positions in type D.

CG4. The number of large compounds in the natural language was increased by restoration of syncopated syllables. Because large compounds had become more common, the complexity of the corresponding foot patterns was reduced and there was freer experimentation with reversed heavy patterns.

a Large compounds like *môdgithâhtio* were sometimes treated as two words because they overlapped the most highly favoured verse pattern, Sx/Sx. Some other large compounds were treated in the same way.

b Hypermetrical clustering signalled a displacement of the metrical norm, allowing for employment of large compounds as 'giant feet', e.g. in *Hel* 557b, *Ic gisihu that gi sind / eðiligiburdiun.*

c Type A3 was excluded from the second half of the line to avoid overlap with the opening portion of the hypermetrical b-verse.

d An Sxs foot was derived from compounds like *middilgard*, with a trochaic first constituent, and *handgiuuerc*, with a medial infix.

e Compounds like *helligethuuing*, with a trochaic first constituent and an infix, provided models for a four-position foot of the form Sxxs. The enhanced frequency of Sxxs words in continental West Germanic reduced the complexity of the corresponding Sxxs foot, sanctioning a higher frequency of long type B and freer employment of Sxxs word groups.[57] As in Old English poetry, employment of an Sxx/S verse pattern was blocked by the overlap constraint.

f The *Heliand* poet made restricted use of traditional formulaic language, perhaps because its predominantly martial character was inconsistent with New Testament values. As a result, the frequency of alliteration on the rightward arsis of the a-verse was slightly lower than would be expected on purely metrical grounds.

g Experimentation with peculiar reversed patterns in continental West Germanic poems created problems of metrical ambiguity that make it difficult to study syntactic constraints on heavy verses. This is an area for further research.

[57] See above, pp. 144 and 183.

CG5. Weak stress and increased use of obligatory proclitics made it more difficult to implement principles of word-foot metre in *Hildebrandslied* and the *Heliand.* The poets made serious efforts to deal with problems of metrical ambiguity, however. Lehmann's adoption of the five-types system led him to overlook some of these efforts, but his claim that continental West Germanic metre was already in decline seems plausible.

ENVOI

To pursue a reasonably straight path through the comparative issues, we have necessarily bypassed important problems internal to a particular tradition or form. Discussion of North Germanic poetry has been strictly confined to issues of significance for native Eddic fornyrðislag, the Norse metrical cognate of *Beowulf.* Evidence from other Norse metres has been extremely helpful, however, and it seems clear that further study of these forms on their own merits can deepen our understanding of alliterative versecraft, broadly conceived. In the study of continental Germanic verse, many challenges remain. Metrical ambiguity may be more carefully restricted in this tradition than we have supposed, but the strategies employed by the poets are quite peculiar and extraction of the complete system may require considerable effort. In the Old English field, several neglected topics beckon. One of my reviewers pointed out, quite correctly, that *OEM* was rather narrowly focused on *Beowulf* and called for broader studies of Old English metrical practice. The time for such studies has certainly arrived, but it seemed desirable to prepare for them by establishing the extreme limits of traditional variation through analysis of the cognate metres, following the trail blazed by Sievers in *AGM.* Confronted with verse forms as diverse as those of the Edda and the *Heliand,* the word-foot theory has attained a significantly higher level of generality. I hope it will provide a useful framework for further research.

Appendix
Rule summary

DEFINITION OF *word*

D1a All stressed simplexes count as words.

D1b Unstressed prefixes count as function words.

D1c A compound may count as one word or as two.

D1d A function word may count as a word or as undefined linguistic material.

DEFINITIONS FOR METRICAL POSITIONS

D2a The primary arsis (S position) is derived from a fully stressed syllable.

D2b The secondary arsis (s position) is derived from a syllable with secondary stress.

D2c The weak position (x position) is derived from a syllable with less than secondary stress.

FUNDAMENTAL PRINCIPLES

P1 *Foot patterns* correspond to native word patterns. The foot patterns most easily perceived correspond to the most common word patterns.

P2 The *verse* consists of two readily identifiable feet. Foot patterns corresponding to unusual word patterns add to the complexity of verses in which they appear.

P3 Assignment of *alliteration* corresponds to assignment of stress in Germanic compounds and serves to bind smaller metrical constituents into larger constituents. The integrity of the larger constituent is marked by alliteration on its first subconstituent.

P4 The *line* consists of two adjacent verses bound by alliteration. The first of these is the *a-verse*; the second is the *b-verse*.

Rule summary

R1a A syllable with primary stress normally occupies an S position. When such a syllable occupies an s position, the S position of the same foot normally contains an alliterating syllable.

R1b A syllable with zero stress must occupy an x position unless it shares an arsis with the short stressed syllable of a resolved sequence. Adjacent unstressed vowels may share a single x position by elision.

R1c A syllable with secondary stress may occupy an s position or an S position.

BRACKETING RULE (CF. P2)

R2a Every foot boundary must coincide with a word boundary. Note: the internal boundaries of compounded forms count as word boundaries for the purposes of this rule.

R2b In verses with three or more stressed words, assignment of stressed words to feet must respect syntactic constituency. Note: compounds count as two words for the purposes of this rule.

EXTRAMETRICAL SYLLABLE RULE

R3 Unstressed words may appear before either foot (as consistent with P2).

VERSE PATTERN RULE (CF. P2)

R4a A short foot is normally balanced by a long foot and vice versa.

R4b A light foot is normally balanced by a heavy foot and vice versa.

R4c Only one foot may be long.

CONSTRAINTS ON REVERSED PATTERNS (CF. P2)

R5a Reversed heavy patterns may not contain a foot of the form Sxs or Sxxs.

R5b Reversed heavy patterns may not exceed normative length.

217

Appendix

R6a Minimize use of minor function words as light feet.

R6b Minimize use of major function words for anacrusis.

R6c Minimize use of major function words in complex foot patterns as substitutes for unstressed word-internal syllables.

KUHN'S LAWS (CF. R6)

K1 First Law: Unstressed Satzpartikeln must be grouped together before the first or second stressed word of the clause.

K2 Second Law: Any unstressed constituents situated before the first stressed word of the clause must include a Satzpartikel.

METRICAL COMPOUNDING RULE (CF. P3)

R7a When two S positions appear within the same metrical domain, alliteration is assigned obligatorily to the first S position, beginning with the smallest domain.

R7b Assignment of alliteration to a given constituent subordinates all other constituents within the domain of application.

ALLITERATIVE PROMINENCE RULE (CF. P3)

R8a The strongest two metrical positions within the line must contain alliterating syllables.

R8b A weak constituent of a weak constituent may not contain an alliterating syllable.

R8c No alliterating syllable may occupy an x position.

R8d Within a compound foot, the S position has priority for alliteration.

DETAIL RULES FOR RESOLUTION (CF. PI, P3)

R9a Within the word, resolution is most natural under primary stress, less natural under subordinate stress and forbidden under zero stress.

R9b Within the foot, resolution is most natural on an S position, less natural on an s position and forbidden on an x position.

R9c Alliteration on the most prominent S position makes resolution less natural on a subordinate S or s position within the same metrical domain.

R9d Resolution of a short syllable is less natural when the following syllable is long and the resolved sequence would therefore be equivalent to an ultra-long closed syllable containing a long vowel.

R9e On the most deeply subordinated s positions, both resolved sequences and long syllables are unnatural. Such s positions are most naturally occupied by a short stressed syllable (unresolved).

UNIVERSAL PRINCIPLE OF SYNTACTIC INTEGRITY

U1 When identification of verse boundaries is problematic, verses corresponding to natural syntactic units are preferred.

UNIVERSAL OVERLAP CONSTRAINT (CF. P2)

U2 Avoid feet that resemble verses and verses that resemble feet.

UNIVERSAL PRINCIPLE OF CLOSURE

U3 Minimize complexity toward the end of the line.

UNIVERSAL PRINCIPLE OF SUMMATION

U4 Metrical complexity is additive.

Bibliography

Árnason, K., *The Rhythms of Dróttkvætt and other Old Icelandic Metres* (Reykjavik, 1991)

Behaghel, O., *Die Syntax des Heliand* (Vienna, 1897)

Behaghel, O., ed., *Heliand und Genesis*, 9th edn rev. by B. Taeger (Tübingen, 1984)

Bessinger, J. B., Jr, and P. H. Smith, Jr, *A Concordance to the Anglo-Saxon Poetic Records* (Ithaca, NY, 1978)

Bliss, A. J., *The Metre of Beowulf*, rev. edn (Oxford, 1967)

Blockley, M., and T. Cable, 'Kuhn's Laws, Old English Poetry, and the New Philology', in *Beowulf: Basic Readings*, ed. P. S. Baker (New York, 1995), pp. 261–79

Bostock, J. K., *A Handbook of Old High German Literature*, 2nd edn rev. by K. C. King and D. R. McLintock (Oxford, 1976)

Braune, W., *Althochdeutsches Lesebuch*, 16th edn rev. by E. A. Ebbinghaus (Tübingen, 1979)

Althochdeutsche Grammatik, 13th edn rev. by H. Eggers (Tübingen, 1975)

Bugge, S., and E. Sievers, 'Vokalverkürzung im Altnordischen', *BGDSL* 15 (1890), 391–411

Cable, T., *The Meter and Melody of Beowulf*, Illinois Studies in Language and Literature 64 (Urbana, IL, 1974)

The English Alliterative Tradition (Philadelphia, 1991)

Campbell, A., *Old English Grammar* (Oxford, 1959)

'The Old English Epic Style', in *English and Medieval Studies: Presented to J. R. R. Tolkien on the Occasion of his 70th Birthday*, ed. N. Davis and C. L. Wrenn (London, 1962), pp. 13–26

'Verse Influences in Old English Prose', in *Philological Essays: Studies in Old and Middle English Language and Literature in Honour of Herbert Dean Meritt*, ed. J. L. Rosier, Janua Linguarum series maior 37 (The Hague, 1970), 93–8

Bibliography

Chomsky, N., *Barriers* (Cambridge, MA, 1986)

Knowledge of Language: Its Nature, Origin, and Use (New York, 1986)

Chomsky, N., and M. Halle, *The Sound Pattern of English* (New York, 1968)

Cowper, E. A., *A Concise Introduction to Syntactic Theory: The Government-Binding Approach* (Chicago, 1992)

Craigie, W. A., 'On Some Points in Skaldic Metre', *Arkiv för nordisk filologi* 16 (1900), 341–84

Creed, R. P., *Reconstructing the Rhythm of 'Beowulf'* (Columbia, MO, 1990)

Daunt, M., 'Old English Verse and English Speech Rhythm', *TPS* 1947 (for 1946), 56–72

Donoghue, D., *Style in Old English Poetry: The Test of the Auxiliary*, Yale Studies in English 196 (New Haven, CT, 1987)

Dresher, B. E., and A. Lahiri, 'The Germanic Foot: Metrical Coherence in Old English', *Linguistic Inquiry* 22 (1991), 251–86

Düwel, K., *Runenkunde*, Sammlung Metzler 72 (Stuttgart, 1968)

Elliott, R. W. V., *Runes: An Introduction*, 2nd edn (Manchester, 1989)

Faulkes, A., ed., *Snorri Sturluson, Edda: Háttatal* (Oxford, 1991)

Frank, R., *Old Norse Court Poetry: The Dróttkvætt Stanza*, Islandica 42 (Ithaca, NY, 1978)

Fulk, R. D., *A History of Old English Meter* (Philadelphia, 1992)

Gordon, E. V., *An Introduction to Old Norse*, 2nd edn rev. by A. R. Taylor (Oxford, 1957)

Hanson, K., and P. Kiparsky, 'A Parametric Theory of Poetic Meter', *Language* 72 (1996), 287–335

Hayes, B., 'A Grid-based Theory of English Meter', *Linguistic Inquiry* 14 (1983), 357–93

Heusler, A., *Deutsche Versgeschichte mit Einschluss des altenglischen und altnordischen Stabreimverses* I, Paul's Grundriss der germanischen Philologie 8 (Berlin, 1925)

Hofmann, D., *Die Versstrukturen der altsächsischen Stabreimgedichte Heliand und Genesis*, 2 vols. (Heidelberg, 1991)

Hogg, R. M., *The Cambridge History of the English Language I: The Beginnings to 1066* (Cambridge, 1992)

Holthausen, F., *Altsächsisches Elementarbuch*, 2nd edn (Heidelberg, 1921)

Hoover, D. L., *A New Theory of Old English Meter* (New York, 1985)

Hutcheson, B. R., 'Kuhn's Law, Finite Verb Stress, and the Critics', *SN* 64 (1992), 129–39

Jackendoff, R., *Consciousness and the Computational Mind* (Cambridge, MA, 1987)

Jakobson, R., *Selected Writings V: On Verse, Its Masters and Explorers* (The Hague, 1979)

Kabell, A., *Metrische Studien I: Der Alliterationsvers* (Munich, 1978)

Bibliography

Kaluza, M., 'Zur Betonungs- und Verslehre des Altenglischen', in *Festschrift zum siebzigsten Geburtstage Oskar Schade* (Königsberg, 1896), pp. 101–33
Englische Metrik in historischer Entwicklung (Berlin, 1909); trans. by A. C. Dunstan as *A Short History of English Versification* (London, 1911)

Kauffmann, F., 'Die Rhythmik des Heliand', *BGDSL* 12 (1887), 283–355

Kendall, C. B., 'The Metrical Grammar of *Beowulf*: Displacement', *Speculum* 58 (1983), 1–30
The Metrical Grammar of Beowulf, CSASE 5 (Cambridge, 1991)

Kiparsky, P., 'Über den deutschen Akzent', in *Untersuchungen über Akzent und Intonation im Deutschen*, ed. M. Bierwisch, Studia Grammatica 7 (Berlin, 1966), 69–98
'The Rhythmic Structure of English Verse', *Linguistic Inquiry* 8 (1977), 189–247

Klaeber, F., ed., *Beowulf and The Fight at Finnsburg*, 3rd edn with first and second supplements (Boston, 1950)

Krapp, G. P., and E. V. K. Dobbie, ed., *The Anglo-Saxon Poetic Records*, 6 vols. (New York, 1931–53)

Krause, W., *Runeninschriften im älteren Futhark* (Halle, 1937)
Runen, 2nd edn, Sammlung Göschen 2810 (Berlin, 1993)

Kuhn, H., *Das Füllwort of-um im Altwestnordischen*, Ergänzungshefte zur Zeitschrift für vergleichende Sprachforschung auf dem Gebiet der indogermanischen Sprachen 8 (Göttingen, 1929)
'Zur Wortstellung und -betonung im Altgermanischen', *BGDSL* 57 (1933), 1–109
'Westgermanisches in der altnordischen Verskunst', *BGDSL* 63 (1939), 178–236
Kleine Schriften I: Sprachgeschichte, Verskunst (Berlin, 1969)
Das Dróttkvætt (Heidelberg, 1983)

Kuryłowicz, J., *Die sprachlichen Grundlagen der altgermanischen Metrik* (Innsbruck, 1970)
Metrik und Sprachgeschichte, Polska Akademia Nauk, Warsaw; Komitet Językoznawstwa; Prace językoznawcze 83 (Wrocław, 1975)

Lass, R., 'Quantity, Resolution and Syllable Geometry', *Folia Linguistica Historica* 4 (1983), 151–80

Lehmann, R. P. M., 'Broken Cadences in *Beowulf*', *ES* 56 (1975), 1–13

Lehmann, R. P. M. and W. P., *An Introduction to Old Irish* (New York, 1975)

Lehmann, W. P., *The Development of Germanic Verse Form* (Austin, TX, 1956)

Lerdahl, F., and R. Jackendoff, *A Generative Theory of Tonal Music* (Cambridge, MA, 1983)

Liberman, M., and A. Prince, 'On Stress and Linguistic Rhythm', *Linguistic Inquiry* 8 (1977), 249–336

Bibliography

Lucas, P. J., 'Some Aspects of the Interaction between Verse Grammar and Metre in Old English Poetry', *SN* 59 (1987), 145–75

Luick, K., *Historische Grammatik der englischen Sprache* I (Leipzig, 1921)

McLintock, D. R., 'Metre and Rhythm in the "Hildebrandslied"', *MLR* 71 (1976), 565–76

Mitchell, B., *Old English Syntax*, 2 vols. (Oxford, 1985)

Momma, H., *The Composition of Old English Poetry*, CSASE 20 (Cambridge, 1997)

Morris, R. L., *Runic and Mediterranean Epigraphy*, Nowele Supplement 4 (Odense, 1988)

Murphy, G., *Early Irish Metrics* (Dublin, 1961)

Neckel, G., *Edda: Die Lieder des Codex Regius nebst verwandten Denkmälern*, 5th edn rev. by H. Kuhn (Heidelberg, 1983)

Noreen, A., *Altnordische Grammatik* I (Tübingen, 1884)

Pintzuk, S., and A. S. Kroch, 'The Rightward Movement of Complements and Adjuncts in the Old English of *Beowulf*', *Language Variation and Change* 1 (1989), 115–43

Pope, J. C., *The Rhythm of Beowulf: An Interpretation of the Normal and Hypermetric Verse-Forms in Old English Poetry*, rev. edn (New Haven, CT, 1966)

Priebsch, R., *The Heliand Manuscript, Cotton Caligula A. VII in the British Museum: A Study* (Oxford, 1925)

Prokosch, E., *A Comparative Germanic Grammar* (Philadelphia, 1939)

Robinson, F. C., 'Variation: A Study in the Diction of *Beowulf*' (unpubl. PhD dissertation, University of North Carolina, 1962)

Robinson, O. W., *Old English and its Closest Relatives: A Survey of the Earliest Germanic Languages* (Stanford, CA, 1992)

Russom, G., *Old English Meter and Linguistic Theory* (Cambridge, 1987)

'Verse Translations and the Question of Literacy in *Beowulf*', in *Comparative Research on Oral Traditions: A Memorial for Milman Parry*, ed. J. M. Foley (Columbus, OH, 1987), pp. 567–80

'A New Kind of Metrical Evidence in Old English Poetry', in *Papers from the 5th International Conference on English Historical Linguistics*, ed. S. Adamson *et al.*, Current Issues in Linguistic Theory 65 (Amsterdam, 1990), 435–57

Review of Kendall, *Metrical Grammar*, *ANQ* 5 (1992), 165–8

'Eddic Meters', in *Medieval Scandinavia: An Encyclopedia*, ed. P. Pulsiano *et al.* (New York, 1993), pp. 148–9

'Constraints on Resolution in *Beowulf*', in *Prosody and Poetics in the Early Middle Ages: Essays in Honour of C. B. Hieatt*, ed. M. J. Toswell (Toronto, 1995)

'Purely Metrical Replacements for Kuhn's Laws', in *English Historical Metrics*, ed. C. B. McCully and J. J. Anderson (Cambridge, 1996)

Samuels, M. L., *Linguistic Evolution with Special Reference to English*, Cambridge Studies in Linguistics 5 (Cambridge, 1972)

Bibliography

Sauer, H., *Nominalkomposita im Frühmittelenglischen, mit Ausblicken auf die Geschichte der englischen Nominalkomposition*, Buchreihe der Anglia, Zeitschrift für englische Philologie (Tübingen, 1992)

See, K. von, *Germanische Verskunst*, Sammlung Metzler 67 (Stuttgart, 1967)

Sievers, E., 'Zum *Heliand*', *ZDA* 19 (1876), 1–76

'Zur Rhythmik des germanischen Alliterationsverses', *BGDSL* 10 (1885), 209–314 and 451–545

Altgermanische Metrik (Halle, 1893)

Sievers, E., ed., *Heliand*, Germanistische Handbibliothek 4 (Halle, 1878)

Sonderegger, S., *Althochdeutsche Sprache und Literatur*, 2nd edn (Berlin, 1987)

Stanley, E. G., '*Beowulf*', in his *Continuations and Beginnings: Studies in Old English Literature* (London, 1966), pp. 104–40

'Alliterative Ornament and Alliterative Rhythmical Discourse in Old High German and Old Frisian Compared with Similar Manifestations in Old English', *BGDSL* 106 (1984), 184–217

In the Foreground: Beowulf (Cambridge, 1994)

Suzuki, S., 'The Role of Syllable Structure in Old English Poetry', *Lingua* 67 (1985), 97–119

Terasawa, J., 'Metrical Constraints on Old English Compounds', *Poetica* 31 (1989), 1–16

'Old English *here-toga* and its Germanic Equivalents: A Metrical and Lexical Study', *Studies in Medieval English Language and Literature* 7 (1992), 35–51

Nominal Compounds in Old English: A Metrical Approach, Anglistica 27 (Copenhagen, 1994)

Traugott, E. C., and M. L. Pratt, *Linguistics for Students of Literature* (San Diego, CA, 1980)

Travis, J., *Early Celtic Versecraft* (Ithaca, NY, 1973)

Whitman, F. H., *A Comparative Study of Old English Metre* (Toronto, 1993)

Index

a-verse, 2
Árnason, K., 97 n. 2
adjuncts, *see* style, appositional
alliteration, 1–3, 64–9
  in adjuncts, 177–8
  in balanced verses, 80–3
  as boundary marker, 6, 23, 87–8, 131,
    144–51
  compounding rule for (R7), 66
  in early Irish and Italic verse, 205
  on finite verbs, 128–33
  in heavy verses, 73–9
  lack of, on substantives, 85, 190
  in metrical archaisms, 62–3
  in Middle English poetry, 208
  principle for (P3), 2
  prominence rule for (R8), 69
  and resolution on third arsis, 98, 110
  on s position, 78–9
  triple, 129 n. 52
  in ultra-heavy verses, 79–80
  in ultra-light verses, 84
  in verses of normal weight, 69–72
  in warlike epithets, 136
  see also matching, alliterative; word
    groups
ambiguity, *see* complexity, metrical
anacrusis, 45–9, 147–51, 170 n. 167,
    201–2
  constituents used for, 52–4, 132
    n. 73, 156–8
  in *Hildebrandslied*, 188–92

and Kuhn's laws, 54–9, 128–9,
    158–9
  after language change, 49–52
  non-prefixal, 3, 49, 138, 156–8
  in Old Saxon b-verses, 151–6
  perception of, 5, 81
  and resolution, 99
  and reversal, 112
apposition, *see* style
archaisms, 60–3, 106
  morphological, 142
  syntactic, 118 n. 2, 126, 138, 178
  of verse form, 35
arsis, 16, 18, 198–9
  see also Appendix, D2a–b
articles, *see* proclitics

b-verse, 2–3, 68, 86, 106, 165–6
balancing (of feet in verse), 40–2,
    199–200
  rule R4 for, 38
binding, metrical (*úaim*), 4, 65, 205
Bliss, A. J., 50 n. 24, 128 n. 49,
    129–32, 150–1, 194–6
Blockley, M., 52 n. 34, 55, 128 n. 47
bracketing rule (R2), 22
Bragi, 14
break, syntactic, 6
breath groups, 50 n. 24, 150–1

Cable, T., 48 n. 17, 55, 128 n. 47, 163
    n. 128

225

and anacrusis, 47, 50
foot-internal, 49, 53–4, 101
as light feet, 46, 124–5
see also prefixes, infixes
foot boundaries, 21–3
foot patterns
in continental verse only, 190
derivation of, 18
after language change, 168–9
marginal or absent in Eddic verse, 32, 36
perception of, 4, 22–3, 26, 31, 112, 201
principle for (P1), 2
in Eddic verse only, 19–20, 33
foot, Germanic, 16
formulas, *see* style, appositional
Frank, R., 24 n. 46, 85 n. 72
Fulk, R. D., 50–1 n. 27, 98 n. 4, 111 n. 69, 115, 143, 163 n. 128
function words
in balanced verses, 24–5
and consonant matching, 128
definition for (D1d), 13
extrametrical, 25–6
inessential, 10, 32–3 n. 19, 138–9, 142, 171–2
length of, 51
major vs. minor, 52–9, 151, 156–9, 189
clause-final, 21, 89–90
see also anacrusis, light feet

Gallehus inscription, *see* runic horn
Gordon, E. V., 34

Háttatal, 85–6
Hayes, B., 39
head (chief) stave, 86
Heusler, A., 36
hiatus, 61–2
Hofmann, D., 6–7, 11, 12 n. 50, 148 n. 66, 169, 174 n. 14, 193

Hoover, D. L., 97 n. 2
hypermetricality, 95–6, 151–6, 170 n. 167, 186
loss of, in Eddic verse, 34–5, 48–50, 81–2, 198

infixes, 20, 36, 140
integrity, metrical, 66, 85
integrity, syntactic
of b-verses, 123–5, 179
of feet, 90, 94
and Kuhn's laws, 56, 127
principle of (U1), 30
see also style
internalization of rules, 4–5

Jackendoff, R., 4 n. 12, 11–12

Kabell, A., 139 n. 15
Kaluza's law, 98 n. 4, 111 n. 69
see also resolution
Kaluza, M., 98 n. 3
Kauffmann, F., 142
Kendall, C. B., 4 n. 12, 6, 48 n. 17, 88, 91 nn. 23, 31; 94 n. 51, 109 n. 58, 128 n. 49, 129 n. 59, 178
kenning, 93–4
Kiparsky, P., 5 nn. 17, 18; 21–2
Kroch, A. S., 119 n. 5
Kuhn's laws, 54–9, 118–22, 172–3, 201
in balanced verses, 183
in Eddic metres, 8–9
and finite verbs, 128–33
formulation of (K1–2), 54
after language change, 158–9
in one-line clauses, 122–6, 174–6
in plurilinear verse, 126–8, 176–9
Kuhn, H., 14, 24–5, 30–1
Kuryłowicz, J., 64 n. 2, 87 n. 1

labelling rule (R1), 21
Lahiri, A., 15 n. 8, 16, 18
Lehmann, R. P. M., 29 n. 1

227

Verses specially discussed

Atlamál in grænlenzco (Am)
  6/6: 99

Baldrs draumar (Bdr)
  13/5: 33
  14/1: 131
Battle of Maldon (Mald)
  146a: 157 n. 100
Beowulf (Beo)
  19a: 104
  66b: 103
  81a: 6–7
  110b: 112 n. 72
  114a: 6–8
  142a: 104
  164b: 92
  167a: 41
  209a: 103
  278a: 160
  316b: 92
  341a: 104
  350b–55b: 127
  387a: 53
  394b: 92
  399a: 129
  401a: 103
  463b: 110, 116, 166
  487a: 104
  494b: 53
  501b: 31
  511b: 46
  517b: 141

553a: 150
620a: 58
658a: 130
707a: 46
758a: 129
941a: 47
964a: 112 n. 74
1101a: 114
1110a: 175 n. 21
1137b: 31, 129
1163b: 47, 152
1166a: 132 n. 73, 133 n. 80
1210b: 108
1215b: 103 n. 29
1307a: 6–8
1420a: 53 n. 39, 75 n. 31
1429b: 112 n. 72
1492a: 175 n. 21
1543a: 47
1584a: 110 n. 66
1679a: 6–8
1696a: 7, 58
1747a: 162
1987a: 58 n. 52, 159 n. 107
2042b: 49
2047a: 181 n. 61
2048a: 102
2093a: 58 n. 53
2288a: 129
2356a: 107
2430b: 107
2600b: 53

Heliand (Hel) *(cont.)*	*Hildebrandslied* (Hld)
1890a: 142	2a: 179
1994b: 155	4b: 179
2001b: 185	5b: 180
2037a: 164, 167	6a: 176
2084a: 168	7a: 186
2146a: 163	7a–b: 172
2190a: 161	8a: 180
2213b: 155	8a–b: 177
2268a: 167	11b: 175
2345b: 141	13a: 180
2370a: 168	13b: 182
2382b: 155	14a–b: 177
2505a: 138	14b: 187
2345b: 141	15a–b: 176 n. 25, 191
2597b: 152	16b: 191 n. 120
2870a: 79 n. 48	17a–b: 172, 192 n. 123
2871a: 33 n. 19	18a: 183
2995a: 167	20a–22a: 173
3052a: 183	20a: 188
3105a: 147	21b: 180
3123b: 187	26b: 176
3301b: 152	28a–b: 172, 174 n. 14
3399a: 162	30a–b: 177
3473a: 138	31a–2b: 172
3530a: 158	34a: 187
3697b: 166	34b: 185
3772a: 142	37a–b: 174–5
3837a: 167	39b: 185
3939a: 147	41b: 190
4003a: 162	42b: 180
4356b: 165	43a: 182
4423b: 142	44b: 180
4483a: 33 n. 19	47a: 185
4617a: 144	48a–b: 174
4667b: 150	49a: 182
4827b: 160	49a–b: 171–2
5021a: 168	49b: 185
5045b: 142	50a: 188
5148a: 187	51b: 190–1
5485a: 149 n. 69	53a–b: 174
5704a: 165	56a: 176
5939a: 156	58a–b: 174

Verses specially discussed